A N

YOUR FATHER

has

SOMETHING

to

TELL YOU

WHAT KIND OF SHADOW DOES A
FAMILY SECRET CAST OVER THE CHILD?

DAVE RIESE

ISBN 978-1-7320917-2-6 (Paperback)
ISBN 978-1-7320917-3-3 (eBook)

Photographic credits:
Front cover: Sasa Mihajlovic © 123RF.com
Back cover: Dave Riese © 2021

Cover photo is for illustrative purposes only.
The person depicted on the cover is a model.

Cover Design by 100Covers.com
Interior Design by FormattedBooks.com
Editing by Sasha Knight
Proofreading by Laura Kincaid

This is a work of fiction.
The action of the novel and the characters have no resemblance to anyone's family members or history.

Flying Heron Publishing, Wilmington, Massachusetts
First Printing: January, 2021

For Susan and Anne

Other Books by Dave Riese

Echo from Mount Royal
The Blue Dress and Other Stories

Fiction is a lie covering up a deep truth:
it is life as it wasn't.

—Mario Vargas Llosa
Letters to a Young Novelist

A man…might be happier if he had been more fortunate in childhood, but, for aught he knows, if he had, something else might have happened which might have killed him long ago.

If I had to be born again I would be born…of the same father and mother as before, and I would not alter anything that has ever happened to me.

—Samuel Butler
The Way of All Flesh

CONTENTS

CHAPTER 1

"Call Me as Soon as Possible"

I've come indoors after four hours of weeding the garden on Sunday afternoon, and although I've left my dirty clothes on the porch, my face, hands, and knees are filthy. Rachel stands at the front door, ready to leave for her evening shift at the hospital. "Don't touch anything on your way upstairs." I wave to her when she backs out of the driveway.

I'm shampooing my hair when the telephone rings. I stick my head outside the curtain to hear the message. No luck. The voice is too low. Probably one of Rachel's neighborhood friends. I forget the call once I'm out of the shower and in bed, absorbed in a new book.

An hour later, the phone rings again. Leaving the book on the bed, I stand at the head of the stairs and listen to the caller's number as the answering machine clicks on. Why are my parents calling? I talked to them less than three weeks ago. Then I hear my sister's voice.

"Mark, it's Leslie. Call me as soon as possible at Mom and Dad's house."

Leslie never calls me from our parents' home. Doing so now can only mean one thing: one of them has died. I grip the railing and struggle to slow my heart. When she hangs up, I run downstairs. Was it Leslie who called while I was in the shower? I listen to the previous message. Leslie.

I dial my parents' number, but I can't admit I disregarded her earlier call. "Leslie? I just came in the door." I speak as if out of breath, which isn't difficult since I'm prepared for bad news. "What's happened?"

"It's Mom and Dad."

Both of them? The phone is shaking against my ear. Her voice is low as though other people are in the house.

"I drove over to visit them around noon and found them in their nightclothes sleeping in the living room. They're sick—"

My words come out in a rush. "Oh, thank God."

"Mark? Did you hear me?"

"I expected terrible news. How long have they been sick? Have they called the Quack?"

The Quack is Leslie's nickname for Dr. Madison. She's never been satisfied with him as Mom's doctor. "First of all, he's too old," Leslie has told me several times. "He's never acted like he wanted to find out what was wrong with her. Just prescribes pills to keep her quiet." Our attempts to convince my father to get Mom a second opinion have failed.

"Of course they haven't called him," Leslie says. "They're drinking again."

"Damn." Although relieved they aren't dead, I can't help being angry at this news.

"I know. I've been suspicious lately but hoped it wasn't true. I don't think they've had a decent meal in days." She stops speaking for several seconds.

"Leslie? Are you still there?"

"I can't deal with them by myself anymore." She sounds exhausted. "I need help. Can you fly here tomorrow for a few days?"

My mind quickly reviews my appointments at work for the week. Nothing critical. "I'll take a morning flight."

"I'm afraid to leave them alone. Before you arrive, would you pick up some food? There's not much in the house. I hate bothering you—" She sounds on the verge of tears.

"Don't worry. I'll come tomorrow. Hang in there."

The earliest flights from O'Hare are booked, but I reserve one of the last seats on the 10:15. Rachel drives me to the airport, only to be caught in the tail end of rush hour.

"Aren't people at work by now?" Having had little sleep, I'm nervous about the delay. Rachel was late getting home from her shift, and we talked for an hour about my parents. She tried to mask her irritation at my abrupt departure but agreed I had to help my sister. Nevertheless, she wasn't happy.

The traffic clears as we near the airport. Rachel continues to ask me questions I've already answered last night, perhaps hoping I'll have a better answer this morning.

"How long do you expect to be away?"

"I should be back by the end of the week."

"And why are you staying in a motel? Didn't Leslie offer to put you up?"

"If I stay with her, we'll do nothing but talk about Mom and Dad. I need some quiet time to log into work and keep tabs on things. This isn't the best time for me to be away given the problems we had last quarter-end."

"Do you think they've started drinking again?"

"Leslie said nothing about it," I lie once again, not wanting to tell her the truth. Growing up with parents who didn't drink, Rachel has no sympathy for mine. I don't either, but I usually find myself defending them whenever we discuss it. Referring only to their illness helps to lessen Rachel's irritation about my sudden departure.

The flight is uneventful. I haven't flown into Logan for at least fifteen years. As the aircraft banks in a wide circle over Boston harbor to line up with the runway, I look out at the familiar landmarks, somewhat disoriented by the new buildings going up everywhere. Boston is having a real-estate boom similar to that in the Chicago area, with office buildings and condominiums opening every month. Just last week, someone on the news said the economy in the last half of 1998 will continue to improve.

The plane flies low across the harbor. Boats that were barely dots only minutes before are now the size of children's toys. Flying lower still, the plane almost skims the surface of the water. A pier flashes into view, a pile of rocks. Finally, the runway. I always hold my breath, expecting that this time the plane won't reach land.

I rent a car and drive out Storrow Drive toward Route 2. After passing the MBTA car garage at Alewife, I recognize several abandoned buildings with parking lots growing weeds. One boarded-up building with shattered plate-glass windows boasts thirty bowling alleys; another rundown complex has an oversized neon arrow that once beckoned motorists to pull into a dance club. These buildings have been vacant for as long as I can remember.

I make a quick stop in Arlington center. Not knowing what food they have in the house, I buy a three-day supply of groceries and, for tonight's dinner, a chicken pot pie—one of Mom's favorites.

Driving down the hill to the homes built around Mystic Lake, I'm reminded of returning home after a year studying abroad in England. The happiness I felt was tempered by my nervousness about the future. My senior year would be overshadowed by the intensifying Vietnam War lying impatiently in wait for a fresh group of men graduating from college.

Before I ring the bell, Leslie opens the front door, her coat on, ready to leave.

"I was worried. I expected you earlier."

I suppress a flash of irritation. "I forgot about the time difference." I've also forgotten that Leslie told me she had a meeting with clients this evening.

After putting the shopping bags down on the staircase leading upstairs, I signal to Leslie that I'll be with her in a minute and walk into the living room. "Hi, guys."

"Well, if it isn't the prodigal son," my father says.

I ignore his tone of voice. "That's my middle name."

I bend over to kiss Mom. She beams and, pulling me closer, kisses my cheek. "Leslie told us you were coming. I'm so glad. I've missed you."

When she hugs me, I'm surprised by her strength; I reach out a hand to steady myself on the arm of the couch. "You've had your hair done. It looks nice."

"Her hairdresser came to the house last week," Leslie adds. "They had a nice visit."

I sit beside my mother and take her hand. "How are you doing?"

"Not so good, but I think I'm feeling a little better—"

"Oh, Mark, can you—" Dad interrupts.

I keep my attention on Mom. "That's why I came. To help you get back on your feet."

"—close these windows?"

They're wide open, the summer breeze lifting the curtains like party streamers. An unpleasant odor lingers in the house. "It was the devil getting them open," Leslie explains.

"I'll close them in a minute. Let me speak with Leslie so she can leave."

We each carry a bag of groceries into the kitchen. "Thanks for coming." She kisses me. "I'm sorry I was abrupt when you arrived. I've been so upset. When I walked in yesterday, there was a terrible smell." She grips my arm. "I thought one of them had died."

"That's what I thought you were going to tell me on the phone."

"They were asleep on the sofa. I woke them and struggled to open the windows. I got Mom into a clean nightgown. Dad wants to take a shower this afternoon, so I've left that for you. Remind him to use the rubber mat."

Leslie is always organized. That's why she's successful in public relations, but she can be overbearing at times.

"You don't mind staying tonight? I have a dinner with potential clients that I need to win over. I'll be back first thing in the morning." She looks around the kitchen. "I'm sorry to leave you with these dishes. I rinsed them, but they need to be washed. And I haven't tracked down this smell yet." She frowns and bites her lip. "There's something else I wanted to tell you, but I can't remember now. Anyway, here's the story on her meds…"

Leslie kisses Mom and Dad goodbye. "See you in the morning."

At the door, she wishes me luck. "We'll talk tomorrow. Oh, now I remember. Get the clean clothes from the dryer and make sure I haven't left anything in the washer."

She closes the door. I take a deep breath and return to the living room.

My father is struggling with one of the windows. "Dad, I said I'd do that."

"We're catching our death in here."

Why is Dad so cold? It's the beginning of July. The breeze makes the weather ideal for sitting on the back porch in the fresh air.

I need to put all my weight on the windows to close them. They stick from accumulated paint.

"I'll boil some water for tea while I put away the groceries."

From the kitchen I can hear Mom talking, but I can't hear what she's saying. Neither can Dad because he keeps asking, "What, dear?" and "Say again?" He's going deaf in one ear, but even with perfect hearing, I sometimes can't decipher her words. How on earth do they communicate? They're like two people living alone in the same house.

I put the milk, ice cream, and frozen food in the fridge but leave the rest on the counter, no longer remembering where everything is stored.

"I made peppermint tea." I carry in the tea tray, trying to sound cheerful. "Leslie says the doctor wants you to drink eight glasses of water a day."

"Ha!" Dad grunts. "If I did, I'd be on the pot all day."

Mom laughs in agreement. "Me too."

"You don't want your kidneys going on the fritz." I pour tea into the mugs. "Sugar?"

Dad stirs in two teaspoons, spilling a few drops on his bathrobe. He places Mom's tea on the end table beside her and then finds a straw in the drawer. "It's tea, Kat."

"I know that," she snaps.

"It'll warm you up in no time," I say, offering a plate of cookies I hope aren't stale.

Dad slurps his tea. "Ahh… hits the spot. Kat and I came down with a bug this week."

"Why didn't you call Leslie? She would have come to help."

He shrugs. "Thought we'd feel better in a day or two. She's busy with her own life—"

"She's told you to call her whenever you need help. She's practically around the corner." I exaggerate. With traffic, her trip from Wakefield can take forty-five minutes. There is no quick way into Arlington.

"We can't call her every time there's a problem. It's not like you're around to help."

That subject didn't take long to crop up. Once Rachel and I moved to the Chicago area after my military service, we'd only returned east at Christmas, and on half of those visits we'd stayed with Rachel's parents. I'm happy we decided to live half a continent away. Over time, I grew tired of my parents' drinking and my father's aggravating bullying. Chicago provided a refuge. I promised myself I wouldn't grow old and be like them.

Mom tries to cover up the awkward silence. "We thought we were getting better."

"Have you been taking your pills?"

Dad speaks before she can respond. "Of course. We might have forgotten once. Or twice."

"Has Dr. Madison prescribed anything?"

"You're not listening. We *thought* we were feeling better." Dad's annoyed under my cross-examination.

So, they never called the doctor. While preparing the tea, I found a vodka bottle in the trash bin. Why ask for a prescription when you have liquor?

"When you've finished your tea, I'll help you with your shower."

"The hell you will. I'll help myself. I didn't add those bars on the wall for nothing."

Mom is laughing. "He doesn't want you to see his…" But she doesn't pronounce the last word clearly. Sounds like she said…

"His 'binky'?" I ask, before I realize she's making a joke.

"I said *dinky.*"

I play along. "I hope his dinky isn't a binky."

"I'll never tell." Mom gives Dad a dark look. Closing her mouth, she pretends to lock her lips, then tosses the key over her shoulder.

"I should wash both your mouths out with soap." Dad's never appreciated Mom's off-color joking.

Where did she get her bawdy sense of humor? Her mother was not one for risqué repartee. She'd become angry with me as a child if I said anything to displease her. Even "Oh, my God," earned a stern rebuke.

"I'm off to take a shower." Dad carries his mug out to the kitchen. He's tall, almost my height of six feet, but walks with a stoop. One tie of his bathrobe drags on the stairs.

"Let me fix this." I kneel to adjust the tie. I hope he'll shave. He's never missed a day unless he was ill or camping. Now, not shaving tells me he's not been well.

I sit on the coffee table and hold her mug, so Mom can sip the tea through a straw. Her hands shake, and if she tries to hold the mug, she'll spill it. She needs one of those hats with a tube that frat boys use to drink beer.

"I bought a chicken pot pie for dinner. Your favorite."

"Sounds good." She licks her lips.

I want to ask when she last had a decent meal. This is Dad's fault. When Mom cooked less and less over the years, Dad assumed cooking and cleaning up. After fifteen years on the wagon, their situation will be dire if they've started drinking again.

Mom probably nagged Dad to get her a "drinky"—a sherry or a gin and vermouth. In the past, he'd give in—not that it would be hard to convince him. He'd mix himself a drink "to keep her company" and then inevitably switch to vodka or Scotch.

If not for Leslie's visit, we'd never have known they'd broken their promise to stop. Social drinking was always part of their lives. How naïve

Leslie and I were to think one conversation with them fifteen years ago would solve the problem.

When Leslie comes tomorrow, we must sit down and have that conversation all over again. So much harder confronting parents than a teenage child. What if they don't stop? Can we trust Dad with the keys to the car? I can't think about this now. One day at a time.

"I'd better put the chicken pie in the oven. It takes an hour to cook. Back in a jiffy."

In the kitchen, I place the frozen pot pie on a cookie sheet and set the timer. The rinsed dishes from dinner and breakfast are piled beside the sink. Opening the dishwasher, I groan and turn away. That's the odor. I load the washer, add soap, and turn it on, then I wipe down the counters, stove, and table with Lysol.

Crossing the hall, I hear the shower upstairs. Dad closes the shower curtain with one swipe, the hooks rattling in protest. "Damn!" I forgot to mention the rubber mat, but I don't hear him slipping in the tub. He's just getting started, so there's still time. I immediately feel guilty to even think of him falling, but Dad's constant needling drives me crazy.

Mom hasn't moved since I left her. She's the shortest member of the family. With green eyes and high cheekbones, and with her teeth in, she's still pretty at eighty despite the wrinkles. I remember her when she was thin and wore high heels. As a child, I cracked my head on her bureau trying to walk in her heels.

"How about some TV before dinner?" I ask.

"It's Monday. Nothing good's on."

I look for a decent movie but with only basic cable, there's nothing. As a Christmas present two years ago, Leslie and I gave them a subscription to HBO, but I doubt they ever watched it, and after a year the subscription expired.

While I worked on my homework after coming home from high school, the quiz shows' theme songs, Mom's laughter, and the emcees' voices were a familiar backdrop. Her favorite shows were *Password* and *Hollywood Squares*. She always watched them with a glass of wine. Taking a break, I'd join her for the show's final challenge. She was disappointed when I left and returned upstairs after the show ended.

I sit beside the fireplace across from Mom. She stares at me, waiting for me to speak.

"We got a letter from Jon. He's traveling in Japan. He'll study in Tokyo for a year." I drop breadcrumbs, waiting for her to pick up the trail.

She twists her earlobe between her fingers as if trying to find a station on the radio. I wait for my information to catch hold. But she looks at me as if *I'm* speaking Japanese.

"He wants to learn Japanese, doesn't he?" She remembers. Maybe she doesn't have Alzheimer's after all. Leslie suspects Mom is too lazy to try to remember the past. More likely, having difficulty making herself understood, she's given up answering.

"He'll attend the American University in Tokyo for a year, starting this fall."

"Will he come home for Christmas?"

"No, the flight's expensive, and it's such a short time, I told him to travel. Jenn said—"

"Who?"

So much for *There's no dementia.*

"Jennifer. Your granddaughter."

"I know that. You shortened the name. She's in Ireland."

"That's right. She married Declan."

"Did I meet this… Declan?"

"Remember you and Dad came to the church in a limo? You met him at their wedding."

"Their wedding?"

Sometimes talking with Mom is like rehearsing a play by Harold Pinter.

A car stops in front of the house. Are Leslie's dinner plans cancelled and she's back? But it's only the mailman. At this hour? A moment later the truck moves to the next house.

I stand. "The mail's late today."

"Don't bother. Nothing good comes in the mail."

Outside, I stoop to look in the mailbox. A loud voice startles me. "Are you their son?"

The mailman's truck is on the other side of the street now. He leans awkwardly across the front seat. "I was worried. They haven't picked up their mail for days."

"They're sick. I only found out yesterday."

"I thought they were away and forgot to put a hold on their mail. Hope they're feeling better." He takes his foot off the brake, and the truck rolls toward the next house.

The box is stuffed. I pry the mail out, one magazine at a time. Letters fall to the ground. I attempt to carry it all in a single trip, but a catalog slides out, pulling a stack of envelopes with it. I stumble on the stairs. More mail scatters across the porch.

Damn! I'm angry with Dad. What were they doing besides drinking? I open the front door. The shower is still running. If he doesn't turn it off soon, I'll need to check on him.

"What was that noise?" Mom asks from the living room.

"I dropped the mail."

I sit on the front steps, sorting the mail in the sun. During my early teens, I sat here reading mysteries. Neighbors called, "Hi," or waved as they drove by. Forty years ago! Gone is my dead self—the boy I used to be. So too is every neighbor I knew—dead or moved away.

Only my parents are still here.

I've forgotten what's become of all the kids on the street, except for the Robinson boy, two years older than me, who lived on the corner. He died in college. Fell from a dorm window. Drugs. I remember his father walking home from the bus stop in his trench coat and hat, staring at the ground. The family moved away the next summer.

I separate the mail into piles—advertisements, magazines, bills, junk. The shock of time passing claws at my throat and I close my eyes. The neighborhood as it was years ago appears fully realized in my mind. The houses are smaller, without the rooms and dormers added since then. Two oak trees stand in front of our house. The hedges planted between the Waters and the McGhees are only a foot high. I hear the shouts of kids in someone's backyard, Ronnie Stevenson practicing the piano, the clicking of a bike at the end of the street.

I lived in this house from nursery school until college and only returned for holidays and the summer before I enlisted in the Air Force. Those years are a lifetime ago, and this house is no longer "home" for me. Do I feel sadness for the passing of time, or is it for the childhood I wish I'd had but didn't? How cruel to be given life to enjoy, only to lose it, both good and bad, piece by piece as we grow old—

"Thanks for getting the mail." The screen door squeals as Dad pushes it open. "Aren't you uncomfortable sitting out there? Here, I'll take the bills."

I hand them to my father. I don't look up, fearing my eyes are red. I clear my throat, which aches painfully. "I'll bring in the rest."

I stand, and the sadness drains away as fast as it came. It's all chemicals in the brain. I'm healthy and happy, but I'd never relive my life if offered the opportunity. Ready or not, the future is waiting for me in the living room.

Dad is dressed in slacks and a long-sleeve shirt. He's shaved, his face shiny, his wet hair plastered against his skull. I smell the shampoo from where he sits at a card table by the fireplace, wielding a letter opener shaped like a Turkish scimitar. With a swipe, he slits open each envelope, reads its contents, and then tears it up or adds the letter to his to-do pile.

The card table is his "desk" with checkbook, receipts, stamps, and stapler organized by an engineer—everything efficiently aligned without sacrificing geometric symmetry.

"Can I help? Oh!" Something brushes against my leg. It's Snowflake, their cat of dubious lineage, pitch black except for a white spot beside her nose. She jumps onto the card table, landing on the pile of bills. When guests arrived, Dad always enjoyed calling "Snowflake" and watching their expressions when a black cat streaked between their legs into the house.

Mom laughs. "She wants to write the checks." I wish she'd put her false teeth in.

"Say what?" Dad cups his hand around his good ear. Amazing how often he positions himself with his deaf ear toward her. He's examining a bill and hasn't noticed the cat.

"Snowflake wants to write the checks," she repeats.

"I'll write the checks later." Dad raises his voice as if Mom is hard of hearing.

"No, *Snowflake* wants to—oh, never mind." Mom clamps her mouth shut, glaring at Dad, her joke ruined by his inattention. She's testy when he doesn't appreciate her stories.

I pick up the cat and place her on Mom's lap. Snowflake turns in a circle, pushing at Mom with her paws, claws picking at her bathrobe.

"She's trying to soften you up," I say.

Mom twists her mouth to one side. "Dad's too bony. The cat can't get comfortable on him." She strokes Snowflake, who arches her back. Her purr roars like a jet engine. I want to lie on the rug and close my eyes, soothed by the sound.

"They're charging me interest?" In disbelief, Dad throws the bill onto the table. "I paid this on time, dammit."

He searches through his checkbook. Mom and I watch in suspense. "Here it is."

I look over his shoulder and see a carbon copy of the check with a date of two months ago. This will obsess him until it's straightened out. "You finish opening the mail. I'll call the company and find out what's up."

I phone from the kitchen. As I suspect, he missed a month. "My father is eighty-two and gets confused. Please set him up for automatic bill payment." I give her Dad's checking info. "Will you also reverse the penalty?"

A moment of silence. "I've posted the credit. I see your father is eligible to upgrade and earn travel awards—"

"My father isn't going anywhere. Thank you." I hang up before she asks me to take a quick survey.

After checking the pot pie, I return to the living room. "It's all straightened out. You missed a payment, but they waived the fee and interest."

Dad slumps in his chair. I'm about to say I've signed him up for automatic bill payment but decide against it for now. His pride is hurt, but it's not like he designed a bridge that collapsed. Cold comfort for an engineer to whom accuracy to the tenth decimal is second nature. He takes these episodes to heart and will be withdrawn for the rest of the day.

I'm in the kitchen when the telephone rings. Dad answers it on the living-room extension. "Mark, it's for you."

"I'm on my dinner break." It's Rachel. "How's everything going?"

"I'm holding down the fort."

"How sick are your parents?"

"They're over the worst of it, but they're dehydrated and have lost weight. I hope they don't have a relapse."

"Have they seen the doctor?"

"No."

"That might be a good idea, don't you think?" The nurse has spoken.

The timer on the stove buzzes. "Time to get their dinner on the table. I'm pulling the night shift. Gee, that reminds me: I should cancel tonight's reservation at the motel."

"I'll let you go. I'll call tomorrow."

After I serve Mom, Dad cuts her chicken into smaller pieces. "Make sure you chew it," he warns her.

When I return from the kitchen with my own plate, she's eating like she hasn't seen food for days. I'm pleased I bought something she likes.

During the meal, I reassure Dad that having his bills paid automatically from his checking account isn't a scam. "You won't need to write a check every month. The company will withdraw the exact amount." It's my idea, so he remains suspicious.

Mom drops her fork on her plate. When she gags, Dad jumps up to pound on her back. Her throat heaves, she takes a breath, and the food slowly overflows from her mouth like a student's volcano project. Dad grabs a napkin to keep it off the rug. He hustles her toward the sink in the pantry and talks over his shoulder. "We'll be back."

Dinner is over.

The evening is golden. The top of the maple tree is on fire in the remaining sunlight, but the porch is in shadow under the canopy of leaves. Dad plugs in the bug zapper and returns inside to get Mom's sweater. Finally, everyone is seated with coffee, but no one speaks.

These long intervals of silence are not unusual. Dad isn't much of a talker unless the subject is woodworking, camping, model railroads, or sailing. I never shared his interests. Instead, I read novels, acted in plays, and listened to classical music. We lived parallel lives, intersecting at meals, on family vacations, or when I had a question about math or physics.

The breeze picks up, and leaves twirl at the end of their branches. "Looks like rain," Dad says. Mom pulls her sweater closer. "Are you cold?"

With her nod, Mom and Dad return inside to watch TV; I remain on the porch, enjoying the anticipation of rain.

After an hour, they decide to go to bed.

"I'll be up in a sec."

In the basement, I empty the dryer into a laundry basket. The clothes in the washer smell of mildew. I dial a quick cycle to refresh them. Coming up the stairs with the dry clothes, I hear Dad cursing. Mom has stumbled going up the stairs, and Dad can't manage to help her up.

It's not the first time it's happened.

CHAPTER 2

"HER VALUES ARE OFF THE CHARTS"

When Leslie and I were children in the fifties, every grown-up we knew—parents, relatives, and the parents of friends—drank. Seen through the eyes of a child, mixing a drink was a fascinating ritual.

Dad was an expert, measuring each ingredient for a bourbon old-fashioned with a maraschino cherry, double martinis with gin and dry vermouth and a green olive or pickled pearl onion, rye whiskey manhattans, sidecars, Tom Collins, and white and black Russians. Leslie and I knew all the names.

At first, our parents drank socially, but after Dad's service in the war and we were born, they started having a drink in the living room before dinner: a martini or a double martini. Dad arrived home from the office and prepared the drinks. Leslie and I were not to disturb our parents during the next hour.

Sometimes, if we weren't hustled out to play, we asked Mom if we could have a sip. She'd laugh. "It's a martini. You won't like it."

"Yes, we will," we'd say in a chorus.

"All right, but just a taste."

Leslie would take a sip. She'd scrunch up her face. "I hate it."

Then I had my turn. The liquor burned my mouth. "It's terrible."

"I said you wouldn't like it."

We didn't like the olive or green onion either.

We learned only to ask when she drank an old-fashioned with a maraschino cherry. Leslie and I argued over who would get to eat it while Mom fished it out by its stem. If Dad was in a good mood, he'd let the loser take one from the jar. I liked the cherry juice more.

As children, we accepted the fact everyone drank. No one talked about a drinking problem. How would we know our parents' experience was different from that of other parents?

Sometimes after a drink, when resentments boiled over, Mom and Dad argued at dinner, but for the most part they were quiet drinkers. They didn't shout or swear or make a nuisance of themselves. In fact, Dad often became more charming. On the other hand, Mom was silent and harbored the injustices she imagined had been dealt to her since she was a child. As she drank, her eyes glazed over, which only hastened her retreat into herself.

Leslie and I never suffered physically from our parents' drinking. But even as children, we sensed intuitively that drinking had other effects, although we were too young to put this in psychological terms. Later we understood how drinking eroded our parents' self-confidence and belief in themselves.

Rachel and I moved to the Chicago suburbs after my discharge from the Air Force. One year into my master's degree program, I dropped out in 1973. I was sick of school and took an entry-level position in data processing. Our daughter, Jennifer, was born in September 1975. That Christmas, we returned to Arlington, so our parents could meet Jenn for the first time.

We stayed with Rachel's parents. Her brother was also home but without a car. When Rob had an interview in a nearby town, we loaned him our car. In return, he agreed to drop us off at my parents'. When I called ahead to say we were coming, Dad answered the phone and, after some hemming and hawing, said they'd enjoy seeing us.

It didn't take long to realize they had been drinking before we arrived. No wonder Dad had been ambivalent about our dropping by. Rachel's parents didn't drink, and not having grown up around alcohol, she was unforgiving. The visit was awkward.

After dinner, Rachel said Jennifer needed a nap. She called her brother for a ride, but he hadn't returned.

"I'll take you in our car," Dad offered.

Outside, Rachel said she'd sit in the back with Jennifer. We only had a mile to drive. "That's safer since there's no child seat."

Dad took out his keys and opened the driver's door. "Dad, I'll drive." I reached for his keys.

"Why?" He stepped back, insulted. "It's my car, and I want to drive."

"I don't think that's a good idea."

He laughed, trying to make a joke of it. "You think I don't know how to drive, do you?" He threw his arms wide. "In case you forgot, I've been driving since before you were born."

"You're too…" I didn't want to use the word drunk. We had avoided the subject all afternoon. "… too tired to drive."

My father smirked as if I were a coward. He'd dared me to say the forbidden word.

"Mark!" Rachel from the back seat. "He's not driving. Are you willing to risk your daughter's life? I'll walk home before I let him drive."

Halfway behind the wheel, Dad heard Rachel and stopped. He smiled sheepishly. "Have it your way." Getting out, he handed me the keys and walked around to the passenger side.

Before starting the engine, I put on my seat belt and waited for Dad to do the same. He couldn't lock the belt. I twisted around to snap it closed.

No one spoke. Dad, who always drove, looked out at the scenery as if he hadn't a care in the world. At her parents' home, Rachel went straight inside with Jennifer. "You handle your father."

Dad slouched against the passenger door, enjoying my predicament.

"Dad, stay here until Rob gets back with our car. Then I'll drive you home."

"Nonsense." With Rachel out of hearing, he was no longer restrained. "Gimme the keys. I'll drive myself home."

"I won't let you go back by yourself."

He came around in front of the headlights. His expression was frightening, and I was glad the driver's door was open between us. "Gimme the goddamn keys. Go inside with your wife and baby."

I expected him to add, "You sissy." I tossed him the keys without speaking, then stepped aside as he got in and slammed the door. He failed several times to insert the key in the ignition. When the engine started, he turned to me with a grin of accomplishment, once again the genial drunk.

"Call me when—"

He revved the engine, cutting off my words, and backed out of the driveway without looking. He braked suddenly, and the car rocked backward. Then he sped away.

"Call me when you arrive home." My whisper was somewhere between relief and a prayer. Where are the police when you need them? Not that I wanted my father arrested for drunk driving, but I'd hoped their driving by might have convinced him to wait.

Ten minutes later, the phone rang. "I made it home." Before I could reply, he disconnected.

Two months after that Christmas, Mom fell for the first time going upstairs to bed. She lost her footing, but the stairs were carpeted, and she was unhurt. Dad tried to lift her up, but he was also inebriated and didn't have the coordination. He called an ambulance.

She was admitted to St. Elizabeth's and held for observation. Dad stayed with her all night and took a taxi home in the morning. That evening, he called to tell me what happened. "We only had one drinky." I didn't believe him for a moment.

When Mom's lab work came back, the doctor said he was amazed. "Her values are off the charts. I'm surprised she isn't dead." He insisted she remain on the ward to attend the alcoholic treatment program. It wasn't AA. If it had been, Mom and Dad would have had nothing to do with it. *They weren't alcoholics; they just drank too much.*

Dad visited every day and took part in the program. To everyone's astonishment, they dried out and quit drinking cold turkey. Leslie and I were hopeful but realistic enough to wonder how long it would last.

They remained on the wagon much longer than we expected.

Children want to give their parents the benefit of the doubt. We hope certain behavior is nothing more than a one-time failing. Even when it becomes more evident, we justify it by saying our parents have the right to live as they see fit. This all changes when it affects *our* children.

In the early eighties, when we visited my parents, Jennifer and Jon, her brother born in 1981, acted standoffish and amused themselves in another room. We assumed they were shy around Mom and Dad and, frankly, we enjoyed having the children play alone, allowing us time to talk. But an incident opened our eyes.

I was outside with my father, looking at his vegetable garden growing against the back fence. Rachel was upstairs in my parents' room, putting Jon down for a nap. Dad and I heard Mom shout and Jennifer crying. Dad ran into the house. I was close behind.

When we came into the living room, Jennifer was already in Rachel's arms. Mom sat straight up on the couch, her eyes blazing. A children's book lay on the floor, and Mom's wine glass had tipped over, the wine dripping on the carpet.

"What happened?" Dad pulled a handkerchief from his back pocket to mop up the wine.

"The damage has been done," Mom said. "We'll have to send the rug out to be cleaned."

"Never mind." He was brusque, turning aside any distraction. "I want to know what happened."

"Grandma said she didn't want to read to me. She pushed me, and my hand hit her glass."

Mom bristled at Jennifer's accusation. "I told her I wouldn't read anymore and asked her to go play." Mom spoke to Dad as if he were the only person she had to convince.

Rachel soothed Jennifer. I hoped she'd say nothing, concerned that words spoken now could never be unsaid.

"She wouldn't sit still," Mom added, "and she wasn't listening. I asked her to get down."

"She pushed me."

"Okay, Jennifer." I picked up the book, open face down on the rug, and sat on the couch next to Mom.

Dad finished patting the carpet. "I'll put some cold water on the stain."

"Jennifer, come here," I said.

She looked up at Rachel, who nodded. I lifted her onto my lap.

"Grandma didn't realize she pushed you. And you didn't mean to be rude when she tried to read." I didn't believe it myself, so how could I expect to convince my mother and daughter? "The best idea is for you two to give each other a big kiss and be happy."

I waited for one of them to say something. When they didn't, I tilted Jennifer toward her Grandma, making sure my daughter wouldn't press her full weight against her.

She gave my mother a peck on the cheek. "I'm sorry, Grandma."

Mom kissed her on the forehead. "I didn't mean to hurt you, dear."

Jennifer slid off my lap and took the book into the dining room.

The rest of the visit was uneventful. When Jon woke up, Rachel changed his diaper and we left.

"We'll be revisiting this sometime in the future," Rachel said while we got ready for bed.

"You mean what happened today?"

"I mean your parents' attitude toward our children. Your mother's behavior is too erratic. The children don't know how she'll react. It has everything to do with her drinking."

Unbeknownst to me, Rachel talked to Leslie about what had happened. Leslie had noticed the same behavior with her children. Our parents were drinking again, and she was afraid they'd have a car accident. I flew to Boston in the fall, ostensibly for a business meeting, so Leslie and I would have an opportunity to speak to our parents. This would be the first time.

CHAPTER 3

"We Must Talk with Them"

I put the laundry down and help Dad pick up Mom and climb the stairs. She uses the bathroom and brushes her teeth. When our parents stopped sleeping in the same room after complaining they kept each other awake at night, Mom moved to Leslie's old bedroom with the queen-sized bed.

Mom sits in a chair while I remake the bed with clean sheets, making hospital corners the way I was taught in the Air Force. Dad finds a clean nightdress to replace the one she wore at dinner. I lift Mom so Dad can get the old nightgown out from under her, looking away to give Mom some privacy. When she's dressed, I help her into bed.

Mom reminds me again that Dr. Madison prescribed two Ativan tablets for her at night.

"I know. Leslie told me before she left." In her pill tray, the two Ativan are the last pills for today. I pick up the prescription bottle to verify the doctor's instructions: one or two before bedtime. Perhaps cutting the dose back to one pill would, over time, reduce the lethargic fog surrounding her and leave her more alert. I break one tablet cleanly in half.

Dad comes in with a glass of water. While he props Mom up with pillows, I place both halves into her mouth. "There you go. Two pills."

She tests the halves with her tongue, then looks at me with narrowed eyes. "I get two."

How can she tell? I pretend not to hear and turn to pull up the duvet to hide my surprise. How low will a son go to cheat his old mom out of one of her pills?

"I get two pills." She raises her voice. "Big pills." And she holds out her hand.

Dad carries over the pillbox. "Here's the other one." Mom tries to take it out. "Katherine, let me get it." Her fingers twitch, and the tablet flies out of the tray onto the rug.

I inspect the pill to eliminate rug fuzz, then hold it up, and Mom opens her mouth.

"Down the hatch, Kat." Dad is pleased he's solved the problem. He gives her a drink of water.

At least I tried.

Once they're in bed with the lights out, I sit on the stairs, listening to make certain they're settled. I'll buy a gate for the head of the stairs to prevent an untimely descent. In the living room, I click through the TV stations but find nothing to watch, so I open my book.

Before I finish a chapter, a door opens upstairs. I call up in a stage whisper, "Dad, is that you?"

"It's my bladder. The fool thing's acting up."

"Do you need any help?"

"Nooo waaay." He stretches out the two syllables and closes the bathroom door.

While opening the couch into a bed, I hear the toilet flush.

"How come you're still up?" he asks, returning to his room.

"It's only quarter past ten."

"Hell, I thought it must be after three."

All is quiet once again.

I'm exhausted and wonder how many days Leslie and I will need to provide around-the-clock observation. It's not the best time for me to miss work, with quarter-end financial reports due for thousands of customers. I work long hours during this time to solve problems with data errors and automated loads, but now it's all the more stressful thanks to the new vice-president assigned to our department six months ago. That's hardly my parents' fault, but I can't help blaming them for not taking better care of themselves. Rachel and I are determined not to be a burden to our children.

I resume reading, but my eyes close, and after dropping the book three times, I call it quits and turn out the light.

Too much has happened today, and my brain won't resign itself to sleep. I lie awake, my eyes wide open, staring at the gray blur of the ceiling. The hot-water heater turns on with a sound I recognize from years before. But surely it can't be the same one after all this time?

There's no light from the street outside. Wasn't there a street lamp between our home and the Robinsons' next door?

Trees creak in the wind, and raindrops splatter against the windows. The promised storm has started.

I float on the surface of sleep, remembering my nights as a teenager lying in the dark of my bedroom: worrying about SATs, applying to college, deciding to enlist to avoid the draft, and having doubts before marrying Rachel. I've survived all these anxieties and will never have to relive them. That thought calms me as I descend into sleep.

The booming thunder awakens me, but I must have had my eyes open a second before the crash because I'm blinded by the stab of lightning that illuminates the living room.

I swing my feet over the edge of the bed and sit up, taking deep breaths to steady my racing heart. In the kitchen, I fill a glass with water and return to the living room. I stop in the hallway when I hear a sound and wonder if my father is up again. Leaving the water beside the couch, I climb the stairs and listen intently, but all is silent. The door to my childhood bedroom at the end of the hall is closed.

I hated sleeping alone in the dark when I was in primary school. Once in bed, the band of light from the hall beneath the door was a lifeline until Mom, after saying goodnight, returned downstairs and switched it off. Watching the light disappear was like the world turning its back on me. Then I would start worrying about something: in fifth grade, buying the book of birds; in sixth grade, cheating on a history test; and many other insignificant events I laugh about today but at the time threatened me with exposure and humiliation.

I've avoided my old bedroom since I left for the Air Force. At that time, it represented a past that was gone forever, and I wanted to forget the memories of confessions, anxiety, doubts, and fears, many of which I'd brought upon myself as punishment for the guilt I always had as a child. Returning for visits over the next twenty-five years, I had no interest in entering that room. Although no longer experiencing the dark visions of bedtime, I subconsciously avoided awakening any memories, especially the childish ones.

Half asleep, the storm hammering against the house, I walk down the dark hallway. Standing before the door, I open it, enter the room, and close the door silently behind me.

My bedroom is long and narrow. At the far end of the room, three steps rise to a door set in the wall. When opened, one finds the stairs continuing into the attic. I always tested it to ensure the door was locked before saying my prayers. The slightest sound on the steps behind it alarmed me, and I had visions of moaning witches or ogres trying to reach me. And during a storm like tonight, when the wind blew through the attic vents and shook the attic door, I waited, afraid, for it to burst open.

Tonight, the wind pummels the windows and rattles the attic vents, but I hear no groans. I leave the room and close the door. A childish memory debunked is still one of the more durable that lurk in the back of the mind, like walking up the cellar stairs in the dark and the steps creak several seconds behind you. The skin on the back of your neck prickles with cold fingers.

Leslie arrives while we're having breakfast. She enters the kitchen carrying a shopping bag. "Morning, Mom, Dad." She kisses them. "Give me a minute. There are more bags in the car."

I leave the table and put on boots over my slippers and a coat over my pajamas.

"Stay inside. I can manage," she says.

I ignore her and open the front door. "We'll be right back," I call over my shoulder.

We wade through standing water on the front lawn, which is littered with branches.

"Any problems last night? Did the storm keep them awake?"

"I woke up once thinking I heard someone roaming around upstairs."

Leslie opens the trunk. "I thought I was early enough that you'd all still be in bed."

"No such luck—they were up at the crack of dawn."

I hand Leslie a bag from the trunk. She waits while I heft the last two into my arms.

She closes the trunk. "Go and get some sleep. I'm here all day. Can you stay again tonight?"

"Of course. I'll come for dinner."

I open the screen door while balancing a bag on the porch railing. "We must talk with them about you know what."

"I dread it. I thought the last time we talked with them... can't we wait until they're feeling better?"

"Unless you want to do it yourself, we have to get it out in the open today, or we'll lose our nerve."

"Will you start the conversation? I'm not good at times like this."

I'd rather not but agree. Leslie is more decisive than I am, but I rise to the occasion when necessary. The wind pulls the screen out of my hand, and it bangs against the railing.

"We'd better get inside before they think we've run off."

With breakfast finished we stack the dishes in the dishwasher and put the groceries away. Leslie and Dad prepare a list of meals for the next week. Mom and I sit in the living room reading the paper. She examines the store flyers and then reads a magazine Leslie brought her from cover to cover. I start the crossword puzzle, but I'm too distracted about the upcoming confrontation to concentrate.

Leslie carries in a tray with tea and slices of coffee cake. My heart pounds as I wait for everyone to be served. I'm back in high school, acting in a play, listening offstage for my cue.

Tea is poured. Coffee cake served. My cue. Enter stage right. "Mom, Dad—"

Leslie interrupts, "Oh, what's this?" She picks up several pieces of colored and white lined paper tied together with a ribbon. The top page has a child's drawing of a bluebird.

"It's Mark's project from the sixth grade," Mom says.

"Fifth grade," I correct her, irritated with Leslie for cutting off my opening remarks.

Mom doesn't hear me or doesn't want any snag in the story she's telling. "Dad found it in one of the chifforobe drawers while looking for his Army discharge papers. I didn't recognize it at first, but then I remembered it was one of Mark's school assignments."

"I see where you wrote your name," Leslie says, adding a trace of false wonderment to her voice, as she quickly scans the pages. "Here's a section called 'Why I picked the bluebird.' Oh, Mark, you were so clever."

I glare at her. I'm a fan of self-deprecating humor, but not when others use it against me. I'll give Leslie a pass because I know she's desperate to postpone the conversation.

"Did you save any of my school projects?" Leslie asks.

"I don't think so, but you never took your projects as seriously as Mark. He got an A. See, it's on the back cover."

"Of course he did. Mark always got an A."

"Jealousy is such a nasty trait." I give Leslie a sarcastic grin showing my teeth, rather than the finger she so richly deserves.

"Didn't you have to buy a book about birds?" Mom asks. "I remember you took the bus alone to the Center…"

"That's ancient history." I take charge, ending any more of my mother's recollections. I'll always remember that day, although it's not one I want to discuss. "Putting aside that brief visit down memory lane, Leslie and I have something we need to talk over with you."

Leslie is unprepared for my sudden transition, then her eyes widen as she understands.

Dad is instantly alert. "All right." He sounds a little defensive. Mom is in her usual state: happy to listen to whatever we have to say.

"Leslie and I have noticed you've started drinking again."

Our parents say nothing. They glance between Leslie and me, waiting for one of us to continue.

"We've been worried about you." Leslie quietly enters the conversation. "At first, it didn't seem to affect you, and I overlooked it—"

"But it's become a problem again." I pick up the pace. "Leslie and I won't stand by until one of you is seriously ill and you can't help each other. Last week is a good example."

Dad seems surprisingly composed. I expect him to deny it, but he doesn't. "I knew Leslie was suspicious when she arrived unexpectedly two days ago," he says. "We've tried to keep it on the q.t. because we didn't want you to worry. We thought we could handle it"—he glances at Mom, who has a stricken look on her face—"but I guess we can't."

He stops speaking. In the silence, Mom is crying. "We were afraid if you found out, you wouldn't bring our grandchildren to visit anymore."

Leslie and I are shocked by her words and look at each other in confusion.

Mom turns to me. "You said Jon and Jennifer were afraid of us." Tears streak her cheeks. "We thought we'd never see them again."

We did say those words—fifteen years ago when our kids were young! At the time, we believed we were justified. Is Mom reliving an event that took place so far in the past?

Leslie embraces her. "But, Mom, you've seen them many times. We'd never tell them not to see you." She looks over Mom's shoulder at me, her confusion evident in her eyes.

I feel sick to my stomach. Something is terribly wrong with Mom's memory. Has she forgotten the family reunions? Jennifer's wedding? Jon's party before he left for Japan?

"And we stopped," Dad insists.

"We know you did." Leslie reaches over to touch his arm. "And we understand how hard it was."

"We were successful for years," he says quietly, "but little by little we thought we could handle a drink now and then."

"And we'll help in any way we can." Leslie dries her own tears as well as Mom's. "You have to let us know when you need help. I thought one of you had died when I came on Sunday. I was frightened. We don't want you afraid to tell us if something goes wrong."

Later, coming out to the car with me, Leslie is still shaking. "My God, that was scary. Our threat all those years ago must have frightened the hell out of her. I'll ask Dad if this has happened before."

"Why didn't he say something today? Or is he used to it? The future isn't going to be easy. You and I need to talk together soon."

"I'll stay tomorrow night after they're in bed."

Backing out of the driveway, I look up at the windows of my old bedroom. Talk about the past. Are we ever free of it?

The flooded roads are treacherous. I force myself to concentrate on driving and to not replay the last hour in my mind. Instead I think about the book of birds and Miss Callahan, my fifth-grade teacher.

To celebrate the arrival of spring, Miss Callahan assigned a project about birds. "Your first task is to pick a bird and explain why you chose it. Who wants to start?"

Hands shot up. Paul St. Charles grunted, raising his hand the highest to get the teacher's attention.

"Paul? What bird did you select?"

Paul thought he was the best athlete in the class. "A falcon."

A sudden burst of whispering. Stewart at the back of the class wanted the falcon.

"Interesting. What information about the falcon do you want to share?"

"Huh?"

"Why did you pick a falcon?"

"It has sharp claws."

"Oh, my! Nancy, what about you?"

"A crane because it's white."

"What a lovely thought, Nancy. Yes, Roger?"

"Flamingos. They're pink."

The class laughed, and Roger blushed the color of a flamingo.

Peter, a short kid whose belly shook when he rounded the bases, chose a pelican.

Each student tried to outdo the other: a buzzard, an eagle, a vulture. Gerry, who had won the school spelling bee every year since the second grade, took a deep breath. He stuttered when excited. "A f-f-flightless c-c-cormorant."

Wendy was half out of her chair, waving her hand. I thought Miss Callahan was ignoring her on purpose. Wendy sat in the front row and always had an answer. Miss Know-It-All.

"Yes, Wendy. What is it?"

Wendy looked around, confident that she'd chosen the most unusual bird. "The blue-footed booby."

The class erupted into laughter. Miss Callahan clapped her hands to restore order, but the bell rang to dismiss students for lunch. While I ate at home later, I told Mom about the bird project. "Wendy talked about blue boobs in class."

"Oh, that sounds interesting."

I don't think she was listening.

After lunch, Wendy raised her hand as soon as the teacher entered the room.

Miss Callahan sighed and brushed her long hair back behind her ear. "Yes, Wendy?"

"It's about our bird project." She held up a book with a bright-red cover.

"We don't have time to discuss this—" Miss Callahan began when Wendy interrupted.

"It's a tracing book with every bird in it."

"Perhaps there'll be time to tell us about it later this afternoon." Miss Callahan's usual answer. Wendy wouldn't get the time she wanted if she got any time at all.

On the way home, I ran to catch up with Wendy. She was holding the red book with her arms crossed on her chest. She stopped mumbling to herself when she saw me.

"What do you want?" We weren't friends and usually didn't speak to one another.

"Can I see the bird book?"

"Miss Callahan's so mean." Having a willing and hopefully sympathetic ear, Wendy unloaded her grievance. "She deliberately spent all afternoon on stupid history."

I needed help picking a bird and tracing it, so I crossed my fingers and lied. "You're right. History is boring. Where did you get the book?"

"If you must know, Mister Nosey, my mother bought it at Woolworth's."

"Let me see it?"

I was too eager, and she pulled back, flipping the pages to show the pictures. Even with pages passing in a blur, I saw that it was exactly what I needed.

I reached for the book. "Can I use it when you're through?"

She started walking away. "I might need to use it a long time."

"I'll copy my bird and give it back to you tomorrow." I tried not to sound desperate.

She walked faster. "I don't think so."

"Why not? I only need it one night."

"Why should I? You hurt me when you pulled my hair last week."

I did this last week when she wouldn't let me use her pogo stick. I waited and waited for a turn because she promised to let me try it. But as soon as she finished, she walked away. I shouted after her, "My mother said you need to share if you want any friends."

Hiding the book, she turned to walk backward. "Why do I want you as a friend? My mother said this was the last one." She smiled. "Too bad for you." Then she ran home.

Maybe I looked like I was ready to pull more hair.

Whenever a teacher assigned a project, I wanted to start on it immediately. I drove Mom crazy, insisting that she take me to the library for a book or to a store for supplies like colored paper. She didn't share my sense of urgency. "Wait until I go downtown."

I'd only turned eleven, and Mom hadn't given me permission to take the bus alone to Arlington Center for my piano lessons in a musty office above the Co-op Savings Bank. If I asked her to take me to Woolworth's that afternoon, she'd tell me to wait for the weekend. I suspected Wendy had lied about her book being the last one. I wasn't taking any chances.

Opening my bureau drawer, I found the oyster shell holding my allowance. I needed ten cents each way for the bus and twenty-five cents for the tracing book. I'd seen the price on the cover before Wendy ran away. I put a nickel and four dimes in my pocket.

When I reached the bus stop on Park Avenue, the Hudson Bus was rounding the rotary with the water tower. I took out my money to count it again.

I paid my fare and sat in the back by an open window. I was the only passenger. The spring air was cold in the shade, but once the bus turned onto Mass Avenue, the sunlight washed over us. I counted my money again. Now three dimes and a nickel. Thirty-five cents.

The bus stopped across the street from Woolworth's. I got off, crossed at the light, and entered the store. The grit on the wooden floor crunched under my shoes. The wood was scoured white. At the edge of the display cases, the floor was still a shiny yellow from the shellac. Easter was the next Sunday, and the candy counter smelled of chocolate eggs and bunnies wrapped in gold foil. I regretted not bringing extra money to buy a bag of jelly beans.

A counter had been moved aside to make room for a pen holding two dozen fuzzy yellow chicks. A sign said each chick was reduced to twenty cents or two chicks for thirty. Most of them hopped about, scratching for food in the wood shavings, but one was sleeping, its eyes closed. I reached over the barrier to run my finger over the soft feathers on its back. To my surprise, the chick rolled onto its side, still sound asleep. I looked to see if anyone had seen me, but the woman at the register was busy with a customer.

"Goodbye, chicks," I whispered. "Happy Easter."

Standing in front of the racks with comics and coloring books, I didn't see the bird book. Had I wasted bus fare for nothing? I examined each shelf with magazines, but everything was out of order. I decided to ask the cash-register lady if there was a copy in the back when I saw a red cover, half hidden behind copies of *Classics Illustrated*. I glanced through it. Just like Wendy's, the liar. I counted out my money. Exactly two dimes and a nickel.

I walked toward the cash register, then stopped. Where was the other dime for the bus ride home? I searched my pockets twice. Nothing. I looked under the comic-book racks. No dime. I'd had it on the bus because I'd counted the money three times during the trip. Then I remembered the chicks. I rushed to the pen and sifted the wood shavings through my fingers, careful not to disturb the sleeping chick. But it couldn't be there. I hadn't taken the money out while looking at the chicks.

The loudspeaker growled. "Store closing in ten minutes."

I panicked, walking in circles, trying to think. If I bought the book, how would I get home? Tears of rage stung my eyes. *I'll call Mom,* but how much was the phone call? Maybe the cashier lady would let me use the store's phone. But Mom would be angry I'd taken the bus alone.

"Bring your items to the cash register. Store closing in five minutes."

The lights at the back of the store were turned off. I had to leave, or I'd be locked in all night. I had to have the book, but I didn't have enough for the book *and* the bus.

My beating heart made me dizzy. I rolled the book up and held it against the leg farthest from the cash register. I walked to the front of the store with a quick glance to make sure the cashier was serving customers. Staring straight ahead, I held my breath and walked outside.

I forced myself not to run. At the corner, I heard someone shout, "Stop. Police."

I froze, expecting more people to sound the alarm. I didn't dare look and kept walking. My ears were hot and my throat tight. I hadn't taken a breath since leaving the store. I gasped for air at the same time I heard the hiss of brakes and the rattle of doors opening. I was at the end of the line for the bus. I risked a glance behind me. No one had followed me.

On the bus, my hands shook, and the dime rolled under the driver's seat. I didn't care. I wanted the bus to leave as soon as possible. I dropped the other dime into the coin box and turned to find a seat.

"Hey, sonny," the bus driver called after me. How did *he* know what I'd done?

I stopped in the aisle and closed my eyes. A hand touched my shoulder. "This is yours."

Some passengers laughed, enjoying the drama unfolding in front of them. I stared at the bus driver. I wanted to shout, "Go back to your seat and drive away." Any second now the police would bang on the door.

The driver grabbed my hand and gave me the dime I'd dropped. I mumbled thanks and pushed my way past the other passengers. I hid at the back of the bus, trying to convince myself that no one saw me steal the book and no one called the police. The farther the bus traveled from Woolworth's, the safer I felt, and when it turned to climb Park Avenue, I wanted to shout, "I'm home free!" I pulled the cord and waited for the bus to stop.

After dinner, I finished my homework in my room. At eight o'clock, I brushed my teeth, washed and dried my feet, and applied zinc oxide to the toes with athlete's foot. I wanted to forget what I'd done that afternoon. I dreaded being alone in my room in the dark.

After saying goodnight to Leslie, Mom stopped at the bathroom door. "Almost ready? You can read for fifteen minutes. Then lights out."

I stalled for time, wishing she'd stay longer. "Mom, how come I have athlete's foot when I'm not an athlete?"

"The germs just like your feet." She kissed me. "Be sure you clean the sink."

Halfway down the stairs, she paused. "Where did you go this afternoon?"

Her question took me by surprise. I didn't think she knew I'd left. "I walked to the Heights to get a book for a school project."

"If it's something you need for school, I'll pay for it. Remind me when I give you your allowance on Saturday. Goodnight."

The fear I experienced that afternoon returned. If only I'd told her where I was going, I'd have had more money than I needed and none of this would have happened. I didn't want to read but was afraid to turn off the light.

The evening was mild, the sky still light. I listened to the shouts and laughter of the older kids playing in the Donnellys' backyard. But soon they went indoors. Someone turned on the TV in the Lunds' house across the street. Next door, Ronnie Stevenson, who was in junior high, practiced the piano. He pounded on the keys when he made a mistake, which was often. A breeze through the window made me shiver. The branches on the maple tree scratched against the porch roof.

I heard my parents talking downstairs, a rumbling that sounded far away. I no longer belonged in the family. I'd committed a crime that separated me from them forever. I tried to fall asleep but couldn't with the light on. I wanted to crawl across the porch roof, climb down the tree, and run away, but I remembered how frightened I'd been when I heard someone calling for the police. I pressed my face into the pillow and wished the afternoon had never happened. It was all Wendy's fault: she wouldn't lend me her book.

A siren on Park Avenue! I held my breath, waiting for the police to turn the corner, drive down my street, and arrest me. I sat up in bed. My pajamas were soaked with sweat.

I walked to the head of the stairs. If I called Dad, he'd say go back to bed and tell him tomorrow, but I'd never ask him. I didn't want to tell my mother either, but I couldn't stay in my room alone. Dad shook his newspaper, folding the pages to make it easier to read. I heard the faint clicking of Mom's knitting needles. My fear prevented me from making a decision. Could I wait and tell her tomorrow? But the police might arrive at any minute.

"Mom." She didn't answer. "Mom!"

The needles were quiet. She looked over the banister. "Have you had a bad dream?"

"No. Can you come upstairs?"

"What's the matter?"

"Can you come up? Please."

She started up the stairs. Back in my bedroom, I crawled under the covers and leaned against the headboard.

"What is it?" She sat on the edge of the bed.

"I did something bad today."

"What?"

I said nothing, wondering how to begin.

"Tell me."

"I rode the bus alone to the Center to get a book I needed for school, and I lost the money to pay for it and I hid it and walked out..." The story spilled out in a wave of relief.

She listened without interrupting. When I finished, she asked what I thought I should do.

"Give the money to the store?" I asked, hoping I wouldn't have to do that.

"That's one idea, but I have another thought. You've learned your lesson, and you won't do it again. I think you should take the money from your allowance and put it in your church envelope for the missionaries. Okay?"

I said I would and gave her a kiss.

"Goodnight. Don't worry anymore. And don't take the bus alone without asking me first." She went downstairs. I was giddy with relief and started laughing. I pressed my face into my pillow, so she wouldn't hear me.

For the last forty years, I can't carry a bag into a store without thinking the manager is watching me. When I leave the store without buying anything, I'm certain he thinks I've stolen something. I must act suspicious, my face flushed with guilt. Whenever possible, I check my belongings at the front of the store. Doing so, I temporarily unburden myself of a memory, one I will shoulder again when I leave.

CHAPTER 4

"A HONEYMOON IS NO EXCUSE TO BE AWOL"

The next day I'm staying overnight, but Leslie remains when our parents go to bed. I brew coffee for her and tea for myself. When visiting Leslie, I'm always shocked at how much coffee she drinks in a day which she says doesn't keep her up at night. I cut the leftover coffee cake in two.

When Dad closes his bedroom door, we wait five minutes, then go to the kitchen to talk.

"They seem to be feeling better now," Leslie says. "I still want us stay with them until we're sure Dad is fully recovered and ready to take responsibility. You should be able to fly home on Friday. I know you need to get back."

She reaches out and covers my hand with hers. We remain silent for a minute.

"I didn't realize how dependent they'd become. I'm sorry it's been stressful for you."

"I appreciate that. Sometimes I worry they won't be as independent much longer."

"I'm willing to pay for someone to come in when you think they need the help—"

"Dad will never agree to that. He says the person will only be in his way and is adamant against asking for help."

"Except asking for your help."

"I don't want to come across as a martyr. I don't mind driving them places or picking things up as long as they give me notice."

"What would make things easier for you?" I take the smaller piece of coffee cake.

"Take the larger piece. I need coffee cake like a hole in my head."

"I always take the smaller piece. I learned the hard way."

Leslie frowns, not understanding what I'm referring to.

"You don't remember what happened?"

"No, I don't."

"I was in the kitchen cutting a sandwich in two to share with you. I must have pissed off Mom about something before this, because when she saw me take a piece, she exploded, 'You always take the biggest piece,' and she grabbed me by the shoulders and shook me back and forth. Her fingers lost hold of my shirt and suddenly I was flying backward and ended up on the floor against the stove."

"Why don't I remember this?"

I laugh. "It didn't happen to you. I wasn't hurt, but I'll never forget Mom's face. She didn't move, just stared at me as if she couldn't figure out how I got there. Then she ran over to make sure I was okay. She was shocked by what had happened, but ever since then I've always taken the smaller piece."

"How times have changed. Today, Children's Services would be knocking at the door."

"Did that even exist in those days?" I ask.

"Who knows? Once Elaine was giving me some lip, and I was ready to slap her face. She saw the look in my eyes and said, 'Don't you be mean to me or I'll call the people that help kids.' I was afraid she might say something to her teacher, but I recovered. 'Okay, call them. They'll come and take you away to a foster home. I could do with some peace around here.'"

"What did she do then?"

"She blustered and stamped out of the kitchen. I told her to go to her room for the rest of the day. I think she was afraid *I'd* call Children's Services and turn myself in. She never tried that trick again."

"Ask her if she remembers what happened. I'll bet she doesn't."

Leslie shrugs, and I repeat my original question: "What will make this easier for you?"

Leslie looks out the window and sighs. "I'd like them to send their laundry out. I worry every time I think of Mom on the stairs or Dad carrying laundry. And find someone to help Mom bathe three times a week. And convince Dad to sell the house and move to an apartment."

"Will Dad agree to move?"

"You didn't ask what was possible, but I'll discuss it with them after you go home."

"The laundry shouldn't be a problem, or the bathing, but moving will be a hard sell. Don't wait too long. Call me if you want me to weigh in."

"Frankly, it's better if you don't. Dad might suspect it's your idea and that you're trying to railroad him. I'll plant the idea, then let him think about it until he believes it's his idea."

She's probably right, but it's one more job she'll have to shoulder alone.

"How are things between them?" I ask. "They seem to be trying their best to get along. I'm curious about what you think."

With her elbows on the table, Leslie takes a moment to rub her eyes. "Mom is living more and more in the past and remembers things about Dad that once upset her. Two weeks ago, she claimed he was leaving to go to Maine for a month. I asked why she thought that, and she said he was going hunting because he was angry with her and was leaving her home with you."

"Me? How did I get dragged into this?"

"You were less than a year old."

"And Dad was going hunting for a *month*?"

"I asked Dad if he knew what she was talking about, and he thought it was when he was sent to Maine by Stone and Webster to work on a hydroelectric plant. Mom was upset about his going away for a month, but he was a new hire and couldn't refuse. These bits and pieces of the past come up without any reference to what you're talking about with her. It doesn't happen often, but it scares me—like someone else has taken her place. It creeps me out. Oh, there's something I want to show you."

Leslie carries her handbag into the kitchen and takes out an envelope with several photos. "Have you seen these? I don't remember them, but I found them tucked inside one of their wedding announcements."

I take the snapshots. The first shows a table placed in front of a fireplace with a large mirror over the mantel. The table holds a cake and two plates with little sandwiches. Surrounding the food is a collection of cups and saucers, spoons, and forks. Looking more closely at one of the teacups, I recognize an emblem. Jumping up, I go to the living room and stand in front of the cabinet that holds Mom's teacup collection.

"Look." I gesture to Leslie, who's followed me. I open the case and take out a cup and saucer. The cup has the same Army emblem. "Mom showed this to me ages ago and said it was part of the table service at their wedding reception."

The second photo shows Mom in the wedding dress she brought across the country. Dad is standing next to her in his dress uniform. The back of Dad's head is reflected in the bottom of the mirror.

The third photo includes another couple next to my parents. "He must be the best man," Leslie says, "but who's she? His wife maybe?"

"Do you know their names?"

Leslie holds up her hands. "Beats me. We can ask Mom and Dad tomorrow. At least now I have pictures to go with the story of their marriage."

"I know some of the details."

"Mom will tell you tomorrow. Dad too if he's in a nostalgic mood.

Leslie leaves soon after. I clean up the kitchen and unfold the couch. I've left my book in the motel room, so I can't read before going to bed. Instead, I study the three photographs again. I think Mom and Dad were married in 1942, but I look at the wedding invitation to check. The date is April 1943.

When the US declared war, Dad enlisted in the Army in January 1942 as a lieutenant "for the duration."

After officer training, they sent him to Oregon to protect Seattle and its seaport from invasion. He commanded the base artillery at the highest elevation on Whidbey Island. Soldiers positioned guns over bunkers clawed from a shelf of granite overlooking Puget Sound. His men drilled at target practice every day. "They sank the Inland Waterway Ferry four times a day," Mom once told me, "but there was never a need to fire the guns." They saw no action.

Dad proposed over the phone. Mom accepted, having long ago made up her mind while walking home with my father from high school. Wartime had changed society, and parents had less control over the romantic decisions of their daughters. With her fiancé three thousand miles away and unable to plead his case, Mom faced her mother's insistence that they postpone the wedding until after the war, although no one knew when that would be.

Converting to the Protestant faith at university, Dad avoided the major objection of his future mother-in-law, although in her opinion, "Once a Catholic, always a Catholic." Grandma was convinced her daughter was marrying below her station, though Grandpa quietly supported Mom's decision. After all, Dad was a fellow engineering graduate of the University of Maine.

The lovers prevailed, and a date was set. The wedding dress was folded in tissue paper and packed in a trunk with other clothes Mom needed for the Oregon weather. Grandma reserved a compartment for two in the first-class compartment on the Empire Builder, a luxurious streamliner with a retinue of "colored" waiters and attendants. Grandpa remained in Boston.

Their fellow passengers were older, married couples, government officials, and military officers. Two people Mom's age traveled in first class, but, newly married, they were rarely seen. Most of the time, the passengers played endless games of canasta. "What did I expect?" Mom asked sarcastically. "There's no shuffleboard on a train."

Besides enjoying the extraordinary scenery, the only activities to relieve her boredom were books and meals. Most of the passengers were servicemen in third class heading to fight in the Pacific. If left to herself, Mom would have walked the length of the train to discover what was going on. Unfortunately, Grandma was glued to her side every minute.

The train terminated in Seattle, where they stayed overnight. Dad met them the next morning to accompany them on the ferry to the island. Arriving midafternoon, they found Dad's friend, Captain Richard Crawford, waiting on the dock. He and Dad loaded the trunk and other luggage onto the jeep; the bride and mother-in-law followed in a taxi.

The Army base—barracks, administrative buildings, and married officer homes—were built around a grassy parade ground shaped like a saucer surrounded by a forest of evergreen trees.

On their first night, the commander hosted a dinner for Dad, Mom, Grandma, and the other officers and wives. After dinner, the ladies retired, leaving the men and the liquor behind.

"That was your father's stag party!" Mom said when she talked about the wedding. "Why wasn't it held before I arrived?" She had her suspicions. "The colonel wasn't keen on 'mail-order brides,' as he called us, and made sure I knew who was in charge." That night Mom and Grandma stayed as guests of the Crawfords.

The next afternoon, Mom and Grandma attended a tea party hosted by the other five wives on base. They had frosted the wedding cake that morning and were decorating the standard, four-room house issued to the newlyweds. The women were excited their numbers on base were increasing.

"When he doesn't get his way," one woman told my mother, "the colonel is stubborn and irritable. Just ignore him."

"Carry treats with you so you can feed his dog," another wife suggested. "That'll get you in his good graces."

"Sylvia, the cute girl over there, was the last one married on base," a third woman confided, handing Mom a teacup and offering her a tray of sandwiches. "Got hitched two months ago. Hey, Sylvia, tell Kathy about your first day working at the library."

Sylvia came over. "The head librarian met the colonel at the door when he arrived with his dog for inspection. 'Colonel, we have a new girl working here.'

"'What's she like?' he asks, the nasty son of a bitch. 'Your girls are either beautiful and dumb, or smart and homely.'

"When I heard that, I came to the door of the office. 'Good morning, Colonel. Today's your lucky day. You're getting two for the price of one. Beautiful *and* smart.'

"The colonel, surprised, then embarrassed, said we'd passed inspection, and left."

"She's my hero," her friend said.

Sylvia laughed. "The colonel has trained his dog to growl whenever it sees me."

The base chaplain performed the nuptials the following morning in the chapel. Richard Crawford, Dad's friend, was his best man; his wife was Mom's matron of honor. Grandma gave the bride away. Enlisted men not on duty could attend the ceremony, but only if their nails, hands, and uniforms passed inspection. After the ceremony, they were dismissed, and the newlyweds walked with the other officers to their new home for the brunch reception.

The reception and toasts lasted less than an hour. My father had twenty-four hours' leave and a reservation at The Camlin Hotel in Seattle. With his mother-in-law in tow, Dad took Mom on the ferry to the mainland. The best man and his wife accompanied them. They dined in the hotel's Cloud Room, and then, with a bottle of Scotch, they retired to my parents' room for a nightcap. Dad said it was the worst mistake of his life. After two rounds, he signaled to Richard to escort his mother-in-law to her room. "She wouldn't budge and nursed her drink for another hour. Finally, she got the hint."

The next morning, after breakfast, the Crawfords hopped the ferry back to the island. My parents accompanied Grandma to the train station. They didn't wait to see her off. They rushed back to the hotel and caught the last ferry that night. A honeymoon is no excuse to be AWOL.

CHAPTER 5

"Reprieved on The Scaffold With Only a Rope Burn"

"Over here!" Rachel's voice rings out from the line of traffic. She pops the trunk, and I throw in my suitcase. A car behind us honks his horn; he can't leave until we move. I give him a withering look and hold out my hands palms up. "Give us a break."

I sit in the front seat and lock my seat belt. Rachel maneuvers among the cars picking up passengers. "What was his problem?"

"We wasted five seconds of his precious time." I don't speak any more until the Friday traffic clears and we're on the exit road from the airport. "Thanks for picking me up."

"I swapped days with Louise so I could come in. I'll take her shift tomorrow."

"I missed you."

She bends her head toward me so I can kiss her.

"I missed you too. How did everything go?"

"Fairly well considering."

"That sounds ominous. What happened?"

"Leslie and I had to talk to them again about their drinking."

"I knew it. I had a feeling that was the problem—"

I cut her off before she gets started. "Leslie and I think they understand they'll be in serious trouble if they don't stop."

"We can only hope," Rachel says, unconvinced.

We travel a few more miles before Rachel brings up a new subject. "Your boss called this morning. He expected you'd be in today."

"I sent him an email that I'd be out all week with a family problem."

"He wants to see you first thing Monday morning."

"That gives me the weekend to clear up any remaining issues."

"The same ones as last quarter?"

"We never have the same problems. We get a new set every time. What Ed doesn't understand is we have no control over most of the data loads."

Rachel pats my hand. "Remind yourself what it would be like if you weren't in charge."

While we're getting ready for bed, Rachel says, "Your boss is rather a cold fish."

"What makes you say that?"

"Considering I've never met him, he might have taken a moment to introduce himself. When I told him you weren't here, he asked to leave a message."

"Now you know what I put up with every—"

"I could have been the cleaning lady for all he knew. Does he even know you're married?"

"Good question. I don't know. The few conversations I've had with him were strictly about work."

I wake up in the middle of the night, which is disconcerting because I normally sleep until the alarm clock turns on the radio. I fumble for my glasses to see the illuminated time. Ten after three! I try to fall back asleep, but I can't stop thinking about work and Ed's message: "Meet me first thing Monday morning." His request isn't unusual after my being away for a week, but in the early-morning darkness, I can't help but think it ominous.

On Monday I leave early for work, allowing for any jams in the rush-hour traffic, but the commute isn't a problem. I've forgotten that people are on vacation. I forgo buying coffee at my building's cafe, deciding to wait and buy one after my meeting with Ed when my stomach should be more settled.

At my desk I review Friday's report of outstanding problems compiled by the managers of the graphic design, data load, and data integrity teams. After prioritizing those requiring immediate attention, I send emails to each team leader. We'll meet later to collectively prepare an action plan.

I receive the bad news when my second-in-command arrives carrying her coffee and daily chocolate-covered doughnut. Emma pulls her hair back into a severe ponytail that gives me a headache whenever I see her. She's of medium height and constantly experiments with one diet fad after another. Last month she told me she was making an appointment for a gastric bypass. She's tough on the staff when they make mistakes or when they ask the same questions month after month, but she's quick to praise an employee for work well done.

"Have you seen the great pooh-bah yet?" she asks.

"We meet at nine."

She looks at her watch. "That gives us ten minutes." She takes a bite from her doughnut and washes it down with a mouthful of coffee. "There was a big uproar Thursday with Andy's performance sheets."

Andy is the nickname of Andrea, who is a designer in the graphics department.

"She was testing a new version of the single sheets with old data, but in the rush, somehow last month's data was accessed for the production run…"

By now I have my head in my hands. "Don't tell me. And the incorrect sheets went to the printers. Why didn't Compliance catch the error? That's what they're paid to do."

"Compliance was backed up and didn't catch the error until Friday morning." Emma is often in conflict with Compliance. "The sheets were rerun, the review was completed by three, and emailed to the printers… yada, yada, yada… The printer worked overtime on Saturday at time and a half and sent them off to the post office by seven. A day and a half late, but no other complaint expected from users."

I throw my head back, exposing my throat. "Reprieved on the scaffold with only a rope burn around my neck. And the cost of all this is…?"

"That will be totaled up today."

"No wonder Ed wants to see me." I sigh, shaking my head. "I've got to find a new job."

"Maybe you'll have to—"

I sit up in shock. "What? Did you hear something?"

"No, no. You're safe. But a rumor is circulating there's a company-wide restructuring plan in the works. But don't worry. What would they do without you?"

"You mean no one wants my job?"

Emma looks at her watch. "Better get your ass in gear. It's after nine."

The meeting isn't as bad as I feared. Ed doesn't hear about everyday problems that occur each month, and he actually says he believes the quarter-end process is improving. "I suppose you've heard about last week's delay."

"I was briefed by Emma just now."

"Good. Emma took the lead on coordinating the process. I'm impressed by her work. She kept me in the loop." He refers to a paper on his desk. "But I want to discuss another subject."

I've never been comfortable when a conversation pivots on the words "another subject."

"This information must be kept secret. Next week Tom will announce his retirement."

I react with surprise. At fifty-eight, Tom is only five years older than me, and I certainly can't imagine retiring. Rachel and I are still paying off Jennifer's college loans, and Jon is only starting school this year in Japan. Any extra money—if any—is deposited in our 401(k)s.

"His leaving isn't a complete surprise considering his disagreements with the VP," Ed continues. "Tanya has been planning for his departure and has decided to reevaluate the organizational structure of her division. I wanted to give you a heads-up that Tom's department will probably be split into two entities."

He says no decision has been made concerning personnel changes, but that I'm in the running for one of the two vacancies. He anticipates four candidates will be considered.

He acts like the conversation is over, but when I rise to leave, he stops me before I reach the door. I'm shocked when he says I should make a note in Andy's personnel file.

"I don't think that's necessary. It would hurt her chance for promotion." I try to keep my voice calm and reasonable. "She's our best designer, and the team look to her for advice and solutions. The quarter-end process will suffer if she decides to leave. And she's the most efficient person to handle the one-off rush jobs that upper management always asks for."

"Let's discuss this more tomorrow." He looks at me with an enigmatic smile. "I'll review her performance reports before making a decision."

Although he isn't pleased by my opposition, his temporizing leads me to believe his decision isn't engraved in stone or he's ambivalent about the idea to begin with.

That evening over dinner, I discuss Ed's news about the new vacancies. Rachel immediately assumes I'll be promoted. "It's about time you got a break. I've always thought you should be more forceful making a case for promotion. You've said it yourself that other employees your age have moved up the ladder."

Rachel reiterates this view from time to time. I've learned she's not complaining that I've been unsuccessful. Her concern is my salary: we need to save more income to retire comfortably. So, I listen to her, avoid feeling irritated, and let the subject roll off my back.

In the two months after my trip, Dad starts calling once a week. I'm surprised at first because in the past we only talked on the phone every two or three months. I wonder what's caused the sudden interest. My first instinct is a cynical one: what does he want?

Rachel has an innocent reason for his calling more frequently. "Did it ever strike you he might have enjoyed seeing you? Maybe he wants to renew the connection between the two of you."

"Maybe he's buttering me up for help with future crises?"

"Mark, that's beneath you. He's in his eighties. Give him a break. He's old and probably regrets the distance between the two of you."

"That ship left a looong, long time ago."

"It's not like it's been a one-way street. You cut yourself off effectively. I know you had differences with him when you were growing up—"

"The problems were more than differences. When you're seven years old, you don't write off anything as a difference of opinion."

"I'm not trying to minimize your feelings, but are you going to hold on to them until he's dead? You won't feel any better, and you'll have lost your chance to do something."

The telephone rings, and Rachel answers it. "Hi… How are you two doing?… He's right here. Just a minute." She hands the receiver to me, trying not to laugh, and mouths, *"Speak of the devil."*

"Hello? How's everything going?"

Apparently not well.

"Mark. It's Dad. Mother fell down the stairs this morning."

"My God, did she hurt herself?"

Rachel turns from the sink. She frowns. "What happened?"

I wave my hand to say, *I'll tell you in a minute.*

"Is she in the hospital?"

"No, no, she wasn't hurt. It's all Snowflake's fault. That damn cat was sunning herself on her favorite spot at the turn in the stairs. Mom was coming down carrying a pillow instead of holding the banister. When she saw Snowflake, she nudged the cat away with her foot, but inadvertently stepped on her tail. I was sitting in the living room, and the first thing I heard was the cat yowling. Mother lost her balance and fell down the entire flight of stairs. Just as I reached her, the upstairs-hall curtain rod crashed with the cat hanging from the drapes. All hell broke loose."

I'm listening in stunned silence while Rachel tries to get my attention. I mouth the words, "*Mom fell.*"

Rachel closes her eyes and shakes her head. She whispers, "Not again."

"Did the pillow help cushion her fall?"

"No, she dropped it at the top of the stairs. I'm thankful the front door was closed."

"How so?"

"Your mother would have rolled off the front porch."

In the background, I hear Mom calling Dad. "Tell him I just relax. I go limp. That's why I don't hurt myself."

"Let me speak to Mom."

When she gets on the line, she repeats her news. "I just relax. I go limp."

Mom has never won a raffle or lottery in her life, but she's survived every tumble without breaking a bone. Maybe learning to ride a horse at summer camp taught her how to topple off gracefully.

I tell her to be more careful, but before she can answer, Dad's back on the phone.

"How did she get up?"

"She sat on the first step, and I was able to pull her up." Then to my surprise, Dad says, "I'm afraid she won't be so lucky next time."

Imagine that. I agree.

I hang up and tell Rachel what happened. "I've thirty-five-year-old friends who've broken a wrist or a leg falling down in their living rooms," she says. "Call your sister and make sure you got the complete story."

When Leslie doesn't answer, I leave a message that Dad called me.

Leslie phones me at work. "Aren't they the limit? I can't believe she wasn't hurt, but I stopped by just to make sure. I don't know if they were drinking. I hope not. She was lucky, but I told Dad she's used eight of her nine lives. She'll break her hip one of these days."

"They can't stay in that house and climb up and down those stairs every day."

"Mark, I've been after Dad for months to move to a place in the center of town. He wouldn't hear of it. Suddenly he decides they'll move to an apartment. Did he tell you?"

"No, but congratulations. You convinced him at last—"

"The hell I did. If you ask Dad, he's the one who came up with the idea." I hear the frustration in her voice. "I know I shouldn't complain. It was easier than I thought it would be, thanks to Snowflake, my hero. By the way, they're sending out their laundry."

Once Dad decides to do something, he's full steam ahead. Two days later Leslie calls to say Dad's hired a neighbor's daughter, a realtor, to sell their house. The following week, he's picked out an apartment in Arlington Center, opposite the high school. Their house sells four days later, and Dad signs the apartment lease.

I'm happy our parents are finally taking steps to make day-to-day life less dangerous. Dad schedules the move for the end of October. I buy a plane ticket to fly home six days before the move. The next quarter-end will be finished. This time, Rachel will arrive four days after me.

I remind Rachel that often a child is too young and lacks the experience to view a moment in the correct context. One might argue that forty-five years later, I could see the exchange for what it was and get over it. But sometimes life doesn't work that way, and the past remains unfinished.

The incident is one I'll never forget. Many people, if they knew, would consider it insignificant. I have done so myself. And then I think of the young boy, seven years old, climbing the stairs to bed. His mother comes up to kiss him goodnight, but he hardly notices because his mind is in a turmoil thinking about what his father said. This memory has had repercussions all my life.

Although I'm two years older than Leslie, we went to bed at the same time. One evening, she and I were playing on the sunporch next to the living room. I was sprawled on the floor, working on a crossword puzzle, straining my eyes. I needed glasses, but I'd memorized the eye chart and passed every year until fourth grade when I got the lines confused.

Mom looked up. "Okay, you two, time for bed. I'll come up to say goodnight after you've brushed your teeth."

Leslie jumped up and kissed Dad, who was reading the evening paper on the couch. She always wanted to be the first in the bathroom.

I put the crossword away. When I leaned over to kiss him, Dad pulled away. "Aren't you a little old for this?" His words stung, and I blushed as I straightened up. Without meeting his eyes, I mumbled goodnight and went upstairs.

I was surprised and confused. I didn't care about kissing him goodnight. Doing so was simply part of the nightly routine, something I did without thinking. Instead, it was his stern rejection that hurt. If he'd said, "Let's shake hands instead," or "I don't think"—chuckle, chuckle—"we need to kiss anymore," I might have laughed with him, gone upstairs, and forgotten it.

The scene—Dad sitting on the couch, wearing his glasses, reading the paper, the lamp shining beside him—was burned like acid in my brain, an image I'll see at death when my life flashes by. Did I suspect at the time how indelible those five seconds would be? No, I was more worried about myself, wondering if something, deep down, was wrong with me.

His rejection cut like a cold knife. Was he repelled, inferring I was a sissy and not worth his consideration? Or was he reacting to some other concern? I don't know. That's what happened, and it dug deep. I can't remember how many nights I thought about his words. I worried about so many things, it probably soon faded to an occasional thought. What I do remember is that I wouldn't kiss him again for half a century.

About this time the nightmares began. I'd lie in bed, eyes closed, thinking about the next day or the next week, searching and inevitably finding something to worry about. Then I'd become aware of the slightest sound. Every thought crumbled away as I opened my eyes a crack to watch the attic door, so solid in daylight, but at night, indistinct, its features a lighter shade of black.

The wind blowing through the attic vents and rattling the door was no longer necessary. Now even a single creak of the wooden stairs triggered the first whispers of fear that slowly blossomed into a numbing terror. The creatures crowding behind the door of my earlier dreams no longer had to bump against it or moan to one another. I now knew there was only a single creature on the attic steps, causing the stairs to crack when it changed position to stretch, slowly test the doorknob, or lightly scrape a claw, testing for the slightest weakness in the door.

A draft of cold air whistles into the room. The door is open! I stare at something slowly filling the doorway. It grows larger than the door. Despite fearing what might be there, I strain to see if I can tell what it is. It becomes larger as it moves down the steps. With each halting movement, the figure grows more visible and solid.

At the bottom of the stairs, it stops and looks around as if not sure which way to turn. When it bumps against the end of my bed, I'm terrified to see my father dressed in a business suit, his jacket off, and his sleeves rolled up. His eyes are black, and they stare at me over the newspaper he's carrying. Slowly lifting a finger to his lips, he signals to say nothing. Two more steps, and he looks down at me. My arm trembles as it stretches out from under the blanket and points to the closed door of my room. A smile barely glides across his lips behind his finger. He doesn't acknowledge my help but glides up to the door and, fading, passes through it.

Each time the vision appeared, I'd wake later in the night. After tentatively passing my hands down the sheet, I was filled with shame. I'd rock in my bed, the headboard knocking against the wall I shared with my parents, my voice moaning in time with the rhythm of the bed. "Ma-a-a-a-a-m-e-e-e-e."

I'd wet my bed.

CHAPTER 6

"The Burning Sled in the Furnace At Xanadu"

I arrive late in Boston Tuesday evening. Leslie and I told Dad we'd come tomorrow to help him clean out the attic. I leave the motel early; I want to look over the things he plans to throw away.

Except for my mother's teacup collection and my father's trains, my parents have never been sentimental about their belongings. Neither books nor knick-knacks, clothes nor furniture, not even most photographs. Over the years, I've rescued several belongings from their trash and spirited them away.

Once when Rachel and I visited years earlier, I found several boxes in the hall. A quick look determined one box contained china. "What are these?"

"They're for Bill Stevens," Dad said from the living room. "He sells stuff at flea markets."

I unwrapped several pieces in newspaper and found china plates and a teacup. "Isn't this Grandma's Limoges service? You're giving this to him?"

"He's selling it for us. He'll take a seller's fee and give the rest to us."

In another box, I found serving platters and tureens carefully surrounded by old towels. "How well do you know him?"

Dad came into the hall. "The Langfords down by the lake use him to sell their stuff."

"Did you tell this Bill Somebody to set a minimum price before he sells it?" I didn't like treating my father like a child, but a potential scam was obvious. Either he was becoming more careless in old age or he had no interest in possessions that were no longer relevant to his life.

"He said he'd get us a fair price," Dad defended himself, although he sounded doubtful. "But I hadn't thought of that."

"I'll research some of the pieces before he takes them," Rachel said.

"If you want them, be my guest." Dad wanted to wash his hands of the entire business.

And that's how we rescued Grandma's seventy-nine-piece Limoges dinnerware from oblivion.

Leslie pulls into my parents' driveway as I'm walking to the front door. I hear a crash from the other side of the house. The attic window is open, and Dad's pitching out belongings he no longer wants. I turn back and meet Leslie at the front steps.

"Dad's started the heave-ho out the window."

"I'll get up there and see what he's throwing out."

Leslie makes us both a cup of coffee and then climbs up to the attic. I visit Mom in the living room. "Would you like me to make you a cup of tea?" I ask, leaning down to kiss her cheek. "Oh, you already have something." I sit beside her, noting she isn't in a responsive mood. "Today's the big day for cleaning the attic. I wonder what we'll find up there."

She arches her brow and sighs. "Your father never consulted me."

"About what? Something he wants to throw away?"

"No, the apartment."

"He said he took you over to see it, didn't he?"

"Yes, he did," she snaps, "but only after he signed the lease."

"The apartment sounds lovely. It'll make things easier for you, don't you agree?"

"I don't mind moving. That's not the point." Her voice trembles. "I have to give up Snowflake."

That damn cat almost killed you, I want to say, but in fact I'm surprised management would forbid a cat in the apartment. "How would they know if you snuck her in?"

"That's what I thought, but Dad said no. They'd make us give her away."

I almost say, "We'll take her," but I catch myself in time. Although I'm eager to clear away any objection to their moving, I know Rachel wouldn't be happy. Our last cat ran away during a hurricane, and Rachel doesn't want another. Maybe Leslie will adopt her.

"I should go upstairs to find out what's happening in the attic. We'll talk later."

Dad is throwing everything onto the side yard. Fortunately, he's fanatical about financial and legal papers, so I'm not worried important documents will take the plunge. I want to look over what he's thrown out, but for my own safety, I'll wait until we're finished.

Rolls of vaguely familiar wallpaper, remnants of old rugs, a package of unopened insulation, books black with mildew, their covers hanging by threads all take flight. Everything goes. Finding my Boy Scout uniform and Leslie's tap dancing costume in a trunk provides a moment of humor to dilute the sadness of watching our childhood dive headfirst from the third floor. The pile below is a social archeologist's wet dream.

Leslie rescues a box of loose photos. Most of them appear to be stuck together. Obviously, a damp attic is no place to archive photographs. She hopes to find Mom's wedding dress, but Dad hasn't the foggiest idea where it is. She asks Mom about it at lunch but gets a shrug. "It's up there somewhere." When Leslie says we don't see it, Mom squints in thought, then throws up her hands and shrugs. "Beats me."

I discover a stained army knapsack wedged between the wall and a broken floorboard. AHERNE is stenciled across the canvas torn in several places. Looking inside, I discover a packet of letters held together with an elastic band.

"What are these letters?" I ask, holding them up. The elastic band breaks, and the letters fall back into the knapsack.

Before I can look at the envelopes, Dad swipes the knapsack out of my hands. "I'll take care of these." He places the knapsack beneath a desk lamp and fan he's put aside.

Three letters fell through a rip in the canvas. When his back is turned, I slide them with my foot beneath the wooden wardrobe.

For the rest of the morning, I keep my eyes on the knapsack but have no opportunity to see anything more.

Before lunch, Dad carries a metal trash can out of the garage, pours lighter fluid on the knapsack and, shielding himself with the trash-can lid, throws a match into the barrel. There's a *whoomp*, a whoosh of air, and a blast of flames. Scraps of burning paper float up in the draft and fall harmlessly onto the grass.

"Who are the letters from?"

I'm concentrating so hard watching from the dining-room window, I'm startled by Leslie behind me. "I didn't get a chance to look at them, but they're probably from Mom after Dad left for Oregon."

"They must be racy considering how quickly he grabbed them from you."

Watching the flames die back, I decide not to tell Leslie I rescued three of them. Dad stirs the contents of the barrel, covers the can with its lid, and drags it back into the garage. "Those letters remind me of the burning sled in the furnace at Xanadu. Dad's Rosebud."

Leslie frowns. "What?"

"The sled in the movie *Citizen Kane*. A piece of our parents' lives gone up in smoke."

CHAPTER 7

"DON'T LET YOUR FATHER DROWN"

After lunch Dad backs the car down the driveway. He stops when he sees me. "Dump the attic junk into the barrels I've put beside the deck. The town collects the trash tomorrow, and I want that stuff gone. I won't be long." He rolls up the window, backs into the street, and stops again. The window comes down. "There are two cartons in the dining room with odds and ends Mom and I won't take with us. They can also be dragged out to the curb. We don't want the neighbors to see any of it in the yard sale."

Intrigued by what he wants to keep out of sight, I examine the contents of the two cartons in the dining room first. Nothing the least bit scandalous. It's only the detritus found at the bottom of drawers and closets in the bathroom, kitchen, and family room. Disappointed, I carry the boxes outside and then tackle the pile under the attic window.

Back in the house, I find Leslie and Mom looking through some jewelry stored in a wooden box. "See what Dad found on a shelf in my closet. I'd forgotten all about it."

"Where did Dad run off to?" Leslie asks.

"I haven't the slightest idea. He didn't say where he went or when he'd be back."

Leslie grabs her pocketbook and coat. "Okay, Mom. I'm off. I'll be back later to make dinner. Mark's here if you need anything."

I kiss my mother. "Hi, beautiful."

"I am not." She smiles at me, her white hair catching the light. She closes her bathrobe at her throat.

"You are to me. Now what are you and Leslie doing with this jewelry?"

"I want to make sure I don't give away any pieces the grandkids might want."

"Isn't this a cameo I bought for you when I was studying in England? If I remember correctly, the postage and insurance was almost as much as the cameo."

"You sent it to me for Mother's Day. I must save that." She puts it aside, away from the costume jewelry destined for the yard sale.

"Here are some cufflinks that were my father's." Mom holds up two iridescent mother-of-pearl links that look too small to hold anything together. "Do you think Jon would like them?"

"We can ask him when he gets back from Japan."

Mom hands them to me. "You keep them for now."

I smile, wondering if anyone wears cufflinks today. Maybe if you wear a tux.

"I found it," Mom says. "I knew it had to be in here somewhere. This is the cross Jennifer received for Christmas from Grandma when she was six. She lost it at some point, and I found it years later hanging from a splinter of wood at the back of her bureau."

"Remember when Dickie told Leslie she was going to hell?" Dickie was one of our Catholic cousins. "He terrified her by saying all Protestants go to hell, like it or not. She ran looking for you. '*I don't want to go to hell.*'" I mimic a young girl's voice then change to the deeper Dickie voice. "'*You will, and you won't get out.*' He chased her around the house. No wonder she was sobbing when she found you."

Mom stops rummaging in the jewelry box and looks up with confusion. "When did you see him? Where's he living?"

"No, Mom. He died three years ago. Seeing Jennifer's cross made me think of him."

"He was a rascal. Always in trouble." She sits back with a sigh against the couch cushions. "I made your father tell his sister to stop Dickie from upsetting Leslie."

"What did I have to tell my sister?"

I jump at Dad's voice. I never heard the car. "We didn't hear you come in."

"Charles, I hate it when you sneak up on me."

He remains standing and opens his shopping bag. "Guess what I bought?" Without waiting he removes two hats from the bag.

Mom and I speak at the same time. "What are those?" Her tone is one of curiosity; mine is one of unease.

"Sailor caps."

"What on earth…" I turn toward Mom. She looks like she has no idea what's going on.

Dad puts one on his head. The cap is made of a soft, dark-blue cloth with a narrow, shiny-black visor. When he turns his head, I see a red ribbon sewn on the back. What navy did the cap represent? None I recognized unless it was made for sailors on the H.M.S. *Pinafore*.

"Try this on. See if it fits." He tosses the second cap to me.

My mouth has gone dry. I know what's coming. I catch the cap and place it on my head.

Dad looks at Mom. "Mark is taking us sailing for one last spin before I sell the boat."

"I am?" I speak with disbelief. "When was this decided?"

"I think it will make a nice family outing," he says.

"Who's going?"

"We're all going. I'll ask Leslie when she's back this afternoon."

I'm not surprised he'll *ask* her and not take her participation for granted. I doubt she'll enlist. In fact, I'm sure she won't. Leslie and I never enjoyed sailing. "Mom can't get in the boat even if we help her. This is not a good idea."

"Nonsense, it'll be fun. Meanwhile, you can bone up on your sailing skills."

What sailing skills does he think I have? My sailing prowess won't even get the boat away from the dock. He's either delusional or deliberately forgetting the past. Or most likely his scheme is to simply get my goat.

"Come out to the garage. I need help hooking up the trailer." He strides out of the living room humming what I assume he thinks is a jaunty sailing tune.

I shake my head, feeling like I've woken from a bad dream only to find myself living it. I'll go AWOL before I step into that boat. I look at Mom. "Why is he doing this? Is he serious, or is this an elaborate prank to upset me?"

She presses her lips together into a long thin line and shakes her head sympathetically.

In the garage, Dad is removing tools, old paint cans, and scrap lumber from the bed of the trailer.

"I'll do that," I tell him.

"I cleaned out most of it yesterday. You can sweep it out when I'm done."

I step back from the trailer. "This tire looks flat." I walk around to the other side. "This one's not much better."

Dad puts down a box of wooden wedges. "All they need is air." He takes a look. "Hmm… guess I might have to buy a new tire."

"Why don't you take the trailer and let them put the new one on."

"They'll talk me into buying two of them."

"Maybe you should get two. You'll need a decent set if you want to sell it."

"Let me back up the car, and you put the trailer on the hitch."

Once that's done, Dad hooks up the taillights. "Yell when you see them turn on."

The lights are fine, and he drives off. I jog up the back steps and enter the house.

My father built two sailboats, the first one when I was in grammar school. He christened it *Sat'day Nite* since he admitted it resembled a bathtub. He spent hours in the cellar during one winter and in the garage the following summer. Even at an early age, I understood that building a boat was an impressive accomplishment. A minimum of enthusiasm on my part might have brought us closer, but my indifference was impenetrable.

One evening before bed, when I went to the basement to say goodnight, I asked how he made wood bend as it neared the bow. He gave me a detailed explanation, and soon I could barely keep my eyes open. Leslie and I learned that asking an engineer a question would unleash a lengthy explanation.

Family sailing trips on the Upper Mystic Lake bored Leslie and me. We counted the minutes until we docked and were set free. Every time Dad circled the lake and approached the mooring, we held our breath, hoping this was the end, but all too often, he'd say, "The wind's picking up," and turn the boat toward open water for another circuit.

As far as I was concerned, the wind never picked up.

He tried to teach me to sail, but usually it ended with him shouting "You're letting the boom swing around too fast" or "To starboard. Not that starboard. The other starboard." I was self-conscious, and his criticism stung. Even when another boat sailed well away from us, I panicked, positive I was destined to hit it. Once the boon swung around and knocked me on the head, and I was convinced Dad had allowed it to do so deliberately. My nautical experience determined a future reluctance to board a sailboat.

Twenty-five years ago, Dad built his second sailboat. I doubt he's sailed it in the last ten years. Apparently now he plans a swan song for the day after the yard sale.

With Dad out buying tires I sit in the living room opposite Mom. "What's he up to?"

"About what?" she says with an innocent look on her face.

"He said he talked with you about sailing."

"He *told* me."

"Okay. What did he tell you?"

"He said you wanted to go sailing."

"I never said anything of the sort. I've avoided sailing ever since leaving home."

"That's not what he told me yesterday."

I push down on my knees to keep my legs from jerking up and down in anger. "And why did he waste money on those hats? They're ridiculous. We'll look like jerks. Is he losing his mind, or is he doing this to humiliate me?" Once I start ranting, I can't stop. "And that boat. It's twenty-five years old. He hasn't used it in years, and it'll probably leak like a sieve. We'll be lucky not to sink. I didn't fly here to drown in a rinky-dink lake."

Poor Mom. I take all my frustration out on her, and she's just as confused as I am. Tears fill her eyes. "Don't let your father drown." A tear slides down her cheek.

I sit beside her on the sofa and hug her. "Don't worry. Nothing bad will happen. I'll make sure he's wearing a life preserver."

Thinking my words would calm her, I'm shocked when she grips my sleeve and cries against my shirt. I must calm her down before Dad comes back, or he'll want to know what's happened.

"I have to pee now."

I hand her a napkin. "Dry your tears or you'll be leaking from both ends."

I help her stand, and we slowly reach the bottom of the stairs. I prepare myself for her weight, but Mom is already on the first step. She clings to me with both hands.

"Grab the bannister with your other hand." I grip the bannister on my side and haul the two of us up the stairs.

"You're better than Dad. He climbs too fast." She laughs. "You'd think *he* had to use the john."

"Mom, don't keep looking at me. Concentrate on the stairs. If you're not careful, you'll take another tumble."

"Don't worry. I just roll down. I don't hurt myself because I go limp."

"Let's not demonstrate that now. I have enough going on with Dad as it is."

We're watching a game show when Dad returns. "The dealer tried to sell me three tires. Said I needed a spare. He's always been a shifty so-and-so."

Leslie is late, so I make a green bean casserole with onion, beans, diced tomatoes, and hamburger, topped with mashed potatoes. Leslie arrives with profuse apologies and sets the table. When everyone is seated, I carry in the casserole.

"I made this when you were growing up," Mom says when I serve her. "It was your favorite."

"I remember. I looked up the recipe in your cookbook, but I could have made it from memory. I doubt it's as good as yours."

Leslie reaches for the basket of bread. "It's like old times with all of us around the table together."

Just like the old days but without the double martinis.

When we were in school, dinnertime was fraught with land mines. Our parents' relationship in the past was prickly and aggravated by drinking. They fought with a quiet anger and a strong dose of passive-aggression, filling the house with tension. The cause of an argument was often an innocent remark, but with liquor it often turned ugly.

Mom liked to tell a story, but she wasn't good at it. She'd often forget a significant detail and, in a fluster, would stick it in only to ruin the effect of her anecdote. If the story took a wrong turn, she'd go back and start from the beginning. Or halfway through she'd lose her nerve, wish she'd never started the story, and ask someone else to finish it.

Sometimes Dad would make a comment or corrected a minor detail, a distraction that caused Mom to lose her place. She'd stop talking and press her lips together so tightly you'd think her jaw was locked. She'd say nothing, but her eyes would dart between Leslie and me as if to say, *See what your father is doing?* If Dad tried to apologize or joke her out of it, she would double down, her silence louder than a scream.

Dad could be condescending. I don't believe he was vindictive, but there was something ready to be awakened, fueled by alcohol. He couldn't tolerate us getting the facts wrong or stretching the truth to "spice up" a story.

On the odd occasion Mom interrupted something Dad said at dinner, he'd become irritated to the point where he'd contradict her, roll his eyes, and exhale with a puff of impatience. At these times, Dad acted as if he'd done nothing wrong, which made Mom angrier because she could think of nothing else.

The result was a silence that neither Leslie nor I dared to break. Dinner would continue accompanied by the sound of silverware scraping plates.

Tonight, Dad eats his casserole quickly. When I ask him if he wants another serving, he says no and pushes his plate away. He clears his throat.

"Leslie," he says, turning to her. "Mark and I are going sailing the day after the yard sale. Just a couple of turns around the lake. I called the boat club, and they said I can use their ramp at a nominal fee considering I'm a former member—"

"That was a long time ago," Mom interrupts. "I'm surprised they still remember you."

Dad ignores her. "All they did was look me up on their computer."

I must have a look of disbelief on my face because Dad raises his eyebrows. "What? You don't believe they remember me? I was a paid-up member for years."

"I don't doubt they have your membership records, but all those years ago your information was on paper. Personal computers weren't even thought of back then."

He stares at me as if I don't know what I'm talking about. "They asked if I was still living on Lake Shore Road."

"Where did they think you lived?" Mom asks, not wanting to be left out of the conversation. "We've lived here ever since Mark was three years old."

Dad glances at her as if her question is too obvious to answer. I'm delighted that Mom remembers when we moved. Leslie reaches over and squeezes her hand.

"I'm looking forward to a couple of spins around the lake with the family on Sunday before Travis buys the boat early next month."

"Who's he?" I ask, suspicious that a stranger has taken advantage of my father.

"The nephew of the people who bought the McGhees' house."

"Don't forget I have a Sunday afternoon meeting with clients," Leslie reminds him. "They give a presentation Monday morning. I'll need to be at that too."

"You won't be here the day we move." Dad acts like they can't leave if Leslie is absent.

"I'll meet you at the apartment after my meeting and bring lunch."

"Then we'll sail Sunday morning and be back in time for your afternoon meeting." Dad gets up from the table and helps Mom onto the back porch.

I rinse the dishes, and Leslie fills the dishwasher. "When did the sailing trip come up?"

"The first I heard of it was this morning," I tell her. "Mom said he talked to her about it last night. Will you go?"

"Not on your life. Will the boat even float?"

I shrug. "Your guess is as good as mine. Dad wants help checking for leaks after I'm through in here."

"I'll take care of the dishes," Leslie says, waving her arms to shoo me from the kitchen. "You finish what you have to do with Dad. I hope he won't be too disappointed when I tell him the client meeting has been rescheduled earlier."

I knew she'd wriggle out of it. I walk out to the porch. "Okay, Dad. Let's finish up with the boat."

"We can wait and do it tomorrow. Besides, it'll be dark soon."

"We'll be too busy pricing everything for the yard sale."

Dad grumbles as he stands and gulps down his coffee.

I check the hardware on the mast and the boom, hoping it's rusty or missing. No such luck.

Dad hooks up the hose and fills a bucket. "Give the hull a good wash with a generous helping of bleach. Most of these stains will go away after scraping them with this brush."

I find a pair of old rubber gloves and pour on the bleach. I look away to avoid the fumes.

Dad removes the orange life preservers from the bottom of the boat. His preserver looks too large for him but perfect for me. My old life preserver will be suitable for Mom if she goes, which I doubt. But that leaves Dad without one. Leslie's and Mom's are too small for him. No worry, I think, isn't it a maritime custom for the captain to go down with his ship?

With the boat empty, Dad covers the bottom with two and a half feet of water. "We'll see if it leaks." The garage rafters and ropes holding the boat off the ground groan ominously from years of neglect. He struggles to rock the boat from side to side.

I help him, but the weight of the water makes moving the boat difficult. I also test for leaks by pushing down on the bow and sloshing the water to and from the stern. Then we wait. I'm hoping water will gush from a crack in the hull, but there's not even a drip.

"We'll leave it overnight just to be sure," he says.

I return to my bleach and water and brush away the years of mildew from the wooden sides.

Back at the motel, I have only enough energy to take a shower. Not even the purloined letters can convince me to stay awake. Lying in bed, I feel like every joint and muscle is aching.

I was never effective in standing up to my father. When I was a child, any opposition I verbalized was ignored, as if my point of view was insignificant. I learned at a young age to keep my disagreements to myself and endure whatever hand I was dealt. A psychiatrist once said that the older child of alcoholic parents constantly tries to keep everything running smoothly and to avoid conflict at any cost.

Growing up, this behavior became part of my personality, except in a few notable cases: the time when I refused to join my father's old scout troop in order to join the troop with my friends; and the time when I argued to go to England for junior year abroad. Dad was against my going. A girl in his high-school class had come back from studying in Germany with nothing but praise for Hitler. I asked if he was afraid the Queen was secretly preparing to declare war. But usually, if I didn't agree with him, I kept silent and did what was expected of me.

In grammar school I was also careful to follow every rule. Except once in sixth grade, I stood up for myself and challenged my teacher about a grade I received. I was unsuccessful, and it wasn't worth the humiliation. Nevertheless, the sixth grade was a turning point...

I have no energy to think more about it. I give in to my aches and pains and fall asleep.

CHAPTER 8

"I ALWAYS GET AN A"

The sixth grade wasn't business as usual. As hard as I tried, I was unable to overcome the teacher's perception that I was no more special than anyone else in the class. Miss Kuesik rarely called on me, no matter how high I raised my hand. She never asked me to run errands. When my first art project earned a C, I was indignant, and during the mid-morning break for milk and graham crackers, I went to her desk to complain.

I held up my work. "I always get an A in art."

Looking over her glasses, she pointed at the drawing. "What's that?"

"That's a cow." I was mystified that she didn't recognize it.

"Why is its head behind a tree?"

"I couldn't draw the head."

She positioned her glasses farther down her nose so as to see me better. She then pointed to four pictures displayed on the bulletin board. "Those are As and Bs."

Everyone in the class was listening to our conversation, made more enjoyable by eating their snack. All eyes turned to inspect the pictures.

She examined my work without saying a word and looked at me again. "Are you saying your work is as good as those?"

Of course I was or I wouldn't be standing there.

"You think your work is worth more than a C?"

I didn't care if mine was better or not. I wanted an A. I always got an A. I shrugged.

"It's not." She handed the picture back to me. "You'll have to try harder next time." And then she spoke the cruelest words: "You can't be good at everything."

I trudged back to my desk. I *was* good at everything. She was just too blind to see it.

Miss Kuesik was one of a new generation of teachers who began teaching after the war. My former teachers had been unmarried ladies of a certain age. To me, they were old. They wore dresses, black or grey, with high necklines. They used little make-up and permed their hair within an inch of its life. They preferred solid black leather shoes with laces and medium heels. These old-lady shoes, as Leslie and I called them, looked like they came with a lifetime guarantee. I knew how to charm myself into their good graces.

Instead, Miss Kuesik—young, unmarried, a recent graduate, with no tolerance for a teacher's pet—was immune to the charms of a prepubescent boy. At the time, I didn't understand that she judged males as marriage material and not as the son she wished she'd had. She had short, stylish blonde hair. She often checked her lipstick in a pocket mirror.

On the first day of school, I got off on the wrong foot. After the allegiance to the flag, we recited the Lord's Prayer. When Miss Kuesik, a Catholic, reached *"but deliver us from evil,"* she ended with an emphatic *"Amen."* Some of us continued with *"For thine is the kingdom,"* but we became self-conscious after *"and the power,"* then more stopped speaking— *"and the glory"*—now only two of us—*"forever and ever"*—and my final squeak, *"Amen."*

Had I earned her disapproval? For the rest of the year, I became a temporary Catholic and adopted the *Reader's Digest* version of the Lord's Prayer.

During the first week of December, the sixth-grade teacher assigned students each day to tape holiday decorations on the school windows. Years before, students had cut the decorations from sturdy, white cardboard—a Christmas tree, star, gas lamp post, swag of holly, and eight different carolers. Some singers faced forward and were featureless, while others cut in profile had noses and open mouths. The display followed a strict pattern, repeating itself around the school.

In the first grade, I was in awe of sixth graders, who seemed so grown up, ready to transfer to junior high the next year, a place as mysterious and frightening as the darkest jungle of the Amazon. Our teacher continued the lesson, but sitting in the row next to the windows, I listened to the two students whispering as they attached the cut-outs, working from the back of the room to the front. I wanted to do this and couldn't wait until I was in the sixth grade. When the students finished, the class erupted into loud applause.

On the first Friday in December, we waited for Miss Kuesik to read the decoration assignments for the following week. She reminded us that only those students with satisfactory grades would be selected, so I was confident I'd be one of the first chosen.

"These students will decorate the windows at the front of the school and those on the side of the building facing the town hall." After she read each name, the student clapped or laughed. I was not on the list. Surely Miss Kuesik had overlooked me when I should have been one of the first selected.

"The second group of students will be announced next Friday." That beam of hope helped overcome my disappointment.

At dinner that night, Mom asked, "Were you chosen to decorate the windows?" I think she hoped my selection would end my continual harping on the subject.

"No, I wasn't." I couldn't admit that the prestigious windows at the front of the school were already assigned. I didn't tell her the only windows remaining were those overlooking the playground and those at the back facing the woods.

"I'm sorry." Mom left the table to bring in dessert.

She was sorry? I had nothing to look forward to except a weekend of homework. All week, I dreamed about Friday. Each day, I suffered watching two students load a stack of white cut-outs and the heavy tape dispenser on a cart and leave the room.

The next Friday, Miss Kuesik stood at the front of the class with her schedule. The class was immediately quiet. Ten students would be chosen, but I suspected most of my classmates didn't have grades high enough to make them eligible. I settled back in my chair.

The windows at the back of the school were assigned first. I wasn't chosen. Only the school's side windows remained, but I would still be a sixth grader held in awe by the kindergarten or the first and second graders in those classrooms. Miss Kuesik read the next names on the list. By the time she reached the last day, I still hadn't been selected. Surely, I would be one of the last two assigned.

"Thursday's the end. We aren't decorating the kindergarten windows on Friday."

Class resumed. I was in a daze. At noon, when the class stopped to eat lunch at our desks, I'd lost my appetite. School ended at two o'clock. I walked home alone, stunned that my five-year-old dream was dead. There would be no next year.

I'll always be thankful to Miss Kuesik for cutting me down to size. I was a better person for understanding I wasn't as special as I thought, but I will never forget—or forgive—the consuming disbelief of not being chosen. This disappointment will be one more death-bed memory flashing through my mind at the end.

A simple history test, hardly worth studying for. Despite the lie I'd told Wendy, history was one of my favorite subjects. I always got an A. I had almost finished the exam and would be the first student to hand in my paper.

That question on the last page! I didn't know the answer. I read the question over and over, positive I'd read it wrong, then closed my eyes, trying to visualize the answer. Nothing. Panic prevented me from focusing. I completed the rest of the exam, but the thought of handing in my exam with a missing answer was unacceptable. I remembered reading the answer in the textbook and knew the exact page where I'd find it. Why couldn't I *see* it?

If I'd had to raise my desktop to get the book, I wouldn't have cheated, but our desks were open in the back. I reached in, touching each book, until I found one the correct size. I inched it out of the desk. The science text! On my second try, success. Leafing through the pages, I searched for the one I remembered. After several attempts, I located the answer.

I brought the test to the teacher's desk, relieved to be rid of it. Turning around, I found Paul St. Charles staring at me, a smirk on his face. When I returned to my desk, I saw him form the words, *I saw you.* I looked away, pretending to ignore him, but when I couldn't stop myself, I saw him mouthing the same words.

"Mr. St. Charles, do you have something to say to the class?"

Heads turned toward Paul. Frozen with fear, I stared straight ahead. What would he say?

He mumbled, "No."

Safe. For now.

"Have you finished your test?"

Paul blushed and looked down.

"I can't hear you."

"No." The word was a loud burst. He was angry now.

"Then I suggest you keep your eyes on your desk and finish it. Ten minutes everyone."

By the time I arrived home for lunch, I regretted what I'd done. I might have remembered the answer if I'd only relaxed. Too late I realized I didn't have to cheat. One wrong answer wouldn't affect my grade. I'd made a terrible decision and would have to live with it. Forgetting the answer shouldn't have mattered. But it did.

Returning to school, I didn't run ahead to walk with friends. I tried to convince myself that I'd nothing to worry about as long as Paul kept his mouth shut, but I didn't want to spend the afternoon wondering what he planned to do.

To my relief, Paul wasn't in class. While taking attendance, Miss Kuesik asked if anyone had seen Paul. No one had. When a student was absent, the principal was notified, and the secretary would call his home.

"Mark, take this to the office please."

I was flattered she'd picked me. Perhaps she'd graded the history tests already and chose me because I had the highest score. I left the room in triumph.

When I returned, the first person I saw was Paul speaking to Miss Kuesik at her desk. They both watched me as I took my seat. He'd told her!

Instead, Miss Kuesik said, "Bring a note from home tomorrow. Don't be late again."

After school, Paul sauntered behind me down the street. "I saw you cheating today."

"No, you didn't." But my guilty face betrayed me.

"You better help me with my book report, or I'm telling the teacher."

He left before I could respond. I didn't believe him. Paul was the last person to accuse someone of wrongdoing. The teacher often kept Paul after school for talking in class, passing notes, and, most importantly, peeking at someone else's paper during a test. Nevertheless, I was worried.

On Saturday, he stopped by with his book report. "Make it better."

I took it without complaining. He said he'd be back before dinner on Sunday, so he'd have time to copy it in his own handwriting.

"Now we're even," I said on Sunday when he collected his report.

He laughed. "We'll see."

I shrugged, not trusting my voice. My throat ached with the dull thumping of my heart.

When Miss Kuesik returned the reports, she stopped at Paul's desk. "Good job. I saw a great improvement in your work."

"Thank you, Miss Kuesik."

The snake! If I'd been brave enough, and if he wasn't bigger than me and if we weren't in school, I'd have punched him in the face.

That was only the beginning. For a month, my life was hell. Paul had a sadistic nature. I'm sure he killed small animals in his spare time. Every day, he caught my attention in class and mouthed the words, *I'm telling*. Sometimes he'd then walk to the teacher's desk. He enjoyed seeing the fear on my face. But he only asked to go to the bathroom, or see the nurse, or pester Miss Kuesik with a question that made her impatient. He didn't care if she reprimanded him. He already had the satisfaction of knowing I was miserable.

Soon Paul was the prodigal student, at least as far as his written reports were concerned.

The last straw was when Miss Kuesik praised him in front of the class. "I wish some of you would learn from Paul. He's been working hard to improve his writing, and it shows."

I seethed. Miss Kuesik had never congratulated me in front of the class. I was still angry when Paul gave me another paper to rewrite.

"One more, but this is the end."

"Just try it," he sneered. "By the way, keep up the excellent work."

Over the next two days, I completed his report. At enormous risk, I worked out my plan and looked forward to the results. Miss Kuesik returned the papers a few days later, but she skipped Paul. Instead, she asked him to stay after school.

He found me on the way home. "You double-crosser. You're in shit now."

He hadn't read the textbook and didn't recognize my improvements were incorrect. I also threw in a few misspelled words I knew he wouldn't notice. Miss Kuesik caught the spelling mistakes; she also knew what he'd written was nonsense.

"She gave me a D minus and suggested I rewrite the report for a better grade." He pushed me up against a tree. "This time you'd better give me an A, or else."

"No, I won't, because I'll tell her you've cheated on all your reports." I escaped past him. "Write it yourself."

His blackmail stopped, but I hadn't counted on my own conscience. I now had two problems to worry about: my original crime plus helping Paul cheat. Revealing this would ruin my reputation with Miss Kuesik. My former teachers would hear about it in the teachers' lounge. That was worse.

My peace of mind didn't improve over time. Paul lost interest in sadism, but the damage was done. Looking back now, I see that my greatest enemy was always myself. I still remember the agony of that year. I might be distracted over the weekend, but on Sunday night I'd assume the cloak of guilt, dreading the return to school.

One evening after riding through the neighborhood with friends, I returned my bicycle to the garage. Walking back to the house, I saw a light in the living room and the top of Dad's newspaper. I was cut off from my family. I didn't deserve to be loved. I'd be haunted by my mistake for the remainder of the school year. Maybe forever.

As June approached, I decided to come clean. If I didn't, I'd never be free of it. The safest way to tell Miss Kuesik was to arrive early before the other students arrived. But time was running out. While other students looked forward to summer vacation, I dreaded it. I couldn't live another day without confessing. My cheating had become an unredeemable sin. Confession and forgiveness are two blessings of the Catholic Church. If I'd been Catholic like my cousin, I might have been spared a year of worry and remorse.

The night before the last day of school, Mom stayed at the hospital overnight when Leslie had her tonsils removed. I slept at Grandma's. I told her I had to leave early the next morning. Her housekeeper made my breakfast, and I set off for the bus stop, faint from anxiety but also eager to lay down my burden.

Two boys were playing catch on the school playground. I walked to the door where every class lined up to enter the school. Locked! I looked in all the ground-floor windows but saw no one. Back at the door, I knocked as loud as I could. No one answered. Giving up, I began walking to the swings. The door opened behind me. A custodian stood in the doorway. "Were you the one knocking?"

I slowly nodded, wondering if I was in trouble.

"What do you want?"

"I need to go to my classroom to finish a project."

"Sorry, kid. No students allowed in the school until the first bell rings." The door closed with a crash. But today was the last day of school!

All morning, I watched the clock inch its way to twelve o'clock. Miss Kuesik collected our textbooks. She removed all the art projects from the walls for us to take home. We cleaned out our desks and threw away old papers, broken pencils, and eraser crumbs. Miss Kuesik placed all her plants in a box. When the bell rang, everyone lined up, except for me and Larry Fitzwilliam, who was repeating sixth grade. Some of our classmates frowned at us not joining the line. The teacher walked them down the stairs to the first floor.

Both Larry and I were too wrapped up in our own misery to speak. I kept wiping my palms on my pants. When Miss Kuesik returned, she acted puzzled to see me. "I'll speak to Larry first."

She sat at the desk in front of him. All I heard her say was, "Don't worry… it will be easier next year… have a good summer… see you in the fall." They both stood up, she patted him on the back, and Larry left the room.

"Mark? We'll talk on the way downstairs." In the corridor, she asked what was on my mind.

"I have to tell you something."

"Oh? What is it?"

"I cheated on a history test. I shouldn't have, but I did."

She said nothing for a moment. "You must be relieved to get that off your chest."

"I am."

"You've learned your lesson the hard way. Now go home and enjoy your summer. Good luck in junior high."

I left school light as a feather. The world was beautiful with the whole summer to read and play. My shoulders were unburdened, and my stomach was no longer twisted in a knot. I didn't look back.

I've driven by the Brackett School on Eastern Avenue a half-dozen times in the forty years since that day. Each time I pull over to park, my eyes rise to the windows in Miss Kuesik's classroom. I don't know whether to laugh or cry.

I wonder what Miss Kuesik thought during those last minutes. I doubt there was any *Goodbye, Mr. Chips* sentiment on her part. As she left me to turn her keys into the principal's office, she probably wondered, *What the hell was that all about?*

CHAPTER 9

"The Chore I Hated Above All Others"

I'm up early the next day, much to my surprise. I was so tired the night before, I expected to sleep half the morning. I wait in the motel's dining room until the busload of tourists ahead of me are seated. In the confusion I'm almost swept into the room set aside for the tour buffet. Instead I escape and enjoy a quiet breakfast, watching the early news.

Driving to my parents' house, I detour through Arlington Center and stop at the apartment building. Their unit is on the fourth floor. I introduce myself to the building custodian, who assures me the elevator is in good condition and inspected every year. "It's out of service during the annual inspection, but only for a couple of hours. We notify residents in advance to give them time to plan ahead."

"Another question. I'm surprised management won't allow residents to keep a cat in their unit."

The custodian looks at me like I'm speaking nonsense. "We allow cats. And small dogs that don't bark. It's the yappers and big dogs we keep out."

"Interesting. Thank you."

So that's Dad's plan. He's tired of the cat always underfoot, endangering Mom, and decided the move is his chance to be rid of it. He'll be lucky if Mom never learns otherwise.

Nine granite steps in an embankment lead from the back door up to the parking lot. That will be a problem for Mom. Dad should have found a building with no outside stairs, but he'd made up his mind and signed the lease.

He's sitting on the front porch with his coffee, reading the morning paper, when I arrive. I hear the trash-collection trucks grinding up and down the neighboring streets.

"You're early," he says, as I walk up to the steps.

"Woke up early. Any water leakage from the boat?"

"Not a drop." He rubs his hands together. "Have a cup of coffee and then give me a hand with the sail."

"I had enough coffee at breakfast."

I follow him to the cellar. The builder divided the basement in half with two rooms on one side for Dad's workroom and the laundry. The other half is the family room.

Dad's second passion is model railroads. His father had been a train engineer, and this was the genesis of a lifelong fascination. Over time, Dad added buildings, a turn house, and a water tower until the diorama grew too large for the family room. He solved the problem by breaking through walls and building shelves with tracks on multiple levels circling the perimeter of the basement.

I step carefully because I no longer remember the layout of the tracks. Tripping over a piece of wood lying on the floor, I reach out to steady myself, almost breaking off a section of track.

In the laundry room, he turns on the light. "The sail should be in here." He opens a warped wooden door three feet up the basement wall. "Remember how you crawled in here to collect oranges for Mother?"

Of course I remember. The chore I hated above all others.

A Florida company shipped us a crate of oranges every three weeks, which Dad stored in this cold, dark room called a root cellar. The room smelled of earth, oranges, and decay. When I climbed into the room, the low ceiling prevented me from standing upright, and I imagined spiders dangling from their webs, waiting to cling to my hair.

Sometimes an orange went bad, and my fingers pierced the black, moldy skin. I hated the stench on my fingers that took half a day to wear off.

Now I'm two feet taller and less athletic. I gingerly climb the wooden steps Dad constructed years ago. In the room, I'm bent in half and can barely turn in any direction. The room still smells of earth with a slight essence of orange.

The sail is the only object in the room and lies on a low table wrapped in a waterproof bag. I try lifting it. "This weighs a ton. We'll never get it up the stairs."

"Stop complaining and just pull it out. We'll haul it through the window."

I drag the bag off the table. It lands on the floor with a smack, and dust puffs in all directions. While Dad opens the window over the dryer, I drag the bag from the room. He ties a rope around it, fashioning a loop at each end. He still remembers his knots from scouts. Dad throws the other end of the rope out the window.

"I'll pull from outside," he says. "Keep it straight and don't let it buckle. At the end you'll need to lift the bag off the floor. Careful you don't bump the train tracks on the shelf."

He wheezes climbing the stairs.

"Are you sure you're strong enough?"

"I'm fine. I set up a pulley."

Hauling the bag out takes all our strength. There's a moment of suspense when Dad loses his grip and the bag teeters on the window frame, ready to fall back inside and crush me. Finally, the bag scrapes over the sill.

"We'll spread the sail on the grass after I take a breather." He heads for the kitchen, inspecting the rope burn on his hands.

While Dad is occupied, I return to the basement and inspect the damage caused when the bag slid sideways and knocked down a section of the countryside. The scene looks like Godzilla passed through. With a piece of wood, I prop up the part hanging on a hinge and lay two smaller pieces on top of the dryer.

I walk around the basement, remembering how excited Leslie and I were when Dad sent a train on its journey. Leslie and I ran from room to room to keep up with it as the locomotive raced through his workshop, past the furnace and hot-water heater, through the laundry room, across the top of the bookcase in the family room, and onto a large plywood platform with a river and bridges in the countryside, and buildings and homes in the town.

I was spellbound watching the train circling the mountain Dad built in the empty coal cellar. If the train was long enough, I saw the caboose disappear into a tunnel at the top at the same time as I saw the engine reappear from a tunnel at the base of the mountain.

My favorite section was the length of track running under the cellar stairs. If I stood on a chair and leaned against the bookcase, I could look through the hole and see the headlight of the oncoming train. In the darkness under the stairs, the red warning lights on the road crossing blinked and the rattle of barriers lowered into place. Finally, the locomotive burst out of the tunnel in a cloud of smoke, blowing its shrill whistle.

I look over the entire landscape. Dad's patience and skill renews a sense of awe.

Meanwhile, Leslie arrives and sets up her pricing operation on the back porch.

"Good morning," I say, coming up from the cellar. Holding out my hands, I wrinkle my nose to warn her they smell. "I need to wash before I can concentrate on a conversation."

"How's it going?" I ask when I return.

"It'll go faster once you lend a hand. How much longer will you be tied up with Dad?"

"I should be free after lunch. We have to unfold the sail and check its condition. Can Mom do anything to help?"

Leslie gives me a look that says, *Are you kidding?*

"Maybe she can stick on the labels."

"I tried that yesterday, and it was more trouble than it was worth."

When Dad comes from the house, he has a bandage on each hand.

"How deep is the rope burn?"

"Not bad. The bandages will prevent it getting dirty."

"Let me do the heavy work. Give your hands a rest."

I shake the sail from its canvas bag onto the grass. The rancid odor coming from the bag makes me gag. I gingerly pick up one end of the sail and feel a slimy coating of I-don't-know-what.

"Whew, that's unpleasant," Dad says as the smell from the bag wafts in his direction.

I spread the sail section by section on the grass. The canvas is stained with dark blotches of mold. The sail looks unexpectedly small given its weight.

"A day in the sun will help dissipate the odor of mildew." Dad wipes his hands on his pants. "Soapy water with bleach will take care of the stains."

I connect the hose and turn its nozzle to full blast. Once one side is rinsed, we pull the sail over and spray the other side. I wonder if scrubbing with bleach will reveal holes or other weaknesses in the canvas.

After lunch, I examine the sail. The scrubbing with bleach and the sunlight has minimized the areas with mold and water stains. No other damage.

When I climb the steps to the back porch, I find every table covered with items for sale. Leslie is behind the picnic table, sticking labels on the smaller items. Periodically she throws one of them into a carton labeled ten cents.

I'm quick to criticize my parents for having no sentimental feeling for their possessions, but for once I'm grateful. The yard sale and then the move Monday will be less traumatic.

"Making any headway?" I pick up a pair of ceramic bookends I used in my bedroom. Too lightweight, they couldn't keep heavy textbooks from falling over onto the floor.

Leslie's too busy sticking on labels to look up. I raise the tarp covering the smaller furniture that will be displayed in the children's section.

"Done," Leslie says with satisfaction. "Pricing is going faster now than it was this morning."

"I'm at your service. What can I do to help?"

Leslie gestures toward the tarp. "You can fold that up and start pricing the furniture. Dad began putting stickers on some pieces, but after we told him his prices were too high, I took them off." She nods toward the cellar. "At some point, ask Dad what he wants carried up."

Later that day, I find Dad in the garage where he's cleared a space to sell his lawn and woodworking tools. "I need help carrying the table saw up from the basement. If you give me a minute, I'll take it apart to make it lighter. I don't want a stranger down there messing with my train set-up. I haven't packed it yet."

"You're taking the trains to the apartment?" I'd expected he'd sell his train collection.

"I'm not selling them until I decide what can be set up in the apartment."

When did he last use them? I doubt they still run, but it's the only possession he won't part with. Everything else, except what's needed in the new apartment, is up for grabs.

"Why don't we do this? If someone wants to see the saw or the washer and dryer, you go with the customer, and I'll watch the garage."

"You'll do that?"

"It's better than trying to move something that heavy upstairs. One of us will break a leg if we try."

After finding a piece of cardboard for a sign, I locate a black marker on the back porch.

Leslie is pricing a hammock, still in its original box. "While you're at it, Mom wants a sign for the curtains and drapes. They need to be cleaned, so we can't ask much."

At six thirty, the evening is too dark to see what we're doing, and we move into the dining room. There's always one more thing that needs to be considered. At eight thirty, Dad calls it quits. Mom has fallen asleep on the couch, and he can hardly keep awake himself. Leslie and I help get them into bed.

"We'll finish the pricing tomorrow. Pray it doesn't rain," is Leslie's last statement before closing my car door.

Back at the motel, I place the attic letters on the desk. All three are addressed to Dad on Jason Street, where he and Mom lived from the end of the war until I was three years old. They weren't from Mom; she was living with him, so I rule out love letters. Who else would have written to Dad? Harriet, his mother, or Ruth, his sister? But the handwriting doesn't look feminine. I decide the letters must be from a friend he met in the service.

The first envelope has a three-cent, purple stamp displaying the Statue of Liberty. No return address. I try to read the postmark, but the ink from the rubber stamp is smudged. The postmark says "Fitc" with a date of "1949." Well after the war.

I remove the flimsy pages from the envelope. The date is 8/24/49, two months before my third birthday; the salutation is "Charlie." Is that Dad? It must be, but he always disliked Charlie and preferred Charles. I skim the two-page letter:

Charlie   8/24

Julie's pregnancy is proving difficult. The doctor ordered her to stay in bed. Birth is hopefully the first week in Oct. Julie's OK with the trip in Nov now that her sister said she'd stay with her while I'm gone. I've been the perfect hubby while she's been pregnant and she says I deserve time off. The trip is my furlough.

Anyway the trip is all set for the second weekend in Nov. Hunting lodges are hard to come by at this late date but I snagged a good one, I think. The two guys who run the lodge will act as our guides. We go up a day early so they can check our guns and make sure we're familiar with gun safety. Drinking is verboten. Meals in the lodge. Lunch will be packed for us every day.

The letter continues on the second page:

> The only accommodation they had was one room with bunkbeds but we'll have it all to ourselves so we should have lots of fun.
>
> On that subject I have some bad news although I'm not too surprised. Remember Steve who came with us ice fishing over a year ago? He was down in North Carolina on business. One night after work he was driving back to his hotel and pulled into a rest area to take a leak. The police

The rest of the page is torn off, and I'm left wondering who wrote the letter. I know Dad occasionally went hunting with a friend who sold us our dog. Is this the same person?

Turning my attention to the second letter, I discover it's an empty envelope. The postmark and date are illegible, but the handwriting is the same as on the first.

The third envelope is similar to the other two except in one respect: the postmark is clear: "Fitchburg" with a date of 11/30/47. I should have read this letter first:

Charlie   11/29

> Good to see you last month in Maine. Thank God for the two extra days to drive to and from East Millinocket. That's a long trip from Fitchburg.
>
> The 3rd weekend in Jan is definitely on. Let me know as soon as possible if you're able to come. If you can get Monday off, you can go up with me Friday night and leave your car at my place. I have all the fishing gear we'll need.
>
> Jerry is coming with his friend Steve. There are two bedrooms in the cottage so that will work. Told Jerry to limit the booze. The

last thing I want is to be up half the night with two drunks next door and a full day of fishing on the ice the next day.

Rick

Dad never talked about ice fishing. Maybe Mom will know who this Rick character is. I'll have to think of a way to question her without revealing that I've seen the letters. It would be just like her to say something to Dad. But will Mom even remember?

CHAPTER 10

"I Didn't Want You to Know"

The next morning, Dad is at the doctor's for his annual check-up. Mom and Leslie are upstairs looking through the box of photos recovered from the attic. After visiting for a while, I return to the kitchen to prepare lunch, opening a can of tomato soup and pouring it into a double boiler, then adding a cup of shaved cheddar cheese and a squirt of Dijon mustard.

Leslie comes down. "Mom's content looking at the photos. After we eat, I'll take her lunch upstairs." She looks in the pot. "Welsh rarebit. I haven't had that in years."

"It's one of my favorite lunches. Careful, it's hot," I warn her as I pour the rarebit over the toast on her plate.

"All in all, they seem to be doing okay now," Leslie says. "As much as I love having you here, I don't think you need to stay once they've moved."

"Is there anything you need done before I leave? Has Dad set us up as secondary health proxies for each of them?"

"He said he's taken care of that, but I haven't seen the paperwork."

"Will he be irritated if we ask to see it? It's not like I'm asking to see his will—" Another thought stops me. "He's made one, I hope."

"He brandished one around last year when I mentioned it."

"He's so touchy about his privacy, I'm reluctant to ask. In the past, he'd have all the paperwork in order, but the way he's been acting lately I wouldn't count on it."

"After you leave, I'll ask him where he keeps the documents. I don't want to tear the place apart in the middle of a real emergency."

"I once asked about their funeral arrangements." I shake my head. "You'd think I was signing him into a hospice. We need a frank discussion about their end-of-life plans."

"*That* will be a problem. He expects to outlive us all. I could call his lawyer."

"He'll say he can't discuss anything without Dad there." I rinse my coffee cup in the sink. "Which is what he should say, but it puts us back to square one."

"For someone so intelligent, Dad certainly has his head in the sand."

"Look, I'll list everything I can think of, and then we can start with the easiest ones first. He must get invitations from lawyers offering a free dinner if he listens to what they have to say."

"Like the seminar he attended about vacation deals? We know how that turned out. He'll say it's a scam and put his foot down."

"And that proves my point. He can be suspicious about one thing, but turn him around and he'll fall for a bad investment."

Leslie carries Mom's lunch upstairs and leaves to prepare a presentation for a client's meeting. She'll return later, and we'll finish the pricing for the sale.

After cleaning up, I hear Mom roaming around upstairs. I run up to make sure she's not coming down by herself.

Mom is leaving her room and, surprised to see me, acts guilty, as if she shouldn't be there. "I had to get some things from my bedroom."

"Leslie's left your lunch in here where it's warmer." Built over the deck at the back of the house, the three-season porch has wicker furniture, which adds a summery feeling even in winter. The cushions are soft and comfortable, and beside each chair, there's a side table and footstool. It's my favorite room in the house, although it wasn't added until my senior year in high school.

Mom points to the tray. "Can you bring that over here? After lunch, I'll read for a while."

I remain in the room and work on the newspaper's crossword puzzle. Mom is fidgeting over her lunch, and I wonder if we've forgotten one of her pills. I find her watching me with an expression that seems to say she'd rather I wasn't there.

"Are you okay? You seem restless."

"I am not." Her rebuke startles me. "You don't have to stay here with me if you have some work to do."

"Actually, I want to write up something for Leslie."

"Go then. I'll be fine up here. I promise not to come downstairs without your help."

"When Dad gets back, we'll put up the gate. I'll rest easier once that's done."

I glance at her before leaving the room. She's nervous about something. "You're sure you're okay."

"I'll just relax before reading."

At the dining-room table, I collect my thoughts and jot down a list of paperwork Dad should have. When I'm finished, I listen at the bottom of the stairs. It's quiet, but I assume she's dozed off over her book. I make a mental note to ask Dad when she last had her eyes examined.

My list for Leslie:

Will
Revocable Trust
Health Proxies
Power of Attorney
Cemetery Arrangements
Funeral Expenses

When will she have time to make sure all this is completed? And if she consults the lawyer, she'll need to take Dad. I think of the millions of people who have to learn the ins and outs about investments, social security, and Medicare to have enough money to retire. How many know what to do, and how many are victims of unscrupulous professionals?

I'm willing to help, but if Dad is determined to push back on everything I suggest, then I'll step aside. It's hard enough to do this for someone who wants help and won't resist.

All's still quiet upstairs. I decide to check on Mom now and not wait until there's a problem. She's reading her book. I smile and turn to leave when I stop and look again.

"Mom?"

I've startled her, and she quickly hides the cigarette. But she can't hide the haze of smoke, its smell conjuring a host of memories.

"Mom?" I enter the porch, feeling like a child who's interrupted an intimate moment between parents he shouldn't see. "Are you smoking?"

She stares at me with a guilty expression, the way I must have when I was up to some mischief. She shakes her head but can't hold her breath. Smoke pours out her nose.

I sit on the hassock in front of her. "I didn't know you'd started to smoke again."

She nods, still unable or unwilling to speak. I reach out to take her hands. "I'm not angry. I'm just surprised. Do they help you relax?"

"Yes."

At that moment I'm aware of two things. With her hands in mine, she's no longer holding her cigarette, and at the same time I see a curl of smoke coming from between the cushions. I pick up the cushion next to her, and the lit cigarette rolls free.

"My God. It's on fire." I speak more from shock than from a sense of danger. It's obvious the flame can be easily extinguished with a cup of water. "Don't worry."

I grab the cigarette and put it out on a glass coaster. In the bathroom I hunt for a cup but can't find one. The same with a soap dish. I find nothing to hold water. In desperation I fill my mouth and run back to the room. The smoke has stopped, and there's no fire that I can see, but I spray the cushions with the water from my mouth and take a deep breath.

Staring at each other, we laugh from relief. I move her to another chair and shake off the water beading on the cushion. Only a dime-size spot of singeing is visible.

"It was an accident," she whispers.

"I know it was. I certainly don't believe you wanted to burn the house down. Promise you won't smoke unless someone's around. I would have stayed up here with you."

"I didn't want you to know."

"Mom, I hope you're not afraid of me. I know I can be stern at times, but I love you and don't want anything to happen to you."

I replace the cushion, hiding the damage. "Good as new. No one will know. Let me help you downstairs. Bring the cigarettes if you want to."

"I don't want them now. Put them back in my bureau drawer."

On the way downstairs, I wonder if Dad has also started smoking again. I don't think of myself as the disapproving parent. Instead I think that, once again, I'm the disapproving son. I'll say nothing to Dad, fearful I might cause a tempest in a teapot.

Our parents smoked until their sixties. All our friends' parents smoked. Everyone smoked everywhere: offices, restaurants, airplanes, movie theaters, and hotel rooms. No one complained or questioned it. After the war, the tobacco companies suspected smoking damaged the lungs, but as capitalists only concerned with their profits, they concealed their findings. Leslie and I didn't like our parents' smoking, but not because either of us had asthma or breathing problems. We hated the smell and the smoke.

They each smoked more than a pack a day. One time when Mom ran out of cigarettes, she asked me to walk down Park Avenue with enough money to buy a carton of Camels at the corner drugstore. Since I was only ten years old, Mom wrote a note to the druggist stating I had her permission to purchase it. I didn't like this errand—the store owner always quizzed me—so I coerced Leslie and one or two friends to go with me for moral support.

On the way, we stopped at the Ben Franklin and examined the postage stamps displayed in glassine envelopes to find any we needed for our stamp collections. We hemmed and hawed at the candy counter, deciding what to buy. My favorites were Atomic fireballs and cough lozenges. Finally, we checked the revolving comic-book rack for new *Classics Illustrated*. We swapped dozens of them among friends. Nothing like these exciting stories were on TV.

Eventually, I couldn't put off going to the drugstore any longer. I trudged down the street, followed by Leslie and our friends in single file. Leaving our friends outside, Leslie and I entered the store. The bell hanging on the door was a sound I hated. At the register, I mumbled, holding up the note. The druggist read it and shook his head. "That's too many. I can't sell a carton to kids."

"But I have a note."

"How do I know your mother wrote it?" He saw our friends pressing their faces against the front window. "One of your friends could have written this."

"She did so write it." Although shorter and younger, Leslie was more defiant, especially when she thought a grown-up was unfair.

I was angry with Mom for putting me in this embarrassing position. A woman huffed impatiently behind us.

The druggist leaned over the counter. "Tell your mother to buy her own cigarettes."

Leslie burst into tears, as if he'd accused Mom of a crime. I took Leslie's hand, and we left. The woman behind us spoke loud enough for us to hear. "Imagine a mother sending her children to buy her cigarettes."

Too upset to try another store, we returned home empty-handed. Mom was irritated with the druggist, but after she heard what the woman had said, she never asked us to buy cigarettes again.

CHAPTER 11

BABY READY TO TRAVEL HOME, 1918

The sale is scheduled to open at nine, but by half past eight, dealers hover around the tables examining vases, lamps, china, and other knick-knacks.

Leslie sets up a patio table with calculator and notebook to record sales. "See that lady over there? She's got her eye on that ugly vase. When did ugly become a collector's item?"

"Actually, I think it's art deco, but don't tell Dad. He'll want to reprice everything."

Mom plops herself down on a lawn chair beside Leslie. "I got that vase as a wedding present. Never liked it. I'll guard the cash box."

I step closer to Leslie. "If you want, I'll snag that vase for you if she ever puts it down."

"Where would I put it? Let her have it. That vase has made her day."

Dad comes over. "Are we ready to raise the curtain?" He sees Mom. "Leslie, be sure to let people know that lawn chair is for sale. Okay, let's go. I'll be in the garage."

The dealers line up to pay for the items they've already picked up. In five minutes, they're gone, off to another yard sale. Leslie isn't happy. "I should have done more research. Three dealers didn't bother to bargain, so you know I priced the stuff too low."

Mom acts unconcerned. "I'd give them away for nothing."

There's a lull with only two women and a man looking over the tables. I prop up the signs about the draperies, the table saw, the washer and dryer, and the tools in the garage.

One woman claps her hands. "May I see the washer and dryer?" I walk with her to the garage. "My daughter is getting married in a month. How old are they?"

I tell her Dad has every owner's manual in a binder with serial numbers and purchase dates. He and the woman go to the basement, where I can see them through the window. On the way out, they settle on a price. "Let me call my daughter and make sure she wants them."

While she's on her cell phone, Dad rubs his hands together, proud of his first sale.

"Rachel and I are each buying a cell phone when we go home. It's high time we joined the modern world. Dad"—I try to get his attention—"you should buy one for the car in case of a breakdown." But he's too busy listening to the woman talking with her daughter.

The woman closes her phone. "My husband and future son-in-law will come by in an hour to move them."

I return to the front of the house, surprised to find a dozen cars parked on both sides of the road. People are lined up, waiting to pay. Mom helps by putting the purchases in boxes or bags, but she's agitated by the rush of customers. Leslie handles the breakable objects.

I help a man load four chairs from the dining room into his truck. My parents will keep the table and two of the chairs. The family arrives for the washer and dryer. While the son-in-law-to-be is in the basement, he decides to buy the table saw.

A woman stops me. "I'll give you thirty bucks for all the books. You can keep the *Reader's Digests*. I can't even give them away."

I pack the books and carry the carton to her car. When I return, I stack the condensed novels into a box labelled *FREE*. An hour later, the manager of a retirement village takes them. "If nothing else, they'll fill the bookshelves."

Dad is gleeful whenever there's a sale. He's happier the less he has. Unlike clearing the attic by chucking everything out the window, he now makes money every time something is purchased.

I'm despondent watching the familiar objects disappear. Our house is a theater, and one by one the props are removed from the stage. However, I'm not ambivalent when a man takes apart my bed and loads it into his station wagon. Good riddance! I hope the next child has happier memories.

Around lunchtime, the crowd thins, and Dad looks worried. Leslie reassures him, "People will be back around one." He and Mom go inside for lunch.

"We'll cut prices in half at three. Maybe earlier," she says. "That should clear out most of what's left."

Leslie counts the change and fills a roll with nickels. She puts an elastic band around the twenty-dollar bills and tucks them under the coin tray. "That's four hundred and eighty dollars in twenties alone."

"Where did those come from?" I point to two large coins that stick up above the quarters in the coin tray.

"The woman who bought most of the Christmas decorations. She complained that the weight of the coins was stretching her coin purse. I had to look at them to figure out how much they're worth. Only fifty cents. Not much considering their weight. Why wouldn't you change them for two quarters?"

She takes them out of the coin tray and hands them to me. I heft the coins; their weight is familiar. "I haven't seen coins like these since the fifties. If you don't mind, I'd like to keep them. Here's a dollar." I tuck the coins in the glove compartment of my rental car. I'm excited to look at them more closely tonight.

Leslie is cashing out a man who's buying the fire screen and andirons. When she's finished, she sits back with a sigh. "That's done. I'd call this yard sale a success." She closes the cash box. "I need to wash my hands before I eat anything. By the way, how much did Dad get for his train collection?"

"He's keeping it."

"All of it?"

"Yup."

At three o'clock, Dad announces that all items are half price. The shoppers quicken their search, afraid they'll miss the last bargain. They cash out and depart.

Dad ends the yard sale a half hour later. Two customers remain, still picking over what's left. Leslie heads inside to prepare dinner, while Dad takes an empty carton and brushes off the picnic tables, which we carry to the back of the house, each one with a label identifying the neighbor who lent it to us. The front lawn looks like the floor of a store at the end of a week-long, going-out-of-business sale. Despite my aching back, I pick up the debris, finding two quarters hiding in plain sight on the grass.

One of the women scurries around with her bag, picking up knick-knacks she once considered and put back. "I don't know what I owe," she says, coming over to pay. "I was never good at math."

I glance in her bag and pretend to weigh it. "Hmm… this feels free to me."

"Free? Oh, then I'll take another minute and find some more things."

I consider sitting on the front porch and letting her take whatever she wants, when the second shopper asks if I will give her a better price.

"How does free sound?"

"You've got yourself a deal." She heads for her car.

The first woman agonizes over two stuffed animals.

"Take all of them," I call to her, carrying over an empty bag. With my right arm I brush everything off the table and hand the bag to her. Happy with her bargains, she drives away, honking once and waving to say thanks. Another car coasts by, the driver looking to see if we're still open. When she sees us cleaning up, she picks up speed.

Dad takes the cash box inside to count the money. I finish clearing the tables.

At five thirty, Leslie announces dinner.

Dad comes into the dining room with the final results. "Seven hundred and ten dollars and thirty-eight cents." Sitting at the head of the table, he heaves a sigh of relief. "This is the first time I've sat all day except for lunch. And even then, I ate my sandwich standing up."

After the dishes are rinsed and put in the dishwasher, I still have an hour before I need to pick up Rachel. We retire to the living room to look at some more photos.

The most interesting is a framed photographic portrait of the Wisdom family with a date on the back of 1899. They're Mom's side of the family. The parents sit at a small table in a studio setting. Their son, Edward, is twenty-six, the oldest of the three children. Elizabeth stands to the right of her parents. Ellen, the younger daughter, is on the left.

Elizabeth had several beaus in her early twenties, but her aloofness and a sense of propriety had not encouraged a passionate proposal. Shortly after the picture was taken she fell in love with Walter Cargill, a recent engineering graduate from the University of Maine.

When Walter visited her family, he met Ellen, younger and prettier, with a captivating figure. Unlike her sister, Ellen was the life of the party and the most sought-after dancing partner. She took a childish delight in flirting with her older sister's beaus.

While courting Elizabeth, Walter became a frequent guest of the family. His visits became a convenient excuse to see Ellen, whose allure triggered an unsettling dilemma. When he decided in favor of Ellen, her sister was devastated, throwing the household into chaos. Walter's reversal violated the societal custom that the elder sister had the privilege of being the first to marry. After several days of quarrels, sibling threats, and secret negotiations, her father came to his elder daughter's rescue and, to settle the matter, bought a home for her and Walter as a wedding gift.

"Don't you have to leave to pick up Rachel?" Leslie says to me.

I check my watch. "Damn! I'm already late. Hopefully, her plane is delayed. We'll stop by for a while before going to the motel."

Driving to Logan Airport, I feel a pall of sadness. The wind is shearing the last leaves off the trees, and the darkness is as black as midnight. The end of the Indian summer proves that winter's weather is tightening its grip.

In the early spring of 1918, my grandmother became pregnant with my mother. One Sunday, during a church social, a rumor spread, creating a minor scandal. My grandmother was middle-aged with a thirteen-year-old son. "Did you hear? The Cargills are having a baby!"

My grandmother suffered from allergies and asthma. When the allergy season began, Walter took her physician's advice and sent her to stay at a ranch in the hot, dry air of New Mexico. Her sister accompanied her.

I was six and shopping with Aunt Ellen when she treated me to an ice cream at Brigham's and first told me the story. At that age, I wouldn't have suspected there was more to the story than what she told me. The part about the blizzard that covered the prairie and trapped their train was my favorite part.

"The train was luxurious. We had a compartment all to ourselves. The journey took eight days. One day a spring blizzard roared across the plains, stranding passengers and train in deep snow. The snow stretched as far as the eye could see," she told me. "The snow crust looked like frozen waves. I'll never forget it as long as I live. All the young men got off the train with shovels to clear the icy snowdrifts off the tracks. In two days, the men had cleared a mile. We celebrated with a banquet. After dinner, the men smoked cigars and played cards. Meanwhile, the crew attached a plow to the front of the engine. Building up a thundering head of steam, the train roared off, arriving at the next station four miles away.

"Did Indians attack you?" I asked, imagining her hiding under a seat to avoid the arrows.

She laughed. "Good heavens, no. We saw Indians at the ranch, but they were friendly. They sold beads and moccasins…"

She stopped speaking and stared out the window of the ice cream parlor. I thought she'd forgotten the rest of the story, but with no Indian attacks and no cavalry coming to the rescue, her story wasn't as exciting as I'd hoped. I finished my ice cream and wiped my sticky fingers on a napkin.

Halfway to the airport, driving becomes more dangerous. The heavens open and rain thunders on the roof, gusts of wind pinning leaves against the windshield. The weather report has said this was the wettest October on record. The lower deck of the highway provides some protection, but traffic slows when the right lane merges to the left, and rain falling from the highway overhead triggers cascades of water, causing cars to suddenly brake.

Looking for Rachel outside the terminal, my eyes smart with tears. Aunt Ellen was quiet and distracted when she reached the end of the story, but it didn't last long. She blew her nose, and we left the ice-cream parlor. It wasn't until college when I learned this story was the beginning of a lie that was hidden until Ellen's death.

I see Rachel standing at the end of the drop-off/pick-up lane. I hop out to load her luggage in the trunk. Struggling with her bag, I tease her, "Planning to stay for a month?"

"You know me. Whenever I finish packing, I always think I need more stuff. You should know me by now—I always pack several pairs of shoes."

Back in the car, we pull out into traffic.

"And if I'm going to set up the cupboards in the apartment and organize the basement storage bin, I need old clothes. You don't plan to stay long at your parents', do you? I need a shower after that miserable flight. The golden age of luxurious flying is long gone." Rachel turns sideways in her seat. "How was the yard sale? You're lucky the rain waited until tonight."

"I've been working flat out since I got here."

"I'm sure your father appreciates your help."

"Oh, he does. That's why he's put me in charge of a sailing trip tomorrow. He's determined to go. Somehow he thinks I have all the skills needed to successfully navigate sailing around Mystic Lake without running aground or hitting another boat."

"You don't know how to sail."

"That's what I'm saying. He's either delusional or trying to humiliate me. He must remember I know nothing about sailing. I'm not going out in that damn boat to have him belittle me all day."

"I don't understand why you didn't just tell him you're not going and be done with it."

"And then listen to him complain about how his own son won't take him on his last sailboat ride?"

"Tell him to go to an amusement park."

In spite of myself, I hoot with laughter.

"That's better," Rachel says. "You can't let it get to you."

"But it does. It's ingrained at this point."

"Well, it's time to out grain it. You can start tomorrow and ixnay the sailing trip. Concentrate on the good times you've had with him."

"I don't remember the good times. I'm not kidding."

"Is Leslie going?"

"No, she has a convenient meeting with clients, sometime tomorrow."

"You've been having a paranoid episode the last few days."

"What's new?" I'm silent while I pass an eighteen-wheeler spraying water like a fire hose. "By the way, we must talk with Leslie about getting someone to stay with Mom when Dad's out. He takes Mom with him now, but getting her in and out of the car is exhausting, and someday he might be tempted to leave her home by herself.

"Last week, Leslie was staying with Mom while Dad went to the doctor's. She was pricing things for the yard sale on the back porch when a neighbor came up the driveway. Mom was with her. The neighbor said she was walking her dog and saw Mom coming down the front walk in her nightgown. The neighbor asked where she was going and Mom said, as ordinary as can be, 'I want to take a walk, and Charles isn't here.'"

"How often has this happened?"

"Leslie asked Dad, and he said it had never happened before. He swears he doesn't leave her by herself, but Leslie and I wonder if he's telling the truth. She feels terrible about not being in the house to prevent Mom from going outside."

"Frankly, you and Leslie need to start looking at nursing homes before she hurts herself. And how the hell did she get down those stairs? I thought you said your mother had problems getting around by herself."

"That's what's so frustrating. Some days she acts like she's ten years younger, getting around and remembering everything. Sometimes she remembers too much. Just yesterday I asked why she and Dad had never let me stay overnight at a friend's house. I recalled feeling they were very unfair. Mom pipes up and says it's because I wet my bed."

"We can guess the reason for that." Rachel assumes a singsong voice: "Father issues."

"It didn't happen that often. And I'll thank you to keep a lid on that."

We arrive at my parents' house at nine. Rachel's enthusiastic, greeting Mom and Dad with a kiss. "I'm getting you all wet," she says, taking off her raincoat. "Mark's been telling me about all the photos you've been looking at."

Leslie brings some cheese and crackers to the living room. "Rachel. Good to see you." They kiss. "Coffee and tea will be ready shortly."

"You must be excited about the move. I can't wait to see the apartment. Mark says it has lots of room."

Mom looks off into the distance and says nothing.

Dad is undeterred by her silence. "It's close to everything, and the extra space will make it easier for Kat to maneuver."

"I can't take Snowflake with me." Mom's lips tremble.

"Mom, I told you I'd take her," Leslie says. "You'll get to see her when I visit."

Mom isn't mollified. She screws up her mouth and stares at Dad, who busies himself cutting a slice of cheese and pretending he hasn't heard. He deliberates over his choice of cracker.

Leslie changes the subject. "We were talking about the trip out west and Mom's birth just before Mark left to pick you up. It just so happens I found an interesting photo in the box that Dad found. I'd never seen it before." She holds up a piece of black cardboard with a small black-and-white photograph pasted on it for me to see. It shows two middle-aged women, one of whom is holding a baby.

"Let me see," Mom says, intercepting the photo before I can take it. Without her glasses, she holds it close. The purple veins on her hand look like earthworms beneath the skin. Someone wrote in white ink on the back: *Baby ready to travel home, 1918.*

"That's me," Mom says, pointing to the baby. "I was born in a small hospital near the dude ranch. There was only one doctor in his eighties. He took care of farm animals when the vet wasn't available." She passed the photo to me. "Before the sisters left, their father sent a telegram. Edward—my uncle—had died from the Spanish flu. Their father told them not to return until the epidemic had died down—"

"It was a pandemic, Kat," Dad corrects her.

"I learned about the Spanish flu in nursing school. More people died from it than during a hundred years of the plague. People became sick in the morning and were dead by the end of the day. There was nothing the doctors could do. Hospitals ran out of beds. Bodies piled up everywhere. It must have seemed like the end of the world after all the deaths in World War I."

No one speaks as we pass the photo around.

Leslie breaks the silence. "I never knew the sisters had a brother until I saw him in that other picture."

"They were upset for a long time," Mom says. "They idolized their brother. No one wanted to talk about him. Too painful."

Mom often talked about her childhood when I arrived home after a high-school date. She'd get out of bed, come downstairs, and pour a glass of wine, all set for a late-night chat. "My mother never told me stories about her life. We never enjoyed a close relationship. She favored my brother Neal. I never felt loved by her and never understood what I'd done to deserve it." She spoke with a forlorn wonder. "It was just something that was."

Although I'd found Grandma's attitude hard to believe, I was too young to recognize the deep pain behind Mom's words. I generally ignored her remarks but nodded sympathetically when appropriate and tried to get to bed.

On the ride back to the motel, Rachel falls asleep, her head lolling forward and her mouth open. I'm grateful she took time off from work and flew out for a few days. The emotions dragged up in the last week have exhausted me. I'm driving fast and almost miss the exit. Rachel wakes up, her hand reaching out to grab the door.

"What happened?"

"Nothing. We'll be at the motel soon."

"I must say your family was great at keeping secrets. I have more sympathy for your mother—well, not that much more. I'm surprised you aren't more screwed up than you are."

Rachel often tells me this to tease me when family difficulties crop up. It usually doesn't bother me because she always ends by saying how much she loves me.

"I married you in spite of your quirks. They made you interesting."

"So I'm not as crazy as you thought?"

"I wouldn't go that far, but I still love you."

CHAPTER 12

"'NOTHING' MADE
A LOT OF NOISE"

That night at the motel once Rachel is asleep, I place the half-dollar coins on an undershirt to prevent scratching. They've been circulated and show some wear on Ben Franklin's forehead but still look brand new. I remember when I first saw coins like these. I was visiting Billy. I was mesmerized by them. I only wanted to look at them.

The next morning, I barely recall a dream I had during the night. Billy's father appears at the yard sale. Although he should have been in his eighties, he looks as young as if he hasn't aged since I was ten years old. He holds out his hand. As if she knows what he wants, Leslie looks for the two coins in the cash box but can't find them. I walk across the front lawn and kneel down to dig with my hands under a bush. I unearth the coins—that's all I remember.

I was in my bedroom listening to records when the telephone rang.

"Mark," Mom called upstairs. "It's Billy. He's asking you over to his house."

I didn't want to go to Billy's. I was listening to *Dance of the Hours* by someone my mother called PaunchANellie on my 45-rpm record player. I'd already played it a dozen times at high volume. By now, Dad would have yelled up the stairs, "Hey, Maestro, turn it down," but he was in his workshop where the shriek of the buzz saw drowned out my music.

"Can he come over here?" I shouted, over the music.

Mom climbed up the stairs to the landing. "Mark, turn down that music and talk to him."

Groaning, I rolled off the bed and turned off the record. "Coming." I was bored, but not so bored that I wanted to be soaked walking to his house. All morning, rain had drummed on the porch roof while bursts of wind rattled the windows. I assumed Billy only called because one of his friends from school had gone home.

Mom stood on the stairs, her hands on her hips. She was mad about something. "Ask him yourself. I'm not your secretary."

I followed her downstairs and picked up the receiver. "Billy? What're you doing?"

Seeing Mom listening from the kitchen, I turned my back for more privacy.

"Do yah wanna come over?" Billy sounded like he was chewing a wad of bubblegum.

"I don't know. Wanna come here?"

"My dad says I can't."

"How come?"

"He just says I can't. Anyway, there's something I wanna show you."

I thought a moment, my interest piqued. "All right. See you in five minutes."

I hung up and took my raincoat from the hall closet. Dad was pounding nails in the cellar, probably making another bookcase. "Mom! I'm going over to Billy's house."

"You don't have to shout." She found my rubbers in the closet. I sat on the stairs to put them on.

"Why can't he come over here? The three of us could play Monopoly."

"Dad too?"

"Your father's too busy."

Her tone of voice made me look up. She was angry. Dad wasn't spending time with her, and Leslie was at a birthday party. Now I was leaving. "We can play when I get back."

"Perhaps." She kissed the top of my head. "Okay, go. Have fun."

When I left the house, the wind blew high in the trees, shaking the last leaves to the ground. I hunched my shoulders against the rain.

Billy Melchoir was a friend due to our parents being friends. His father was an English teacher at Browne and Nichols, a private boy's school on the Charles River. Mr. Melchoir once tried to convince Dad to enroll me in the school. "He can ride with me and my boys. It'll do Mark good."

My father laughed. "The Arlington public schools are excellent and a lot cheaper." That surprised me. I didn't know parents had to pay for kids to go to school.

Later, I asked Mom how much it cost to go to school. "Nothing. Except for our taxes."

"How much do the Melchoirs pay?"

Mom raised an eyebrow, which she did when being sarcastic. "They don't pay a dime."

"They don't? All of them? Then what did Daddy mean?"

"It means Mr. Melchoir teaches at the school, and his boys go for free."

The Melchoirs had five boys. Billy, the oldest, was my age, eleven. Stevie was two years younger. A year later, Joan Melchoir had another boy, Robbie. Mom told me Joan had hoped for a girl. Not one to give up, Mrs. Melchoir became pregnant again. Once more, no girl, but nature gave her a consolation prize: twin boys, Tommy and Eddie. The family bought a minibus.

With Billy attending a different school, I didn't see much of him, except during the school year on the occasional weekend when he wasn't with one of his school friends. Billy's father had summers off, and the family vacationed in the Adirondacks at the cabin they'd inherited from Joan's mother. Although good friends with the Melchoirs, my parents must have found their lifestyle galling.

Despite wearing rubbers, my shoes and the bottoms of my pants were soaked. At the Melchoirs, I pulled off my socks and draped them over the hall radiator. Billy wedged my raincoat into the closet already bulging with coats and jackets.

The house was quiet. Not the usual chaos with five boys arguing, making a mess, or fighting over and often breaking every new toy. Sometimes Mr. Melchoir lost patience. "QUIET!" The boys, immediately silent, knew the slightest sound risked punishment.

"Where is everyone?"

"Mom drove Stevie and Robbie to a gym exhibition. The twins are at my grandma's house. Dad's in the basement." Billy seemed happy to keep him down there. He had blonde hair cut in a flat-top. He was six inches taller than me and stronger from playing sports. That was why I didn't *want* to go to his school. With no recess during the day, all boys were required to take part in a sport for two hours after school. I wouldn't last long in that crowd. I only wanted to read books and listen to classical music.

"Let's go to my room. I have something to show you."

"What are you boys up to?" Mr. Melchoir stood at the head of the cellar stairs. He was a tall man and looked like a giant. His arms had muscles bigger than my legs. One summer, when we visited the Melchoirs at their cottage, Stevie and I walked down to the beach with his sailboat before dinner. The wind switched direction and filled the sails of the boat, which swerved away from shore.

"Look what you've done," Stevie wailed.

"It's not my fault." I'd arrived only an hour before and was already in trouble.

"Yes, it is. You let it go."

"What's the matter, Steven?" Mr. Melchoir came striding up the path. "Stop whining."

"My boat's sailing away. It's all Mark's fault."

"I didn't—" I started to protest.

Mr. Melchoir smacked Stevie on the back of his head. "Stop sniveling. Don't be a baby."

Stevie wasn't crying, but I was glad his father didn't believe him.

Mr. Melchoir had pulled his T-shirt over his head and stepped out of his moccasins, then unbuckled his shorts and let them fall to the ground. I was shocked to see he wasn't wearing underwear. He dove into the lake, his arms arced ahead of him. In no time, he reached the boat and swam back. He emerged from the water, shaking his head to throw the hair out of his eyes. I'd never seen a man, not even my father, completely naked before.

"Here you go." He handed the boat to Stevie and ruffled his hair. "Feeling better now?"

All this time I stared at his penis, which was shriveled by the chilly water but still looked enormous. I always turned away when I undressed in front of anyone, afraid that my penis would get hard, for no other reason I could think of except to embarrass me.

Mr. Melchoir put on his moccasins and picked up his shorts and T-shirt. "You two go back to the cottage. I have to see a man about a horse."

Stevie started walking up the path. They were buying a horse? I ran after him, but he was inspecting his sailboat and hadn't heard his father. I looked back once and saw Mr. Melchoir, still naked, striding into the woods. I wanted to go with him and see the horse.

Now, on this rainy afternoon, Mr. Melchoir loomed over us in the hall, his figure reflected in the hall mirror. Billy shrank back. "We're going up to my bedroom."

"Don't make a mess up there." His father returned to the basement.

Billy's bedroom was the only room on the third floor. To reach it, we walked into Stevie's bedroom closet and climbed the stairs that folded down from the ceiling.

Once in his room, Billy pulled the stairs up, turning his bedroom into a hideaway. An opening cut in the floor above the second-floor hallway was covered with a wooden grill to prevent an accident. The opening allowed his parents to monitor what he was up to.

Billy was acting mysteriously. What did he want to show me?

"Ronnie, my friend from school, slept overnight."

I'd met Ronnie once at Billy's and didn't like him. He was in seventh grade, two years ahead of Billy and me. Ronnie had bossed me around the whole time he was there.

Billy was removing a cigar box from a drawer. He opened the box and some photographs fell onto the floor. "Close your eyes and don't look."

When he was ready, we sat side by side on his bed. He showed me the first picture, a photograph of a woman lying on a couch. The picture was dark, but I saw she was naked. Her breasts were small, but she used her hands to push them together. She looked Chinese.

In the next photo, the same woman knelt on a chair with her back to the camera and stared over her shoulder. Her hat was made of straw or bamboo and came to a point.

"She's old," I said.

The next picture was a duplicate of the first one. "If you want this, we can trade."

I didn't want it but knew I should pretend to be interested. "What do you want for it?"

"I'll think of something. Here's another one."

Another grainy picture of the woman standing at attention. She wore a sailor's cap and kerchief. With one hand she saluted; the other held a fan below her waist, hiding what we both wanted to see.

"This one's better." Billy revealed the last photo.

The photo was out of focus. Wearing her sailor's cap with the end of the kerchief between her teeth, she slouched in a chair, her legs apart. She had no hair between her legs, and her fingers pulled the skin apart. We stared at the picture in silence, then leaned closer, bumping our heads together.

Breaking the silence, Billy spoke with awe. "There's nothing there."

"Girls don't have a penis." I spoke with the pomposity of secret knowledge. Billy had no sisters.

"*I know that*. Ronnie thinks she—"

A creaking sound came up through the hole in the floor. "What are you boys doing up there? You're too quiet."

Billy stammered. "I'm sh-showing M-Mark m-my coin collection."

"Stop stuttering and clean up after yourselves." Mr. Melchoir returned downstairs.

Billy pushed the cigar box to the back of the drawer, uncovering the silver disks.

"What are those?" They were more interesting than a Chinese woman showing off her body. The four shiny, circular objects gleamed in the light from the desk lamp.

"They're silver half dollars. My grandmother gave them to me for my birthday."

He handed one to me. I was shocked by its weight and size. It was unlike anything I'd ever held. Nickels, dimes, even brand-new quarters were nothing like these. They were money but were more than mere coins. "Where did she get them?"

"The bank probably."

"They're so shiny." The head of Benjamin Franklin bulged from the surface, and I rubbed his face with my thumb. The other side had a large bell with a crack.

"That's the Liberty Bell," Billy said, showing off.

Mesmerized by the shining silver, I didn't care if he thought I didn't know that.

"My dad said I can't spend them. I can only look at them."

I stared at the other three coins. What would it be like to hold all four in my hands at once? I reached inside the drawer, but Billy stopped me.

"Give it here." He took back the coin and wiped off my fingerprints, then slid all four into a purple velvet bag and closed the drawer. "Let's go downstairs and have a Coke."

We spent the rest of the afternoon playing Monopoly, swapping hotels and play money. When it started to get dark, I said I had to go home.

I dawdled in the hall putting on my shoes and socks, wondering how I could talk my way up to Billy's room. Distracted, I put my rubbers on the wrong feet.

"Billy?" Mr. Melchoir called up from the basement. "Has Mark gone home yet?"

"He's going now."

"Then get down here and sweep up the mess you and Ronnie made this morning."

Billy sighed. "Okay. I'll be there in a minute."

"No. Get down here now. Mark can let himself out."

Billy didn't look happy. When Mr. Melchoir gave his boys a job to do, he wasn't satisfied until it was perfect. Mom once told me that during their engagement, Mr. Melchoir returned the love letters from Joan with the grammar and punctuation corrected.

I put my hat on. "See you later." I opened the door. Billy trudged down the hall like a convict returning to his cell. When he disappeared down the cellar stairs, I closed the front door with a sound loud enough for them to hear then waited in the hallway, listening to make sure no one was coming up.

I climbed the stairs covered with a thick carpet. At the top, I listened again but heard nothing. My heart thudded so hard I could barely breathe. I crossed Stevie's room to his closet and pulled down the stairs to Billy's room. The hinges squealed, and the springs gave a loud twang. I hoped they couldn't hear that all the way down in the basement.

The light on Billy's desk was still on. Taking out the velvet bag, I was surprised by the weight of the money. I fished out three coins, leaving one in the bag. Halfway to the stairs, I stopped and turned back. I removed the remaining half dollar and tucked the bag behind the cigar box.

I left the stairs lowered, afraid they'd slip out of my hand and fly up with a crash. Short of breath, I wanted to get away as fast as I could.

I was halfway down the stairs when someone opened a cupboard. I froze, the air sucked into my lungs. A faucet was turned on; a glass filled. My heart echoed in my throat. The light from the open refrigerator was reflected in the hall. I saw a figure in the mirror and shrank out of sight. The back of my neck sent a rippling shock down my spine. That's when I recognized myself in the mirror. Ice cubes splashed in the glass, the refrigerator door closed, and footsteps descended the stairs. My legs shook. I sat on the stairs until they stopped.

Leaving the house, I held the storm door open with my bum then slowly closed the front door, hearing it click shut. The wind swept away all sound. I crossed the porch to the top of the stairs. The storm door crashed shut behind me and I raced home. Blind to traffic, I ran across the intersection, fled down Cedar Avenue, and turned right on Buena Vista Road.

I waited outside until I'd caught my breath. My parents sat in the living room having a cocktail and a cigarette. Dad was reading his newspaper. When I removed my raincoat, I realized I still held the half dollars in my hand. Turning toward the closet, I dropped two into each pants pocket.

"Did you have fun?" Mom asked.

"It was okay, I guess." How clever to act like it was an ordinary afternoon. After hanging up my coat, I leaned against the archway between the hall and the living room to take off my rubbers. The coins in my pockets clinked together. I walked to the kitchen to be out of earshot.

"Don't track water into the kitchen. I just waxed the floor."

Returning to the hall, I hid behind the closet door. Trying to lift my shoe out of the rubber, I lost my balance and fell against the door.

The coins in both pockets sounded like bells.

Mom sat up. "What was that?"

"Nothing."

Dad lowered his newspaper, now interested in what was happening. "'Nothing' made a lot of noise." He put his paper aside. "I'd like to see 'nothing.'"

I removed the coins from my pockets and walked into the room, one rubber still caught on my shoe. I kept as far as possible from Dad.

"What are those?" Mom leaned forward. "Come closer where I can see." She recoiled in surprise. "They're silver dollars!"

"*Half* dollars," I corrected her.

"Get over here." Dad looked at them and then at me. "Where did they come from?"

I wished I was alone with Mom. She was easier to lie to. Why wasn't Dad in the basement building something? "Billy gave them to me."

"He *gave* them to you?" Dad said those words with accusing disbelief. He stared at me, then glanced at Mom. "I want you to give them back." He returned to his newspaper.

"Do his parents know he gave them away?" Mom asked.

I couldn't think of anything to say to Mom. It seemed pointless to try to convince her the money was mine now. My feet were glued to the floor.

"Did you hear what I said?" Dad's voice came from behind the newspaper.

"Yes."

"Then put on your raincoat and bring them back right now."

"I'll give them back tomorrow when it's not raining."

My father lowered the paper again. "No. You'll do it now."

I took my coat from the closet and put it on. The wet seemed to be on the inside of it now. I sat on the stairs to put on my rubbers. The coins rattled.

I left the house and trudged up the street. What was I going to do? I couldn't bring them back. What would I say? The wind blew hard against me, and the rain ran down the inside of my collar. Walking in circles, I wondered why I'd taken them. I didn't want them now. Why did I always do something that got me into trouble?

Halfway up the street, I came to the Donnellys' house. No lights were on. Their garage was under the side porch. At the bottom of the driveway, a drain gurgled with rainwater. I walked down the incline beside a stone retaining wall holding the earth back. A row of hedges hid the house foundation from view. I stacked the half dollars in a neat pile under a hedge. Giving them a last look, I covered them with wet leaves.

I walked around the block and returned home.

"What did Billy say when you brought them back?" Mom asked.

"Nothing. I said you wouldn't let me keep them."

"I think that's best. He shouldn't give away something that valuable. Don't you agree?"

I shrugged and went to my room to wait for dinner. Sitting on my bed, I listened to the rain beating against the windows. The wind blew the leaves faster and faster in a circle that spiraled up like a cyclone.

CHAPTER 13

"WHEW!
MIGHTY HOT IN THERE"

Rachel drops me off Sunday morning. She has some shopping to do and then she'll drive to the apartment. I spend most of the trip complaining about sailing that afternoon. At my parents' house she gives me a kiss. "Good luck," she says. "Don't drown."

Dad has hauled out another two trash cans of stuff he didn't sell. Cardboard signs are labeled in his distinct handwriting: TRASH—MOVERS DO NOT MOVE.

When I enter the house, I don't see anyone. "Hello. Is someone here?"

"I'm up here," Leslie whispers from the porch overlooking the backyard. "I'll be up in a minute. I'm making coffee."

"There's fresh coffee already made. Bring me another cup."

After preparing two mugs of coffee, I go upstairs.

"Where's Mom?"

"In her room. She's resting on her chaise lounge. The yard sale was a little too exciting."

"The house feels lighter. Tomorrow's the big day."

"Dad put the stuff that didn't sell on the curb for the trashmen. The Salvation Army isn't coming until later this week to pick up the large pieces of furniture that Mom and Dad couldn't even give away."

"Too bad they'll have to move them. Make sure Dad gets a receipt to take off his taxes."

As I speak, I'm scanning the empty driveway through the back window. Something is missing. "What's different?"

Leslie looks up. "The boat's gone."

"Where did it go?"

"Travis called last night to say he wants to take it with him on vacation this week."

"So, all this time Dad planned to go sailing in a boat he no longer owned."

"Technically Travis is buying it today. He and Dad are at the boat club raising the sails."

"That'll take time, even if there are no problems. I won't need to rush over to the club."

"They don't need you. Travis will take him out on the lake."

"What?" I pretend to sound insulted. "I've been thrown overboard?"

"I knew you'd be disappointed, but I'd be prepared. He'll lord it over you."

"I'll always be a disappointment. I was never the gung-ho sailor back in the day. Did Dad bring his sailor hats with him?"

"What sailor hats? They were on the way out the door when I arrived."

"Probably not. He wouldn't dare insist that Travis wear one. It's not the family adventure Dad hoped for."

"It wasn't going to be an adventure for me." Mom's at the door eavesdropping. "What if I had to pee? I'm too old to sit on a plastic bucket." She chuckles with a sly grin. "Mark, slide over that box. I want to check out the photos Leslie's looking at."

A large, dirty carton is perched on the coffee table. "Where did that come from?"

"Dad brought it up from the basement," Leslie says. "It's where I found the photos I showed you last night. He was rummaging around in the cellar and discovered them in the cabinet where he stored his railroad material. I found Mom's high-school yearbook this morning and dozens of photos I've never seen before."

I kneel on the floor and flip through the photos still in the carton. "Here's one of Dad with his scout troop. It looks like it was taken at the old town hall. There's no date on it."

As a teenager, Dad joined the scouts with his friends, a rite of passage for boys in the twenties. This photo is one of the few Leslie and I have of him as a young man.

"Which one is he?" Leslie asks, examining the line of boys.

"There." Mom points to the boy at the far left. "The one in white pants with his hands behind his back."

"He's quite handsome, clean-cut," Leslie says. "How old do you think he is?"

I inspect him more closely. "Thirteen, fourteen years old?"

The boys stand ramrod straight with chests puffed out, their feet shoulder width apart. They're dressed in baggy pants with lacings below the knee, a uniform with an unsettling resemblance to that worn by the doughboys in WWI.

"Aunt Ruth told me a story when Dad first joined the scouts and visited the priest—"

"That's a good story," Mom says.

"I never heard it. When did she tell you this?" Leslie asks.

"Years ago. We were staying with our cousins at their cottage in Maine. I'd joined the scouts that summer and was telling her about working on my Tenderfoot badge. She was laughing before she even started telling the story about Dad. 'When my brother—your father—came home and told us, our mother had a fit.'

"As part of his Tenderfoot badge, Dad needed the signature of his priest to confirm he attended weekly church services. The housekeeper at the rectory told him to wait in the parlor while she went upstairs to tell the priest. When the priest didn't come down, Dad thought he'd forgotten and prepared to leave. At that moment, the priest swept in and asked what he wanted. Dad explained why he needed his signature.

"The priest looked at the card and asked what troop he belonged to.

"'Troop such-and-such, Father,' he said.

"'Which one is that? The town hall? Why aren't you in the troop here at your church?'

"Dad said he wanted to be with his friends.

"'What? You don't have any Catholic friends at St Barbara's?'

"'I mean my friends from school.' Dad and his sister didn't go to the parochial school.

"The priest slapped his hands on his knees. 'I'm sorry. I only sign for boys in the St Barbara troop.' He returned the card and left the room.

"Dad left the rectory, upset and embarrassed. When he told his mother what had happened, she took the bus downtown and gave the priest a piece of her mind."

"What did she say to him?" Leslie asks.

"Aunt Ruth said their mother never told them. Dad's troop waived the requirement—"

Mom interrupted, "Your father was the golden boy, and his mother never talked to the priest again. Dad said his mother lost some of her faith in the church. She'd leave the confessional booth if that priest was in there."

"I wish I could have known her," Leslie says. "She sounds like quite the lady."

"She had a tough life," Mom says. "Money was a constant worry. She earned money repairing evening gowns. She also laundered women's delicate dresses. Everything was done by hand. It's good she made money because Dad's father spent most of his pay on alcohol and gambling at Suffolk Downs. Dad doesn't like to talk about his childhood."

"Was his mother unhappy when Dad became a Protestant?" I ask.

"He converted after he was in college when we planned to get married."

Leslie looks at the photos she's removed from the box. "Here's a larger picture of you in your wedding dress." She holds up a professional photo taken before Mom left home. "And who are these other people?" Leslie shows Mom a smaller photo taken with the best man on the day of their wedding. "Is the woman with him his wife?"

"They're the Crawfords. She was my matron of honor and Richard was Dad's best man. He was a major in charge of transportation."

"Did you and Dad keep in contact with them after the war?"

"Your father stayed in touch with Richard. Don't you remember going to the Crawford house to buy Duchess?"

"I remember being disappointed we didn't get another dog," I say. "Did this Richard like hunting and ice fishing?"

"Oh, yes. He was always planning hunting trips with groups of friends and inviting Dad to go with them. Your father went a couple of times." Mom stops talking and looks away. She twists the cord of her bathrobe around her hand. "He and his wife eventually got divorced. He liked his guns and dogs more than his wife.

"Mr. Crawford always acted a little odd. He was killed while hunting alone shortly after his divorce. They said the shotgun went off accidently, but Dad thought it was suicide. He was terribly upset when he got the news. But as I said, I never liked him that much."

I decided to reread the two letters from the attic in light of this new information. Her intuition about people was often correct after meeting them one or two times.

At that moment, a car stops in front of the house. I get up to look. "Rachel's here."

"Ask her in," Leslie says.

"Not on your life. I'm getting out of here before Dad comes home."

Rachel finished her chores early at the apartment. Once in the car I attempt to keep my eyes open, but the rocking of the vehicle is hypnotic, and it's a losing battle until Rachel brakes for a sudden backup on the highway. My eyes fly open, and I look around, trying to get my bearings.

"Sorry, I didn't mean to scare you."

"I'm more tired than I thought."

She doesn't speak until she merges with the traffic changing lanes for the exit ramp. "I almost forgot. How was your sailing trip? I assume you didn't crack up the boat." When I don't answer, she looks at me with concern. "What happened? Did the crew mutiny?"

"I never went. Nothing happened as far as I know."

"Your father went alone?"

"A neighbor's grandson bought the boat, and he took Dad out for a test run."

"Lucky you."

"After I worried about it all week."

"Be thankful. It could have been—"

"Forget it. I don't have the energy to discuss it." I lean back and close my eyes.

"Are you planning to ask me about my day?"

I sit up and assume the role of the interested husband. "And how was your day?"

"Good and bad. I had to locate the weekend building manager and complain about a few things that should have been done. Nothing major. A bedroom window wouldn't stay open, the filter over the stove—it was awful—was caked with grease, and the vent for the bathroom fan hadn't been cleaned for who knows how long. The maintenance man was nice, and everything was corrected."

"Is that the good news?"

"The good news can wait until dinner. I'm rather proud of myself. I hope your father will be happy."

"Uh-oh. That's the beetle hiding in the rose."

At the motel I take a shower and lie down for a nap while Rachel watches the news.

Once we've ordered dinner at the restaurant, I ask her what her good news is before she bursts with anticipation.

"You're not going to believe this." She smooths her napkin on her lap as if she's setting the stage.

"I'll try. Just don't ask me if I can guess what happens next." I stifle a yawn. "I don't know what *I'm* doing next at this point."

"As I told you, I went to the apartment manager's office, and while I was telling him what had to be done, a young woman came in with a stroller. When I was finished, I stayed and watched her baby while she talked with the manager. The baby was adorable, her arms and legs flailing in all directions. I had my keys in my hand, and when the baby saw the sun flashing off them, she stopped moving and just stared like she'd never seen anything like it. I'm always in awe at how babies react to—"

Interrupting Rachel's peroration of infant psychology, the waiter arrives with our drinks. "Your appetizers will be out momentarily."

I nod thanks and turn back to Rachel. "So, you ended up having a long chat with the mother."

"You know me, I'll talk with everyone. We sat in the library off the reception area. By the way, the apartment building is beautiful. Anyway, we talked about being a new mother. Her husband works all day in Boston, so she feels stranded all by herself. She walks to the supermarket, but without a car she's limited by how much she can buy at a time.

"She said she'd overheard me talking to the manager about my parents moving in. I said no, my parents-in-law were moving in tomorrow. We started talking about elderly parents, and I said she was too young to have that worry, but she said no, she was the youngest of eight kids, all girls, and her parents have just retired. Her father has mobility problems, and it's hard for her mother to care for him when they're outside the home."

"Sounds familiar," I say, while Rachel sips some of her wine.

"That's what I said. How your father has to bring your mother along with him wherever he goes. I said your sister wants to hire a home health aide of some sort, but it's difficult finding someone to come whenever your father needs someone to stay with her while he's away. He doesn't want someone underfoot every day doing nothing. Where would she sit all day? But then this woman said she could stay with Mom when Dad had to go out."

"How serious is she?"

"She said she'd enjoy having company, and I think the money will come in handy. I told her if she wanted to try it, that would be wonderful. I'll talk with Leslie tonight, and then we can talk to your father tomorrow."

"Will she drop out once she discusses it with her husband?"

"It might not work out long-term, but at least it's a start."

The waiter serves the appetizers and takes a step back, surveying the setting. "Is there anything I can get for you?"

"We're fine for now," I say.

He wishes us, "Bon appétit." We take a few minutes dividing up the dishes.

"This is the best calamari I've had in a long time." Rachel closes her eyes as if overcome with the taste. "How are your spring rolls? They look good."

I nod, my mouth filled. I wave my hand in front of my mouth. "Hot."

We concentrate on eating and don't speak. After several minutes of silence, Rachel reaches across and takes my hand. "You seem to be in another world. What's wrong?"

"Nothing's wrong. I'm just tired of this whole business. We've been out straight since I got here. I just want to go home."

"Think how Leslie feels. No wonder she's at a breaking point—"

"That reminds me: when I told the folks you and I were going out for dinner tonight, I saw the disappointment in Leslie's eyes when she realized she wasn't included. I'd like to ask her to come out with us before we head home."

"I was going to suggest the same thing. I want to get up to date with what's going on with her kids. Plus, we need to talk about what needs to be done for your parents. I'm not that confident about the future."

She stops speaking and looks closely at me. "I know you're upset about your parents, and that's understandable, but sometimes I think you're so consumed by the bad times, you can't remember the good ones."

Her sympathy brings tears to my eyes. I nod, agreeing with her.

"What you need to do over the next few weeks… or months is to make a list of the times when you were happy being with your father. But you have to be fair. There's not going to be a perfect time." She shrugs. "I know he's not perfect, but your mother loved him—"

"At least in the beginning."

"You know that's not true. The trouble is alcohol came between them."

"But alcohol didn't create the problems," I say. "It revealed them."

"And you think that couples who don't drink to excess have none of these underlying problems. That's not reality."

My mood improves somewhat over dessert, and by the time we drive back to the motel, I convince her to go for a swim. "The pool is open 'til ten. Maybe we'll have the steam room to ourselves." I wiggle my eyebrows suggestively.

"I thought you were tired."

As it turns out, the motel has no sauna or steam room. You can't have everything.

One Saturday when I was in third grade, my family drove to the countryside near Fitchburg, where Dad's best friend from the Army, Richard Crawford, raised dogs in backyard kennels. This was the first time Leslie and I learned that Dad planned to buy a dog.

When we arrived, Mom and Leslie went into the house; Dad and I walked around to the kennels. Mr. Crawford, dressed in jeans and Wellington boots, was hosing down the cages and cement runways. He held up his hand in greeting, finished the area he was flushing, and turned off the water. He left the kennel, taking off his gloves, and shook hands with Dad.

"Good to see you, Dick. Not the most enjoyable part of breeding dogs."

"I'm the man following the elephants at the end of the parade."

The dogs barked and whined for attention, circling the enclosure and throwing themselves up against the fence. None of them seemed dangerous, but for now, I was happy they were in cages. Their barking was so loud, I had to block my ears.

I walked toward the cages that had already been hosed down, my shoes squishing in the mud. An overpowering stink came from the enclosure. The odor made me gag, and I almost threw up.

"Watch where you're walking, young man," Mr. Crawford called as I picked my way through the muck. "There's dog shit over there."

I stopped in my tracks, unsure what to do.

"Mark, come back before you fall or one of your shoes comes off."

I backed away, wondering if I'd already stepped in dog doo.

Mr. Crawford opened the cages and let out four dogs. Jumping up against him, two of the dogs were big enough to put their paws on his shoulders. "Down, you fool dogs." He was obviously delighted with their affection.

He bent down and picked up two rubber balls, which he lobbed toward the trees on the far side of the yard. The dogs immediately raced after the balls, playfully growling and nipping at each other to gain an advantage. They ran back to Mr. Crawford and dropped the balls at his feet.

"Give it a try." He tossed one of the balls to me. A red setter leaped in the air but failed to catch it. When I fumbled the ball, the setter caught it on the bounce and bounded back to me, her chest heaving from the exertion. She dropped the ball. When I bent down to pick it up, she licked my face. Her body was in constant motion, her eyes fixed on my hand. The ball was slimy with saliva.

The dog and I played with the ball for a long time. I finally got used to the slippery surface. When a brown-and-white dog tried to join our game, the setter growled from deep in her throat, and the interloper jumped away.

The Crawford kids and Leslie ran out the back door. The other dogs followed, darting among them, veering away at the last moment, impossible to catch. The children, two boys and a girl, chased the dogs and, accustomed to living in the country, yelled at the top of their voices. Running with them, I also shouted with abandon. The freedom to run and run with nothing to stop me was exhilarating. The red setter never left my side.

When we stopped, bent over with hands on our knees to catch our breath, the dogs nudged against us, wanting to lick our faces. Leslie was scared at first but soon allowed a beagle to come close enough to lick her hand. If we tried to grab hold of the dogs, they jumped away, barking and looking back at us. The race started again.

I liked the red setter and hoped that she was the dog we'd take home. But when I asked Dad, he said, "No, we're not getting that dog." Instead, he pointed to the white dog with brown spots and a long, thin tail. He said the dog was a pointer. "You take her when you hunt ducks. She points in the direction where the ducks fall."

I turned away to hide my disappointment. Why did we need a dog that pointed at dead ducks? I'd rather leave with no dog if I couldn't have the setter.

Mr. Crawford took Dad hunting one or two weekends a year. Wives weren't invited, so Dad went alone. Not owning a gun, he borrowed one from his friend. I wasn't interested in hunting. I didn't want to be around when Dad brought home dead birds and rabbits.

A large white barn built on a foundation of boulders stood at the end of the lane from the Crawford farmhouse. Mr. Crawford and Dad walked down to the barn after lunch.

I trotted behind them. "Where are you going?"

Dad stopped and turned toward me. "We're going to the barn. Mr. Crawford has a new gun to show me."

Mr. Crawford said something to my father, and Dad nodded. "Stay at the house with the other kids. We'll be going home after I'm finished down here."

I watched them cross the packed earth that stretched from the lane up to the door of the barn. I was tired of running with the other kids. Looking at guns was better than sitting around bored without a book to read. Halfway back to the house, I saw a ledge of granite poking above the meadow. I sat on the rock facing the barn, waiting for Dad to come out. The field had been mowed recently, and the smell of grass filled the air.

When my bum ached from sitting too long on the rock, I walked slowly back to the house. Leslie and the other kids sat on the front porch eating Jell-O, competing to see who could make the most noise sucking it through their teeth.

Mom came out to the porch when she heard me. "Have you seen your father?"

"He went with Mr. Crawford to the barn. They're looking at a gun."

Mom's shoulders sagged. "Run down and tell him we need to leave soon. I promised Grandma we'd stop by on the way home."

I was happy we were leaving. I didn't like Mr. Crawford's kids. I blamed them for keeping the setter. They wanted her for themselves and gave us the dog they didn't like. They acted stuck-up because they lived on a farm, but just because their father raised dogs didn't make them special. One day they'd have to hose the dog doo out of the cages, and that was a job I never wanted.

I ran down the lane toward the barn, then rolled back one of the heavy double doors and walked inside. It was hot and dark. Unable to see where to go, I stayed by the door, waiting for my eyes to adjust. The bales of hay stacked to the rafters made my nose itch. The sun was like a searchlight shining through the dirty windows, particles of dust swirling like clouds of gnats.

I heard Mr. Crawford and Dad talking in a room up a flight of stairs at the end of the building. I walked past the stalls once used to stable horses but were now only storage for broken farm machinery and furniture. Their voices were indistinct, and I wondered what they were saying.

I stopped at the foot of the stairs. "Dad." When he didn't reply, I started to climb the stairs and called again.

A door above me opened. "Mark?"

I couldn't see my father behind the door. "Mom said it was time to go home."

"All right." Dad was impatient. "Run back to the house and tell her you found me."

"I'll wait for you."

"Mark, you can't stay here. It's too dangerous for kids, with guns around."

Mr. Crawford walked across the floor and spoke to Dad. I couldn't hear what he said.

My father was angry now. "Wait in front of the barn. We'll be down in a minute."

I walked outside the barn and paced in a circle, watching my shadow turn around me. After ten minutes, Dad came out. His shirt hung lopsided where he'd missed a button.

"Whew! Mighty hot in there."

"I'm sweating too." I pulled up my shirt, flapping the cloth to cool my chest.

Dad put his arm around my shoulder, which he rarely did. "Let's get our dog."

When it came time to leave, Mr. Crawford whistled to the pointer. She saw the open door of our car and jumped onto the backseat as if she'd been riding there for years. She stepped on Leslie and me until we moved, and she settled down between us.

Mr. Crawford passed a paper bag to Mom. "These cans of dog food will tide you over until Monday."

He closed the back door, then reached in to tweak the dog's ear. "Enjoy your new family, Duchess."

She licked his hand.

"Okay, folks, good luck." He rapped the car roof with his fist.

When Dad turned the car around, Duchess sat up and looked out the back window, whimpering a couple of times. Leslie put her arms around the dog's neck. "Don't cry, Duchess. You'll have fun at our house."

"Of course she will." Mom turned to watch us in the back seat. "Take turns patting her head, but be gentle."

Duchess turned in circles until she squeezed me into the center of the back seat so she could stick her head out my window.

"Charles, I need a cigarette."

Leslie frowned and rolled down her window. Out of sight of the Crawford home, Dad stopped at the curb. He shook two cigarettes from a pack in his shirt pocket. The lighter on the dashboard clicked.

Mom took a long drag. "Thank God. Just because they don't smoke, the rest of us can't? Is it a religious thing?"

Without answering, Dad pulled back into the street.

"Don't forget we're stopping at my mother's."

I fell in love with Duchess on the way home and never once regretted getting the dog I didn't want.

CHAPTER 14

"I'M A SHARK, AND I'M GOING TO BITE YOU"

Moving day runs smoothly. The packers are early. Although a supervisor came two weeks ago to give an estimate, the driver walks around the house to decide how to load the van. Two men are carrying boxes to the staging area outside. "We'll be ready to go in about three hours," he tells Dad.

I load the boxes with the model railroad into the trunk of my parents' car and our rental. I lock the seat belt around a carton of breakable items: Hummel figures, an art deco lamp, and a metallic carousel that revolves in the sun and rings three chimes, an object I always put in a dark corner because it drives me crazy. I call Rachel at the apartment to tell her to expect us before twelve. She's completing the job of lining all the shelves in the kitchen and bathroom before we arrive.

When the movers are finished, my parents drive off. As they leave, I'm amazed that neither of them looks back at the house where they raised a family and lived for over half a century. I shake my head, awed by their nonchalance. I dread the next five minutes.

The movers close the van with a rolling crash. The three men crowd into the cab, laughing at the driver's joke, and are gone.

I enter the house for the last time.

The living room is a stage unrecognizable without curtains, pictures, mirrors, and the Oriental rug. I expect it to seem larger without the furniture, but instead it looks smaller with all the life drained out of it.

The floor shines where the rug covered the wood for decades. The mantel over the fireplace is empty. The balloon lady, a longtime resident, is in the carton of breakables in my car. The day Mom received her as a gift, she warned Leslie and me, "If one of you breaks this, your name will be mud." I never dared to look at it, afraid a glance might cause a tremor and knock it off the shelf.

On the second floor, I cross the three-season porch to the back windows. My shoes rap loudly on the wooden floor, a sound that disrupts the leisurely mood of the room. The furniture will be placed on the deck off the living room in the apartment. The sheer curtains are drawn across the windows.

The sound of a key in the front door. Women's voices, the banging of pails, the thump of a heavy object help me shake off the film of memories running through my head.

"Hello?" someone calls out. "Anyone here?" The cleaners have arrived.

From a bedroom window, I see the real estate agent get out of her car and greet the workers. I'm relieved that life has entered the house again.

The home I remember has set me free. I descend the stairs, startling the cleaners. I smile and nod to them as I leave.

By the time I arrive at the apartment, the movers have unloaded the heaviest furniture. Dad created a floor plan of the apartment to scale, specifying the exact location for every stick of furniture. While studying the plan, the driver waves me over. "What did your father do for work?"

"Engineer."

"That explains everything."

The Oriental rug is already in the living room, and one worker is assembling the beds. The foreman helps the other worker wrestle in the heavy sleep sofa. How will they squeeze it through the doorway and then maneuver it from the hall into the living room?

I wonder if my father is concerned it won't fit, but he's preoccupied with measuring the living room wall to double-check the position of the sofa.

I look back in time to see the movers flip the couch onto its end as if it weighs nothing and angle it through the front door. Once inside, they make a ninety-degree turn, hump it partway down the hall, and then lower the couch back to its horizontal position. They jockey it back and forth into the living room.

The driver arches his back, brushing his hands on his pants. "Now be honest. You didn't think we'd get it in, did you?"

"I thought you had a fifty-fifty chance."

"This is nothing. Last week we moved a piano into a Boston condo. On the third floor, and there was no elevator. By the way, I think your parents have too much furniture for this apartment."

"You think? The consignment shop was scheduled to pick up some of the large furniture last week but cancelled at the last minute. They're coming tomorrow. Anything they don't want will be collected by the Salvation Army."

Mom gets up from her perch on a kitchen chair and walks to her usual place at the end of the couch. She falls back against the cushions. "I'm moved in," she announces.

After an hour, the movers finish moving everything into the apartment. They cut the tape on each box and hang up all the clothes they've packed in tall wardrobe boxes. Dad signs the contract and gives them each twenty-five dollars.

"Enjoy your new home." The foreman salutes my father and closes the door.

Early that afternoon Dolores drops in. A large woman, she cleaned our house for as long as I lived at home. She has a brassy manner, with red hair, a booming voice, and a smoker's raspy cough.

When she arrived to clean every two weeks, Mom reheated the coffee from breakfast, and the two of them gossiped at the kitchen table for half an hour. Mom prepared lunch for her at twelve, and in late afternoon, they had a glass of sherry before Dolores went home. Rachel always wondered how much cleaning she actually did.

Over the years she became less a cleaning lady and more a close friend, acting as a sounding board for Mom. Married three times, Dolores is unfazed by any marital complaint a client chooses to share with her. She's seen and heard it all. In retirement, she often visits Mom for an afternoon.

"I would have been here sooner, but the beauty parlor was behind schedule. By the way, how do you like my new glasses? I especially wanted red frames to match my hair."

"They're big," Mom says.

Dolores helps Rachel unpack the dishes in the kitchen, while I set up the TV. Later Dolores and I make the beds. When we're finished, she pulls me aside. "Your mother can't be left alone in the apartment."

"Rachel has arranged for a woman who lives in the building to come in whenever Dad's away. She can tell you more about it."

"That's good as long as she's dependable." Dolores isn't quite convinced. "In an emergency your father can always call me."

"Leslie and I are looking for someone to come in for three to four hours a day to help bathe and dress Mom."

Dolores leaves the bedroom to unpack the box with the bathroom supplies. Before she starts, Leslie arrives with lunch, and Dad invites Dolores to stay. She takes charge in the kitchen, telling Dad he's done enough for one day. "Go in the living room, Charles, and relax with your bride. The rest of the unpacking can wait 'til tomorrow."

In the late afternoon, walking to our car parked on a side street, Rachel and I see groups of kids going from house to house. "I always liked taking the kids around the neighborhood on Halloween," Rachel says. "Each child tried to be the loudest one to shout, 'Trick or treat.' Our gang of kids were like an invading army."

A little boy in a fish costume comes up to us on the sidewalk and holds up his bag. "Twick and tweet."

His mother hurries up to him. "Bobby, you have to wait until you come to a house."

He frowns at us as if we're the ones playing the trick on him.

Rachel bends over for a closer look. "Goodness, you're a scary fish—"

"I'm a shark, and I'm going to bite you."

"Bobby, don't be rude. You can't go around pretending to bite people. Sorry, folks. This is his first Halloween, and he's confused by the rules."

"I wish I had some candy for you," Rachel tells him and then says to his mother, "This brings back memories. Enjoy it while you can. It's over before you know it."

Bobby and his mother pass us, and Rachel calls after him, "Goodbye, Mr. Shark."

Already growling, he tries to stop and turn around, but his mother steers him toward the steps of the next house.

Rachel says she'll drive, and I relax in the car. I can't wait to have a hot shower. I think back to the time when I took our kids to their grammar school for the costume parade. Jennifer was angry when she didn't win best costume in the sixth grade, especially as Jon had already won second place in the first-grade line-up.

I don't remember much of my days as a child on Halloween except when I was a freshman in high school and had to dress up as a hobo to collect candy because Mom had run out. I picked a street where I wouldn't be recognized because I was too embarrassed to risk having a classmate open a door and give me a look of disdain.

The only memory that's still painfully vivid happened a few days before Halloween. When I was in third grade, Massachusetts organized the Trick-or-Treat for UNICEF drive on Halloween. The PTA president asked Mom to help by introducing the program in the second and third grades. For a week, she studied the speakers' guide, which included a script and a poster displaying the distinctive orange collection box with the UNICEF logo.

The night before, she practiced the two-minute speech in front of me. Mom wasn't used to public speaking but was reassured she'd only be addressing children my age. Her rehearsals were a success. The morning of the presentations, she gathered her materials and said she'd see me later that day. She'd pick up the collection boxes when she received her schedule at school.

During arithmetic drill, there was a knock on our classroom door, and Mom entered the room.

"Class." Miss Kichener clapped her hands. "I'd like you to welcome Mrs. Aherne. She has an announcement about trick-or-treating next week. By the way, she's Mark's mother."

A soft chorus of "Ohs." I beamed with pride.

"Thank you, Miss Kichener, for inviting me." Mom appeared uneasy but tried to act happy to be there. "As your teacher explained, I'm here to talk about the UNICEF fundraiser. All over America, students will ask their neighbors to contribute a nickel or dime to UNICEF when they go from house to house on Halloween. You'll carry a box like this one." She held up the poster showing a narrow box with a coin slot on the top. I noticed the slight tremor in her hands. "When your neighbors come to the door, hold up the box to remind them to contribute to this worthy cause—"

A hand shot up. Mom was taken unawares by the interruption, but before she could react, Miss Kichener spoke up. "Yes, Wendy?"

"Mrs. Aherne, does this mean we won't get candy this year?"

Some grumbling came from other students who'd also heard this rumor.

Mom was unprepared for a question but quickly recovered. "Of course you'll get candy. That remains the same. UNICEF is extra and voluntary."

Wendy spoke up again, this time without raising her hand. "Does that mean I don't have to bring the box if I don't want to?"

"Oh, well, I don't th-think so..." Mom stammered, and her hands shook more.

The teacher intervened. "Wendy, don't be rude. Every student will carry a box. People know about this fundraiser and will give whatever they can." Miss Kichener nodded to my mother to continue.

Mom had lost her place in her speech. She stared at Wendy as if she thought the kid deserved a good smack.

"Mrs. Aherne?" Miss Kichener prompted my mother. "You have something to distribute to the class?"

"What? Oh, yes. Hand these around so everyone gets one." The students passed the stacks of waxed cardboard down each row. "They're easy to make."

I looked at my sheet of cardboard. How did she know? It didn't look simple to me.

Mom showed the class how to fold the cardboard. "You insert the tab labeled A into the opening labeled B." She couldn't hold the box still to insert tab A.

Wendy waved her hand, distracting Mom, who fumbled her box and dropped it. Malcolm, sitting in front of Mom, jumped up and returned it to her.

"Yes, Wendy, what is it now?" Miss Kichener was impatient.

"Mrs. Aherne, why do your hands shake so much?"

No one said a word. I could tell Mom wanted to put her hands behind her back, but she held the half-folded box with both hands and couldn't.

Miss Kichener glared at Wendy. "Miss Fischer, I will see you after school. Now apologize to Mrs. Aherne."

Wendy murmured something unintelligible.

"Read the instructions." Mom no longer hid her anger. She snatched up her notebook. "Ask your parents for help." With a quick "Thank you" to the teacher, she left the room.

I was sorry for Mom. I should have warned her about know-it-all Wendy. But I was also ashamed of her shaking. I'd become used to it and wasn't prepared to see it from the class's point of view. I'd been proud to have my mother there, and now that special occasion had become an embarrassment, something else to live down.

Mom was humiliated. She went straight to her car and drove home. She'd lost her self-confidence. She called the UNICEF coordinator and said she wasn't well. I doubt she told the woman the real reason.

CHAPTER 15

"IT'S MY LICENSE"

Two weeks before the move, Mom received her updated handicap tag for the car. Her limited mobility is a valid reason; nevertheless, she acts like she's put one over on the registry. What she doesn't know is that the state flagged her license. When I visit the day after the move, Dad tells me a letter arrived from the registry the previous week. "I didn't show it to Kat until last night because I didn't want her to be upset just before the move."

"Is there a problem? Are they saying she's not disabled?"

"The registry wants to know if she can still drive. Her license will be revoked unless she passes a driving test." He hands me the letter, adding, "So that's the end of that."

I can't remember the last time Mom drove the car, but I'm relieved. I remind Dad that he must be understanding when talking to Mom. I could add, but don't, that he's at the age when his own driving could be called into question after an accident. Leslie and I are concerned by the dents and scratches on the bumper and side doors of his fire-engine-red Buick. One day soon, we'll have to intervene to save the life of a hapless pedestrian.

Unlike Rachel's mother, who never learned to drive, Mom had always been a free spirit, driving everywhere to shop, visit friends, or take us to doctor and dentist appointments. But when she turned seventy-five, she had difficulty walking and relied on Dad to help her into the car. Her eyesight began failing, and the shaking in her hands limited what little dexterity she had left.

When I see Mom, she's outraged at the Registry of Motor Vehicles. "I've been a customer for sixty years. They can't do this. It's *my* license."

Dad is unsympathetic, having heard this over and over since last night. "You sent a letter from your doctor saying you're handicapped. The registry wants to make sure you can still drive"—he pauses—"safely."

"What if you aren't here and I have to drive someplace?" she asks.

"If I'm not here, I'll be *in* the car, so it won't be here for you to drive."

"Maybe when I go with you to your doctor's appointments, I'll take the car and drive somewhere on my own." Mom smiles triumphantly.

"And where do you plan to go?"

"I haven't decided yet." The conversation is over as far as she's concerned.

Dad goes to the kitchen to make lunch while Mom remains on the couch, pursing her lips and glowering in his direction. She won't let this go without a fight. "Your father..." she whispers angrily. I wait for the rest of the sentence, but she feels those two words say everything.

"Mom, Dad's worried about your safety driving on crowded streets or the highway."

She checks to make sure Dad's not listening. "He doesn't want me going off by myself."

I squash a shout of laughter building in my chest. *Yeah, Dad's afraid you'll be running around with your twenty-year-old boyfriend.*

Dad calls us in for lunch. I take Mom's arm and help her to the kitchen. She looks at her plate and then at Dad, who's rooting around in the fridge. He's forgotten to cut her sandwich into triangles. With her tremor becoming worse, he cuts her sandwich to make it easier to hold. I shake my head to warn her to say nothing. I cut the bread.

Dad sits down with the mayonnaise and spreads some on the inside of his sandwich.

Mom delivers her *coup de grâce.* "How can I get you to the hospital if I can't drive? Have you thought of that?"

He pretends not to hear her and hands me the mayonnaise.

"Have you?" she insists.

"You can't get down the elevator and into the car alone. How are you going to do all that *and* help me?"

"So what will you do? Stay here and die?"

"I'll call an ambulance." Dad is beyond the end of his patience.

Mom is silent. She realizes she's gone down the wrong path and tries another. "How will I visit you in the hospital?"

Dad puts his glass down with a thud. I attempt to short circuit what's becoming a ludicrous argument. "Mom, if Dad goes into the hospital, Leslie will drive you to see him."

"I want to take the test. Just in case. I might need my license, and I want to keep it."

"Fine." Dad's voice is as hard as granite. "I'll drive you to the registry. But once we arrive, you're on your own. They'll test your eyesight first. If you pass, good on you. Then you'll take the road test *if* the state trooper dares to get into the car with you. If you pass, I'll be the first to congratulate you." He stands and takes his plate to the sink. "I'm taking a nap."

In the silence that follows, I realize Dad is, in fact, saying he no longer needs Mom. It's a heartbreaking revelation, and I'm angry that he didn't take my advice to be less argumentative.

When Mom finishes eating, I clear the table and start the dishwasher. I turn around and see a tear running down her cheek, so I move my chair closer and put my arms around her. "Dad doesn't mean to get angry—"

"Yes, he does. He's stubborn. It drives me crazy."

"I don't want you to go crazy," I say gently. "Do you think you can pass the test? Or are you angry because you can't go where you want to?"

She's crying more now, sniffing the snot up her nose. What can I say except, *he drives me crazy too?* I've thought about the day when my kids tell me, "Pops, it's time to give up your license." Part of my life will be over. Another signal that I'm old and coming to the end. Is driving more important than sex? At least with ED, you can fight back with pills and porn.

But driving represents freedom from your parents. Giving up a license is regressing into a mirror of your childhood. Once again, you're dependent on other people. Except now you don't have parents who think you're cute or handsome, you are no longer a darling child with promise. Your children don't think about you every minute of every day the way you thought about them. No wonder some old people give up the ghost, lay down, and die.

I rub my mother's back. She calms down and sags against me. "Do you want to take a nap?"

Her voice is muffled against my shirt. "I need to pee first." She giggles.

How many times a day does she need to pee? "Let me get your walker, and we'll scoot to the bathroom."

Ever since I can remember, Mom told anecdotes at dinner about what she had seen or heard during the day. We broke in at our peril. Most of the time, her stories were funny, and we all laughed. Some included a moment when she believed she'd been wronged. Alcohol aggravated her paranoia and her sense of injustice. We were expected to express unquestioned sympathy or justification.

One day, she dinged the fender of a car belonging to a woman visiting a neighbor. Mom pulled over and, getting out, profusely apologized. The stress caused her hands to shake more than usual. The owner of the car came off the neighbor's porch at full throttle. "What have you done?"

Examining the fender, Mom found rusted dents in several places with no way to tell where she'd hit the car. The woman turned on her. "How could you be so careless?"

Taken aback, Mom couldn't collect her thoughts.

The woman saw my mother's hands. "You've been drinking. I should call the cops."

Here, Mom stopped the story to defend herself. "I'd only had a small glass of wine with lunch. How dare she accuse me of drinking?"

"'I'm not drunk,' I told the woman. 'Look. Your car's ass is sticking out in the road!' That shut the woman up."

Mom looked triumphantly around the table. "She left, and I turned around and came home. I was too upset to go shopping."

"Mom, that woman was mean." Leslie patted her arm.

"She knew she was in the wrong," I said. "That's why she was angry."

Dad put his fork on his plate and leaned forward. "Did you call the insurance company?"

"Oh, I forgot about that. I was upset."

"You'll do that first thing tomorrow." He crushed the sympathy we'd shown Mom. "Where's her information? Did you get the name of her insurance company?"

Dad's sternness caused Mom to doubt herself. "I think so. Yes, I'm sure I did." She didn't sound convincing.

Then came Dad's final shot: "And you shouldn't start drinking until I get home."

Mom calmly placed her silverware on the table. She was determined to get the last word. "A little glass of wine with lunch is *not* drinking." She flung her napkin on the table. "You can get your own coffee." She went upstairs to their bedroom.

At the time, I didn't realize that Mom's account was more of a confession than a story. Her need to unburden herself was a characteristic I shared with her. But now, as an adult, I think she was sending a plea for help.

Later I went upstairs and knocked on the bedroom door.

"Mom, if the woman didn't ask for your insurance info, she probably knows there was no damage. Don't worry. Nothing will happen."

"But what about Dad?"

"I'll speak with him."

I spoke with Dad, but he only grunted a response.

It was an argument about nothing.

CHAPTER 16

"Going Back to Work Will Be a Pleasure"

That evening Rachel and I meet Leslie outside the restaurant at 5:00. We'd hoped to arrange something the previous night, but Leslie had been busy, though meeting this early should give us plenty of time to catch up before Rachel and I have to head to the airport. I'd made a reservation for four earlier in the day although Leslie had told me not to expect Palmer.

"Palmer's not coming. He said he has a paper due tomorrow. Surprise, surprise." Leslie meets us outside the restaurant. "It's almost impossible to involve him with family. He did nothing to help with the yard sale."

She's becoming more and more irritated but suddenly stops and grins sheepishly. "I promised myself I wouldn't get upset, but I'm tired of arguing with him. Frankly, I don't want him to come if he plans to sit around with a scowl on his face."

"That doesn't sound like the Palmer I know."

"He's a teenager now," I remind Rachel. "Remember how embarrassing your parents were when you were his age."

I open the door of the restaurant and follow the women inside. The hostess is away from her reception podium.

"I remember Mom driving me crazy with her complaints about Dad when I came home after dates."

"I'm disappointed he didn't come." Rachel was looking forward to seeing him.

"Palmer was at a friend's house Friday and Saturday. He wasn't worried about his paper then. But he gets good grades, so I shouldn't complain. Now I have to start worrying about alcohol. I laid down the law about not drinking at his friend's house. He agreed all too quickly, but I'm not convinced—"

The hostess rushes up to us.

"Reservation for Aherne," I tell her. "There's just the three of us."

She checks her list. "Yes, sir. Your table is ready." She signals to a woman coming from the dining room. "Sandra will take you in now."

I step aside to allow the women to follow her. Rachel and Leslie resume their conversation on the way to the table. Even deciding where to sit around the table causes nary a blip in their discussion.

Sandra hands me my menu. "David will be your waiter this evening." She pours each of us a glass of water and removes the fourth place setting. "Enjoy your dinner."

I thank her, take my seat, and try to catch up with my sister's story.

"—this fall, he attended a party where there was drinking. Palmer was dumbfounded when I confronted him. He stared at me in disbelief. 'Who told you?'

"'Never mind that.' I was angry—he's fourteen for heaven's sake. I told him he was grounded for the next two weekends. I had no choice. It would be so much easier if Sean were still alive. Palmer wouldn't have dared tell his father to stop poking his nose in his business, but he jumped up and told me just that and stomped upstairs. I shouted after him that he was now grounded for three weeks. He slammed his bedroom door."

"It's important to make sure you stick to that," I say.

Leslie grimaces and holds up a thumb and forefinger an inch apart. "I relented slightly. Palmer didn't come down to dinner, but after he'd cooled off in his room, he came down and apologized." Leslie's shoulders sag as she remembers the conflict. "It's hard being both father and mother, but I want him to be safe. Anyway, to make a long story a little longer, I said because he apologized I'd take the third weekend off the penalty box. I know he was hoping I'd take them all off, but I wasn't doing that."

"No, you're right, you shouldn't," Rachel agrees. "So how did it go?"

"He didn't complain, although he missed out on a movie and pizza party."

"Considering all parents deal with underage drinking at one point or another, we're lucky we haven't had any serious problems." I lower my voice. "This is off the record, but we had an incident with Jenn—"

The waiter stops by our table. "I'm David, and I'm your server this evening. Have you been here before?"

Leslie says she's eaten here several times. "I decided my brother and his wife would enjoy coming for dinner."

"Well, thank you—we're happy to have you."

We give him our drink orders and then spend a few moments looking over the menu. "I know you love eggplant parmesan," Leslie tells me. "I had it last time, and it was the best I've had in years."

"You've convinced me." I close my menu. "That and a side Caesar. Okay, I'm set."

"What are you having?" Rachel asks my sister.

"I'll have the baked stuffed lobster. I deserve it after the yard sale and move."

Rachel returns to her menu—"I need more time"—and I resume the story of Jenn's brush with the law.

"One Saturday night, Rachel's working and I'm home alone. The telephone rings."

"When was this?" Leslie asks.

"I think Jenn was a sophomore in high school. So, the phone rings, and I check to see who's calling. It was the Lexington police station. That made me sit up and take notice. It was Jenn. The police found a keg at the party and arrested all the kids. We went to court the following week. Luckily one of the fathers knew the judge—"

"But they were kids," Rachel interrupts. "Even though you're angry with them, you expect some rough patches." She turns to Leslie. "Don't tell anyone. Jennifer would kill me if she found out we told you, but I don't want you to feel so badly about Palmer."

The waiter comes with our drinks and asks if Rachel is ready to order.

Rachel looks down at her menu. "You two order first. I haven't decided yet."

"They've already ordered," the waiter reminds her.

Rachel begins clicking her tongue to show she's busy choosing. "I can't decide between the halibut or the crabs. The crab cakes sound delicious."

The waiter starts to make a note on his pad.

"Is the fish fresh or has it been frozen?"

The waiter acts like he's taking it personally. "All our fish are fresh, ma'am."

"The cook has to spank them before lunch every day."

Rachel looks at me. She's not amused. I've told this joke before.

The waiter ignores me. He's probably heard some variation of it many times. At least I get a laugh from Leslie.

"Is the halibut baked with a heavy crust or is it light?"

"Baked with lightly crushed breadcrumbs and our selection of herbs, ma'am." He shifts his weight to his other foot.

Rachel gives a few more clicks of her tongue. I look at Leslie to see what she's thinking. She's doesn't seem to notice.

"I guess I'll have the crab cakes after all."

"Certainly, ma'am."

"Oh, and may I have a baked potato instead of the seasonal vegetables?"

"Of course." The waiter leaves.

"I'm sorry if he thinks I'm difficult. But I don't like 'seasonal' anything. I want to know exactly what I'm getting."

Leslie asks about our kids. "Is Jenn coming back from Ireland anytime soon?"

"She'll be home before Christmas," Rachel says. "Jon's already in Japan, travelling with the other students. We've told him once he starts college he'll have to take out student loans like Jenn."

"Not much more than one or two thousand," I add, "but I think it focuses the mind when they have some skin in the game."

"Elaine's a freshman," Leslie says. "Palmer graduates high school in three years. They'll overlap for one year. Elaine got a partial scholarship for field hockey, but she's upset at all the time it takes. Palmer is interested in photography, so I'm encouraging him to pick a college with scholarships in the Midwest."

There's a lull in the conversation as if Leslie considers talking about college costs will ruin an otherwise enjoyable dinner.

Over coffee and dessert, Leslie tells a funny story about her attempts to have one of Sean's brothers discuss sex with Palmer. "Obviously, I wasn't going to do it. I looked at some books in the library, but they seemed like they were written for sixth graders. I thought, really, do they learn this that early?"

"But Palmer's fourteen. It's a bit late at this point," Rachel says.

Leslie laughs. "This was two years ago. I talked with Ralph, but he and Bridget have three girls, so he's had no experience talking with a son. He said I should speak with Ronan. With four boys, he said he'd be willing. When Palmer was staying with them—it was the summer before eighth grade—Ronan broached the topic, but Palmer said he knew all about it. Apparently, his oldest cousin beat Ronan to the punch. Ronan and I had a good laugh. Kids these days know more than I even thought of at their age. What happened with you and Jon?"

"I thought I was being proactive. I had a couple of books, but they reminded me of the filmstrip I saw in school. Anyway, just as we were getting started, Jon said, 'Oh, this is what Scott's father told him.' That took the wind out of my sails, but Jon sat down, and we went through one of the books. I don't know what he'd heard from Scott, but he wasn't surprised by anything I said. When we finished he stood, said, 'Thanks, Dad,' and ran out to play ball. I was left with the library books, feeling like I'd been run over by a truck. I put the books in my briefcase, returned them to the library, and that was it."

"How did Dad handle it with you?"

I looked over my glasses and gave Leslie my what-do-you-think expression. "I attended a meeting at school with Dad. All I'll say is I was shocked by the info. Totally took me by surprise. But then I was hopelessly naïve."

The waiter brought the bill, which I paid over Leslie's objections. "We owe you. Don't worry about it."

At the cars, we kiss each other, and she thanks us once again for dinner. "Mark, I appreciate all your help. I couldn't have done it without you."

"I'm relieved they're in a safer place. They should be all set for now. Let me know how the paperwork review goes."

"I will. Bye, Rachel. Love you both. Keep in touch."

Rachel drives the car. "Get some sleep. I'll wake you when we're near the airport."

"I'll be glad to get home." I yawn. "Going back to work will be a pleasure."

CHAPTER 17

"If You Have Any Questions, Come and Ask Me"

My seventh-grade teacher, Mr. Robertson, separated the boys from the girls when we lined up to walk home for lunch. When the bell rang, he dismissed the girls. This was unusual, and we boys looked at each other, wondering what was up. As we filed out of the room, he handed each of us an envelope. "A signed permission slip is due by the end of the week."

Outside the school, we stood in a large group, the rules governing schoolyard cliques suspended. Several girls joined us, wondering if we were in trouble. We showed them the envelopes addressed to our parents. Usually when a notice was sent home, the flap was tucked inside the envelope. These envelopes were sealed.

Dwayne, an older boy held back to repeat the seventh grade, said the letter was about sex. He reminded us that girls in our class had received a similar envelope two months earlier. "It's about the facts of life. Girls learned about their periods."

What was he talking about? The only periods I knew about were at the end of sentences.

I hoped that Dwayne was correct. I'd learn something to fill in the blanks. When Dad was home from work, I'd ask him to sign my permission slip.

Back at school, the classroom buzzed with details from the letter. Some boys had asked their mothers to sign their letters at lunch, and these circulated around the class. The letter explained that a meeting for boys was scheduled to show a filmstrip about human sexuality.

"I know all about it," Dwayne bragged. "I went to the meeting last year and don't need a refresher course." He acted much older than us, and I wondered if he'd been kept back before.

A local doctor was scheduled to lead the meeting. The school administration encouraged fathers to attend with their sons. I wondered what Steve Bushnell would do. His father had died two years ago. Surely his mother wouldn't come. Maybe an uncle would stand in for his dad. The meeting was the first Saturday in March, two weeks away.

I knew about erections and their inevitable habit of occurring at inopportune moments. In fact, they were a nuisance because, when I had one, I couldn't pee. I grew up with a sister, so the physical difference between boys and girls was no mystery. I also learned that certain things shouldn't be done around girls. Last year at the cabin my parents rented each summer, my sister and I were dressing after swimming. As a joke, I demonstrated holding up a towel with my erection. And it was a *damp* towel.

I learned too late that my sister couldn't keep a secret. She was convinced she'd go to hell if she didn't tell Mom everything. That evening, Mom asked to speak with me. Alone. She wasn't angry, but as the disciplinarian, she made it clear that my behavior was unacceptable and shouldn't happen again. Perhaps Dad hadn't yet heard about the incident, but even if he had, he always left the unpleasant discussions for Mom to handle.

At twelve, I was clueless about sex, and what I'd overheard didn't make sense. Despite my As in school, I never questioned *why* boys and girls were different. I was sure there was something I needed to know, but even if I'd been able to formulate a question, I didn't have the courage to ask it. Instead I assumed the difference in anatomy was a quirk of nature that adults no longer found relevant. The bits of information I overheard listening to older boys only confused me more.

During recess, if the playing fields were muddy, the older boys separated into cliques to discuss sports, girls, and sex. Those of us not in a clique due to age or low social standing made do talking with each other or with girls, playing marbles, or swinging two ropes for girls to skip double Dutch.

Whenever possible, I wormed my way into the outer circle of a clique and picked up some whispers about sex before I was discovered and kicked out. But hearing information piecemeal only created more confusion. Once, I heard Dwayne recite a poem:

> *In days of old when knights were bold*
> *And sheiks were not invented,*
> *They wrapped a sock around their cocks*
> *And babies were prevented.*

I laughed with the other boys, but what did Arabs have to do with a sock to prevent babies? Did a man walk around all day with a sock in his pants? A valuable lesson I'd learned early in life was to play along and not ask. Ignorance was preferable to ridicule.

And now the letter from school promised to change everything.

Human Sexuality Saturday arrived: a mild spring day with the sound of water dripping from roofs into gutters. Dad dressed in a business suit, white shirt, and tie. He wore a pair of boots with metal clasps. I was in my Sunday school clothes and a sweater Mom had knitted for me. At the last minute, I couldn't find my boots, so I borrowed Leslie's. They were dark blue with a pink band around the top. When I pulled my pant leg over the boot, the pink didn't show.

I assumed Dad would drive the car, but instead we walked the quarter mile to school. I worried that we'd be late. I hated walking into a roomful of people staring at me.

The school playing fields were at the end of our street. Drifting fog swirled around us as we kept to the cement path to avoid the pools of standing water. My father and I didn't speak, and I had to run at times to keep up with him. My sister's boots clomped on the asphalt. They were too small and hurt my feet.

The meeting was held in the combination gym/auditorium. Several classes of seventh-grade boys from neighboring schools were also attending. I'd never seen them before, and the prospect of anonymity was a welcome surprise. Most seats were taken. I wanted to sit in the back, but Dad walked to the front where there were two empty seats on the aisle. I avoided the eyes of anyone I knew, as if caught someplace I shouldn't be. I wanted to be invisible.

The gym was quiet without the shouts of boys, the thump of the ball, and the squeak of sneakers on the wooden floor. Although tall for my age, I didn't enjoy basketball. I hated playing on the skin team, which played without shirts. I was embarrassed at how skinny I was. Why didn't I have hair on my chest like the older boys?

A young man in the center aisle threaded a filmstrip through the projector. I was always disappointed when a teacher showed a filmstrip rather than a film because they were never interesting, and with the shades drawn, I fought to keep my eyes open. When the man turned on the projector, a hush of expectation swept through the room. He focused and leveled the projector, using a bullseye displayed on the screen. Across the aisle, I saw my teacher, Mr. Robertson, talking with his son. Before he noticed me, I turned away and slouched in my chair.

An older man with white hair and a wispy beard stood at the lectern, scanning his notes. When he was ready, he cleared his throat. "Can everyone hear me?"

A boy seated in the last row shouted, "No."

He adjusted the microphone in its holder and tightened a screw. "Now can you hear me?"

There was a chorus of "Yes" and a few whistles.

"Good morning," he said. "I'm Dr. Wellman." He cleared his throat again and glanced down at his notes. "As you young men grow up, your body changes—" The microphone shrieked with feedback, and he made a further adjustment. "As I was saying, your body changes, and you develop secondary sex characteristics."

Pictures of the female and male reproductive organs were cartoons. Rats. I'd hoped for photos. A drawing of a cross section of the male organ was unsettling and looked painful. The shuffle of feet were men and boys crossing their legs. Then we saw a photograph of tadpoles. They had long tails but hadn't grown legs yet.

"These creatures are called sperm," the doctor said. "They whip their tails back and forth, racing toward the egg."

Cut to a cartoon of the egg waiting patiently in something called a fallopian tube. The egg was drawn to represent a wistful princess atop a castle. The drawbridge was down. The next diagram showed a mob of invading sperm. Then a close-up of one sperm, dressed as a prince, crossing the moat.

"Once a sperm enters the egg," the doctor said, "the egg prevents other sperm from entering."

In the next cartoon, the drawbridge was raised, and the princess was smiling. I found all this hard to believe. Surely the other sperm were smart enough to find another way inside. And what if two sperm princes raced across the drawbridge at the exact same moment? These were good questions for the doctor, but I wasn't asking them. And where did the sperm come from anyway?

After a few photos showing the fetus developing in the womb, the instructor turned up the lights and asked if there were any questions.

Silence. The radiators along the wall hissed and clanged. A few coughs.

Before the silence became unbearable, Mr. Robertson stood up. "Doctor, some boys may not know how the sperm gets inside the woman. Would you address this?"

The speaker hesitated and swallowed. "Of course." He took a deep breath. The audience leaned forward, as if sucked toward the front of the auditorium. I held my breath and listened.

You do what? You put it where? Does he know what he's talking about? And then what happens? I was dizzy with facts, then I remembered to breathe. And Mom was worried about what I did with a damp towel!

Leaving the gym, a few boys ran ahead, shouting and laughing as if the lecture was old hat. How much had they known before today? Other boys, acting cool and nonchalant, chatted with friends as if saying, "That was interesting, but let's get together for soccer this afternoon." The rest of us were silent, concentrating on thinking and walking at the same time. I nodded to the boy who sat behind me in class. His eyes widened, but he said nothing. I wasn't the only one speechless.

Dad and I crossed the field back the way we'd come. The sun had burned off the morning fog, leaving the trees, fence, and houses in sharp relief. I saw the world with new eyes. My questions had been answered, but more were wasting no time crowding offstage. The facts made sense in theory, but what do I *do* now?

Dad spoke once on the way home. "If you have any questions, come and ask me." His tone was perfunctory. These words were the beginning and end of our discussion about sex. I was scornful; this was something he had to say. If we'd never discussed the simplest emotional issue, how would we ever talk about this? I'd never ask him any question about sex even if my life depended on it.

At home, Mom asked me how it had gone. I ignored her and went to my room. "Did you learn anything?" she called after me with a laugh.

Very funny. I silently mimicked her tone of voice and stuck out my tongue, before I changed out of my Sunday clothes and adjusted bicycle clips around my jeans.

"See you later." I went straight to the front door, avoiding her and Dad. "I'm collecting for my paper route."

I closed the door with a bang before they could reply. I was angry. I'd been deceived and kept in the dark.

It reminded me of adults justifying their lies about Santa Claus: "All done to bring joy to children at Christmas." But I also remembered walking home one day in second grade, when Kathleen, the girl across the street, told me Santa didn't exist.

"Of course he exists." She's nuts, I thought.

Kathleen laughed and told me to ask my mother.

"We planned to tell you after Christmas," Mom said. I was stunned by her deception. Humiliated that I'd fallen for a story that, looking back, was an obvious hoax. And been laughed at by a girl I wanted to kiss who thought *I* was crazy for still believing such nonsense.

All this time, sex had hidden in plain sight behind a flimsy curtain of silence. Only after wallowing in ignorance and tormenting myself for months had the curtain been pulled aside with a smirk and a laugh. Hoodwinked once again.

I stayed out the whole afternoon. After collecting, I sat on the fence facing the highway, waiting for the delivery van with the afternoon papers. When an older boy rode by on his bicycle, all I could think was, *He already knows about this*. Or when watching a man getting out of his car, I was amazed: *He's known about this for years*. And when I threw a newspaper onto the porch of a house where young children played on the lawn, I looked at them for a moment, then shook my head. Another generation of suckers!

CHAPTER 18

"It Was the Wrong Decision"

With no traffic delays driving to the airport, we have plenty of time to return the car, check our bags, and walk to the terminal. After boarding the plane, I settle back to sleep during the flight. I barely drop off when I'm jolted awake. "Did we hit something?" I ask in shock.

"Yeah, the runway." Gathering her magazines and pocketbook, Rachel stares at me. "We've landed in Chicago."

"Already? What time is it?" Looking at my watch, I'm surprised it's so late. "Why'd it take so long."

"Your watch is still on Boston time."

We ride the bus to the regional transportation center in our town and walk to the long-term parking.

"I'm amazed I used only one week of vacation to do everything we did," I say, starting the car. "I'm exhausted."

"I noticed. You were asleep before the plane took off."

"By the way, while you were in the bathroom, Leslie said she's getting Life Alert buttons for each of them."

"Hopefully, they'll use them."

The mail on hold will be delivered tomorrow. Newspapers are piled on the doorstep. The call light on the phone is blinking furiously. "I'll listen to them," Rachel says. "Go upstairs and get ready for bed before you fall asleep standing up."

Coming upstairs, she tells me one of the calls is from my boss. "You're to see him first thing tomorrow."

"Got it." Once in bed, I fall asleep immediately.

Next to being fired, the worst fate in the corporate world is being passed over. Walking out of Ed's office after hearing the news, beset with conflicting emotions, I need to leave the building. I can't face my staff today, some of whom must have heard rumors I wasn't promoted; the rest will soon find out. Before I leave, Emma arrives and, seeing me, acts unusually distant. I tell her I've already heard the news, and she sighs with relief and commiserates with me. I ask her to cancel the group meeting this morning.

I cross the street and turn into the anonymity of the city's Public Gardens. The lawn crew is vacuuming up the last piles of leaves, the swans have been relocated for the winter, and the swan boats are covered with tarps until spring. I find a secluded corner where I can quietly think and compose myself. Surprisingly, I'm not as disappointed about not getting the position as much as I'm embarrassed by being passed over.

The first thought I have is why. What do I lack? Where am I deficient? I can't remember much of Ed's explanation. After getting the bad news everything else was blah, blah, blah. Hopefully, I'll remember more before I tell Rachel. Just not tonight.

My next thought is worse. The company has been facing declining revenue since the beginning of the year and, suspiciously, haven't been replacing departing staff. Are they slimming the organization to make it more attractive to potential buyers? I've heard nothing to prove I'm correct, but in my current frame of mind, I have a premonition that I will be gone by next summer. My sense of invulnerability is gone.

A group of tourists are taking a guided tour with a docent of the PG. I'm too far away to hear what the guide is telling them, but when she points to a group of autumn flowers, everyone bends over for a closer look. Two tourists are photoholics, unable to stop taking pictures. I hear the clicks as they repeatedly press the button, as if afraid the plants might bloom and walk away.

The docent walks toward me; I shrink back, trying to be invisible. I imagine she's describing me as vegetation that has evolved into an invasive species that must be eradicated. I'm shocked when the tourists move closer and stare at me. Their cameras sound like those of paparazzi. Only after they move do I realize I'm sitting in front of an unusual variety of ferns.

In the end it comes down to money. Not only did I lose the promotion, I also lost the increase in income. Our lifestyle won't be greatly affected. Rachel and I can still travel, and day-to-day expenses can be paid without much thought. But our schedule of saving for retirement must be ramped up. It's true that no matter how much money one earns, one never feels it's enough. I haven't talked much about the potential promotion with Rachel, but soon she will want to know the who, what, when, why, where of the entire situation.

I return to the office to use the bathroom. I'm not inflicting a porta-potty on myself in my current frame of mind. Then I empty my inbox into my briefcase, shrug into my jacket, and sneak out of the office like I don't belong and if found might be arrested.

I spend the day at the Boston Public Library and catch the subway to the parking lot before rush hour. Pulling into the driveway, I notice Rachel's car is gone; she's on the evening shift. I carry the mail into the living room and turn on CNN. In the refrigerator I find a frozen eggplant parmesan that Rachel bought this morning from the local Italian restaurant. Dinner will require no clean-up, which makes the meal more enjoyable. I turn on the oven and only then realize I had this meal yesterday in the restaurant. Oh well, one can never have too much eggplant parmesan.

While waiting for the oven to preheat, I call Rachel. The ward secretary places the phone on the counter, and I hear her ask someone if they know where Rachel is. Suddenly, she answers, "Rachel Aherne."

"It's me. Thanks for buying the eggplant."

"See what a good wife I am?" She turns from the phone and tells someone, "No, the patient is in room fourteen," then resumes our conversation. "It's crazy here. One of the nurses is sick, and the nursing office sent us a sub who's only worked here one week. Like we have time to train her."

"Okay, I'll let you get back to work."

"See you later."

I hang up and put my dinner in the oven, then glance through last week's Sunday paper and find the magazine with the crossword puzzle. It's hard to concentrate because I still see Emma arriving at the office. When she saw me, she acted subdued and didn't voice her usual critique of the latest office controversy.

"I've seen Ed already and got the bad news," I'd told her. "He left a message on my home phone asking to see me first thing today. He didn't want me taken by surprise if I met a team member before he told me."

"I was shocked by the announcement that Richman was promoted. I predict he won't last long. He doesn't know the first thing about the job and doesn't have the respect from the members of his new team." Emma turned to hang up her coat. "I want you to know how we feel."

"What can I do?" I said, lifting my arms. "Easy come, easy—"

"As much as we'd hate to lose you, the team agrees it was the wrong decision."

"Thanks. That softens the blow somewhat. By the way, I appreciate your handling things last week. Incidentally, do you know if anyone was hoping to snag my position?"

"You know I wouldn't take your job if it was offered on a silver platter. As for anyone else"—she'd shrugged—"I don't know, but if I did, I wouldn't tell you."

She probably knew but was protecting the staff. "You're right. Your discretion is noted."

And I'd made my getaway.

The oven buzzes: dinner's ready. I begin sorting the mail while eating and watching TV.

"How are things at work?" Rachel asks the following night while clearing the dinner table.

"The same."

When I say nothing more, she looks up from wiping the counter. She raises her eyebrows and tilts her head; she expects more of an answer. "Nothing about the promotion?"

"Oh, that ship has sailed. I wasn't chosen."

"When were you going to tell me?" She sits at the table. "When did you find out?"

"Yesterday."

She reaches over and strokes my hand. "I'm so sorry. It must be a disappointment."

Although it is, I raise my shoulders in a half-hearted shrug.

"And that's the end of the matter? No other possibilities?"

"The company is downsizing as people leave. I think they're looking for a buyer. I've searched the company website for open positions, but there's nothing at my level."

"Isn't there someone you've worked for who might know of some other positions?"

"The unspoken rule is you talk with your manager before contacting someone in another department."

"Surely that doesn't apply when you have a casual conversation. You're not applying for a job."

"I doubt Ed would entertain the idea of my leaving to work elsewhere in the company."

"What if you say you're thinking of leaving, would that make a difference?"

"With the downsizing, they might jump at the chance to let me go. You can't threaten to quit if you don't have another job."

"Then look for one. At least you'll see if your skills are in demand."

"It won't be easy. I'm almost fifty-four. I don't have much time to be switching jobs."

"Better to find out now. You don't have to take the job."

"I may need to take a cut in pay to get in a company with long-term prospects."

"You've done that before, and your pay went up as they quickly realized your value."

I sympathize with Rachel when she expresses her outrage. "As if you didn't deserve it," she says the next morning. "Are they crazy? They don't know how good they've got it."

Her disbelief helps distract me from a sense of failure.

After a week, I've accepted the reality, and become irritated when Rachel won't. I listen for a while but eventually tune her out. I'm tired of her criticizing an organization to which I've dedicated many years of my life.

As the days pass, her words are like the drip, drip, drip of water that over time erodes my rock of confidence. I begin to believe I'm not measuring up to what's expected of me. Maybe they were right not to promote me.

I still enjoy seeing the people I work with every day. They make the job worthwhile, and I look forward to the socialization during work. My staff is dedicated, and I feel a surge of pride when, during the yearly performance review, an employee expresses his appreciation of my management style. Of course, I'm a realist and understand there's an ulterior motive to their praise, but nevertheless I appreciate the thought.

On the weekend, a change comes over me: work no longer provides me with a challenge, and my satisfaction of accomplishment is gone. I'm easily annoyed with minor admin changes made by upper management. A new HR procedure becomes an irritant. A decision to replace a software product only marginally better is a waste of time. I must watch my tongue in meetings when I'm about to verbalize a complaint.

Once this dissatisfaction takes root, it's almost impossible to return to my former positive attitude. I make the decision to leave almost without knowing it. I begin looking at the help-wanted section of the Sunday newspaper and fantasize about what I'd like in a new job. The fantasy becomes a plan, and the resentment at work grows more intolerable.

I avoid thinking about how my team will miss me because I understand this feeling is a mirage and rarely true. One might be missed for a week or at most a month, but like a death, the world keeps spinning, and everyone goes on with their life without looking back.

I find my résumé in an old folder in the bottom of my desk, but it's out of date by twenty years. The text describing my first job after grad school will be reduced to the name of the company and one line. I must start from scratch.

It's a challenge to summarize my work over the last two decades. After writing two pages, I try to create some order to my work history. Some of my achievements also should quantify the money and time savings gained by the company. When I finally admit suffering from writer's block, I spread out the ads I've cut from the newspaper and work on the letters I'll send with my résumé to prospective hiring managers.

At work the next morning, I locate copies of my last ten performance reports. They identify several achievements I'd forgotten. Too bad I didn't have these reports last night. For references I call former bosses, some of whom work at other companies, to ask if I may include their names. Few are surprised by my decision to leave. That evening I finish the first draft of my résumé.

On Wednesday I mail résumés to four companies and over the weekend fantasize about who will respond and what they have to offer. On Sunday I cut out a new set of ads.

I'm worried about the interviews; I haven't done one in years. I'm not the glad-handing type of person who immediately establishes a rapport with an interviewer. All the anxiety I felt after dropping out of grad school and looking for my first job returns. I find a set of index cards I once used to review before an interview. Each card has a question an employer might ask. My answer is written on the back of the card.

Two companies invite me in for an interview. After my second meeting, I panic. I haven't presented the best impression of my past responsibilities. I'm depressed. I'll need to practice my delivery and act like I'm an actor playing the part of an extrovert.

In the back of my mind I remember the last years of my father's job. He ended up feeling he'd failed in some way. Our situations are different, but there's always a way a job can turn into hell on earth.

When Dad returned home after World War II, he looked for his first job. Trained as a mechanical engineer, he joined Stone & Webster in Boston. He considered himself fortunate to find a job in a world-renowned company with attractive benefits. In the forties, it wasn't unusual for a man to work at the same company for his entire career. Dad was no different: he remained with S&W until his retirement.

In the early fifties, Mom and I visited Dad's office on what must have been the hottest day of the summer. The large room held rows of desks and drafting tables. Every window was opened at the bottom and the top, and large standing fans swung back and forth, fighting to keep the temperature down. I knew nothing about what he did at work except for one thing: He used an inexplicable object called a slide rule.

In the late seventies, the company faced tough times. Nuclear energy was the future of S&W until the moratorium on nuclear power plants. Oil embargoes also delayed contracts to build new electrical generation plants.

Dad never spoke of an interest in upper management or never had the ambition to pursue it. Several of his contemporaries became senior managers, one even becoming president of the company. Once I enlisted in the USAF and moved away, I lost touch with the day-to-day routine at home. I wasn't there when, as Leslie told me, Dad, in his late fifties, lost faith in the company and his work. Young engineers straight from college were hired with salaries comparable to his after thirty years of experience. Perhaps he didn't upgrade his skills to use new technology and found himself left behind.

He suffered from anxiety and ulcers for years. Mom often found him pacing the living room in the mornings while waiting for his ride with a neighbor into Boston. I knew he was experiencing a rough patch in his life, but I assumed his ulcers were the primary cause. Plagued with indecision about my master's degree program, I was too consumed with my own problems to take much notice.

At work, Dad was reassigned as Manager of Administration. On one of my rare visits home, I remember him saying at dinner, "Can you believe I spent the afternoon checking every emergency exit on each floor of the building? Effective use of my time."

His stomach trouble became worse, and he missed work several days at a time. During his tests, the doctor found the *H. pylori* virus which, at that time, was an unsuspected cause of ulcers. He also discovered a cancerous tumor in his digestive tract, and a surgeon removed a significant section of his colon.

Worries about his health and disappointment at work aggravated his physical complaints. As Dad became absent from work for longer stretches of time, the doctor finally wrote a letter, and S&W granted him early retirement and his pension in 1978. He never talked about the end of his career to me, but I suspect he believed he'd not lived up to his potential or had failed in some way.

Over the years, he lost interest in his hobbies. He filled his days with reading, watching TV, visiting family and a few friends, and eating out with Mom two or three times a week.

Remembering his experience, I'm determined to avoid that fate. I don't have his physical ailments, but I know if I stay at my company, I'll eventually resent being passed over. I'd better move on before I become older and bitter.

CHAPTER 19

"WE SHOULD BE THANKFUL
WE GOT ANYTHING"

I must admit that moving my parents into an apartment wasn't as difficult as I'd expected. They're safer now and Leslie and I feel a sense of relief. That's easier for me to say because I'm not the one on call. As I worry about my job search, I feel more and more guilty about Leslie shouldering the burden of caring for our parents. Despite the incident with the boat, I'm no longer allowing Dad's bullying to upset me when he calls. And my anger, which I've always considered justified, no longer seems as reasonable in light of my parents' need for help. I can no longer justify continuing my self-imposed estrangement without considering the effect it has on Leslie's quality of life.

When I'd told Rachel about my not getting the promotion, she'd agreed I should look around to see what was available. Nevertheless, I want to keep my search for a job out of the general conversation at home for the time being.

After sending out another dozen or so résumés, I'm surprised to receive only three replies. Two of them asked for a telephone interview and in each case it was soon evident that further discussion was unwarranted: the salary was too low, or I didn't have the exact experience they expected. The third reply was a telephone call from a secretary to come in for an interview. This was one of the companies I believed would be a good fit for me and I carefully prepared the day before.

The meeting was successful until the last ten minutes when the man had a telephone call. At first he seemed to brush it off, but looking once more he decided to take it. He listened and then hung up after saying, "I understand." He explained he was only the first manager to interview a candidate; a second meeting would be with the hiring manager. He then made it clear that he wouldn't recommend me for the second round. I was so shocked I couldn't think of anything to say. The secretary outside his office smiled and wished me a good day.

I kept my cool until I was out on the street before I exploded with a rush of anger that caused several pedestrians to give me a wide birth. I was furious that I hadn't demanded to know the reason for this abrupt dismissal. Had the hiring manager only just read my résumé and called to say he wasn't interested? But after all the encouragement and interest from the first man with whom I'd spoken, I doubt I would have received a reason that made sense. I'd have been embarrassed to listen to him stuttering a reason. At that moment I decided the time had come to work with a headhunter. And it was time to look to the East Coast for a job.

That evening I talk with Rachel and tell her about my experience that afternoon as well as the outcomes of my interviews. She's shocked by the rudeness of some of the hiring staff. I explain they see so many people they forget that we're human and not pegs on a board.

I don't tell her that my focus is no longer to work in Chicago. But changing my job search to the Boston area is unlike signing on for a new job here. I can't state my demands and say take it or leave it. Everything will require careful negotiation. I must talk with Rachel before going much further. She won't agree if moving back recreates the former tension with my father. And will she look favorably on moving back east with the obvious result of spending more time with my parents? I'll wait to see what happens before I say anything.

I meet with a Mr. (call me Ted) Wooken in his office in a local office park. Like a banker, he has nothing on his desk except a pad of paper and a telephone. With a genial manner that puts one at ease, he soon gets down to business, his questions crisp and direct. We have a long conversation about why I want to leave, what kind of position I'm looking for, the range of salary I expect, and the area where I want to live.

I tell him I need to find a job west or north of Boston. I ask about his familiarity with the New England market, and he quickly assures me that's not a problem. "The process is the same, and I have colleagues in that area who will be part of your team." But what did I expect him to say?

"The only difference is the interview which, of course, will require travel. We'll ask for a telephone interview first to identify any positions that don't fit." He isn't encouraging about the time of year for a job search. "The upcoming holidays, you know. The job market in IT is in a holding position in the Chicago area, but it may be better in the Boston market."

"I've heard the economy is doing well. I see dozens of cranes erecting office buildings."

"Different professions, different cycles. Hiring will improve after the holidays. But it doesn't hurt to put your résumé out there and be ready when the positions open."

"I'm somewhat in a hurry because my parents are elderly and need support. My sister has assumed responsibility for their care for too long."

He sees the desperate look on my face. "Cheer up. It always seems daunting when you start looking, but I've many contacts I can call to get a complete lay of the land."

He gathers the papers on his desk and puts them in a folder. "I'll get started on this right away. First I'll review your résumé to see what can be beefed up to catch their eyes."

On my way back to the office I wonder if I would have been better served engaging a headhunter in the Boston area. I call the *Boston Globe* and have the Sunday paper delivered to me at work.

I'm concerned that I've not kept Rachel up to date with my plans and I struggle to think of a way to tell her. I know she won't be happy when she learns that I want to move back to Massachusetts. I must tell her soon.

A week passes before I hear anything from Ted. But first I receive a letter.

Most of the mail is advertising. We often get two copies of the same catalog but have no success trying to eliminate duplicates. I throw bills and letters to the side. I rip the junk mail in half for recycling. As usual when I'm alone at night, I eat dinner in front of the TV. My fork is halfway to my mouth when I see an oversized, cream-colored envelope with the embossed return address of a law firm in Boston. I put the fork down, look at the envelope more carefully, and open it. Each of the three pages is thick like the paper I once used for résumés.

> Mr. Mark Cargill Aherne:
>
> I am sorry to inform you that Mrs. Alice S. Cargill, the widow of your uncle, Neal W. Cargill, died in Charlottesville, Virginia on July 6, 1998.

I stop reading. Dad mentioned she'd died, but he didn't know when. Aunt Alice must have been almost eighty.

> As you may know, your uncle had established a trust during his lifetime, known as the "Neal W. Cargill Trust."
>
> Under the terms of the trust instrument, upon the death of Mrs. Cargill, the property is to be distributed in equal shares to the two children of Katherine Riese and to the two nieces of Alice

Cargill. At this time, each of you is entitled to twenty-five percent of the trust property in the amount of $123,789.54.

I review the last sentence several times to make sure I've read the amount correctly. I realize my mouth is full and stop chewing. I swallow and turn to the next two pages.

Enclosed herewith is a statement of the securities held in the trust. At your earliest convenience, please contact me at the above address with instructions as to how you wish us to disburse the payment to you.

Very truly yours,
Casandra McDermont

With my legs shaking uncontrollably, I fall back in the chair, still unable to believe my eyes. I grab the first page and reread the salutation to ensure the letter is for me.

I run to the kitchen and call Leslie. While the phone is ringing, I have a troubling thought and almost hang up. I don't want to spoil her surprise if she hasn't received her letter yet. Should I wait a day to call? Before I hang up, Leslie answers, "Hello?"

"Leslie, did you receive a letter from a legal firm in Boston?"

"Thank goodness, you got yours. Mine came yesterday, but I decided to wait until you contacted me. I called Mom and Dad to tell them."

"What did they say?"

"Dad said he hadn't received a letter and wonders why. But the lawyer told me that he's not part of the trust."

"You called the lawyer? Is he allowed to give you information about the estate?"

"It's like a will, and we have a right to see it. I called the lawyer this morning, and the facts are interesting. There are two trusts. We share one trust with the nieces of Aunt Alice. Remember them? We met them once."

"They're the ones who live in Virginia. Neal and Alice lived with one of the nieces after leaving Boston."

"Right but get this: The second trust is shared only by the two nieces, from which they could withdraw money for their aunt's care."

"That's fair. There must have been many expenses caring for her over the years."

"Fair, my ass. The two of them could take money out of either trust for her care. Guess which one they used?"

"Son of a bitch. The trust the four of us shared together."

"Bingo!"

Before Leslie hangs up, she says, "I've been riled up all day thinking about it but finally calmed down and told myself we're lucky we got anything at all. When Uncle Neal severed all ties with Mom and Dad, I remember thinking any money from that side of the family went up in smoke, so we should be thankful we got anything."

I return to the living room and turn off the TV. While reheating my meal. I think about what Leslie said: *We should be thankful we got anything.*

She's right. Neal suffered from dementia in his old age and believed Dad had been unfair to him and Aunt Alice. The reason for the break seemed so insignificant at the time I've forgotten the details. Neal's anger was also directed at me. When visiting my parents, I called to schedule a visit with them. Aunt Alice answered. She talked very quietly as if Neal was hovering nearby.

"Who's that on the phone?" he snarled.

"It's Mark. Your nephew," Aunt Alice told him.

"Hang up. HANG UP! We don't talk with the Ahernes."

"Oh, Neal. He's done nothing—"

"Hang up the damn phone."

Click. I was cut off.

When Neal married Alice Leland, a girl from Virginia, fifteen years his junior, they moved to a posh suburb of Boston. Alice never considered herself prejudiced. She fondly remembered the "Negros" who worked on her father's farm, at least those who remained farmhands and lived with their own kind, didn't attempt to improve themselves, or complain about their wages. Friction between the tolerant regard for blacks in the North versus the paternalistic attitude toward them in Virginia was unavoidable.

Despite having only a high-school education, Neal was given Walter's engineering business upon his father's retirement. When Walter died, Mom inherited some stock, Grandma Bess was bequeathed a sizeable sum to live on, and the remainder of the estate went to Neal. Mom never accepted the unfairness of it all, especially since she'd had a close bond with her father. But the attitudes in the forties were still stacked in the son's favor, and there was nothing she could do.

Neal once offered my father a part ownership in the company. When Dad hired a lawyer to look over the contract, he was told that after Neal's retirement, my uncle's share of the company would revert to Aunt Alice. The lawyer warned Dad that he would be supporting her until her death. Dad refused, and words were exchanged.

Neal retired in his late fifties after running the business into the ground. He had all the money he needed to retire at that time. This episode and Aunt Alice's prejudice fueled a tense relationship between my parents and Neal, which everyone papered over to preserve familial equanimity.

One Sunday after dinner at Aunt Ellen's house with my family, Grandma, and Neal and Alice, Mom made an unfortunate comment. In my great-aunt's candy dish, she found licorice jellies shaped like gingerbread men covered in sugar. "My favorite." Mom helped herself to four of them. "I love nigger babies."

Aunt Alice bristled and attacked. "We never called our Negroes niggers. Growing up, I loved our cook and my nanny and the yardman. We took care of them, and they were happy. They wanted to be part of our family."

Mom meant nothing insulting by calling the candies nigger babies. That's what they'd always been called, and she felt unfairly attacked. Leslie and I, at five and seven, were unaware of the gathering storm. Words, then opinions, and finally accusations were flung back and forth, criticizing the South's treatment of blacks and the North's hypocrisy. The Civil War was relitigated, and the Southern social order was challenged. Whatever was said, the words stung.

Bursting into tears, Mom retreated with Dad to a bedroom, while Aunt Alice and Uncle Neal hunkered down in the kitchen. Leslie and I were confused and alarmed. She fled to be with Mom while Aunt Ellen comforted me, assuring everything would soon be better. We left shortly thereafter. The subject of race was never mentioned again.

During a summer arts festival before I was a senior in high school, I had the role of Roderigo in *Othello*. My family left on vacation before the play's run ended, and I stayed with Aunt Alice and Uncle Neal in Weston where the play was performed at a local school. My uncle and aunt graciously offered to host a cast party after the last performance on Saturday night. "But you can't invite the Negro."

"The Negro," a Harvard law student, was both the director of the play and the actor playing Othello. I said a cast party was already scheduled at the school and the matter was dropped.

CHAPTER 20

"DON'T START WITHOUT ME"

Rachel often told me early in our marriage that I shouldn't try to get away with anything, because she'd find out. The first time she mentioned this, I thought it was the typical warning a new wife tells her husband in order to forewarn him about thoughts of future indiscretions.

"What's the occasion?" Rachel sees the champagne flutes on the dining-room table. "A party? I'm all excited."

I grab the letter from the Boston lawyer off the table, stand behind her, and speak in a seductive voice. "Are you ready for a big surprise?"

"How big is big?"

"Very big, if I do say so myself."

She leans backwards against me. "You've always had a high opinion of yourself."

"If you're going to be sarcastic, I won't show it to you."

She reaches down and gropes me. "Ah, gee, I guess that ain't it." She turns and puts her arms around me. "I suppose I'll have to take you as you are." Her playful tone of voice is cut short when she sees the letter. "What's that? An excuse? I know. The dog ate your penis."

"Read it. I'll uncork the bubbly."

She removes the pages from the envelope while I take a bottle of Asti Spumante from the freezer, where I've put it to chill quickly.

"Who's this from?"

"Read it."

"Give me a moment. I need my reading glasses."

She reads the first page with a frown on her face, which disappears a moment later. "Holy cow! Did you expect this?"

"I'd always hoped but gave up after all this time."

"You always said Neal was a lost cause."

"That's what Leslie and I—"

"A hundred and twenty thou?"

"And change." I hold up the bottle. "Time to celebrate, even if it's only left over from the brunch we hosted a month ago."

"Only the best. It was a very good year."

We clink glasses and take a sip.

Rachel looks off into space. "I've already thought of three things I want to buy."

"Hang on there. I hate to burst your bubble, but it is my name on the trust."

"That's right. Think only of yourself."

After a couple of glasses, I suggest we go upstairs. "It's late. I can't stay awake much longer." I climb into bed while Rachel brushes her teeth and performs the interminable feminine things she does before bed.

Under the covers, she leans against me, her head on my chest. "This must have been a surprise, especially after the news about the promotion. Did you tell your parents? What did they say?" She lifts the covers. "What's going on down there? I didn't know he was invited."

"He just showed up."

"And what does he think is going to happen?"

"Time for you to start earning that money you want to spend, but he may not stick around too long."

Rachel bounces out of bed. "I'll be right back." She stops in the doorway. "Don't start without me."

"I'll try not to."

Rachel can go overboard with the repartee she likes to play at times like this. On our honeymoon, as an eager husband, I wasn't in the mood for playful banter that dragged on too long.

"What should we call this young man who's always coming between us?" she said in the hotel one night.

"I don't know."

"Well, we have to give him a name. What do you think?"

"Can we baptize him tomorrow?"

"Ah-h-h, c'mon, don't be a spoilsport. What's a good name?"

I thought for a long moment. "Hmmm… DICK. That's what we'll call him. Dick."

And so it came to pass…

I'm awake long after Rachel falls asleep. I decide to say nothing about the two trusts. Leslie will, I'm sure, tell Rachel in good time. The financial windfall will soften the loss of income, but I hate to think the trust money is taking the place of a higher salary. When we have to move, the inheritance will pay for that and help put our retirement savings back on track. Now is the time. I'll tell Rachel tomorrow night.

I proposed to Rachel over the telephone from Kansas two weeks before Thanksgiving. We were twenty-two years old. When I flew home for Christmas, Mom showed me two rings that she'd had cleaned and evaluated by a jeweler. We sat on the edge of her bed. "Elizabeth's ring is larger, but Ellen's has a unique facet cut." I chose the latter. The next day I officially proposed on bended knee to Rachel.

After Christmas, I flew back to hospital administration tech school in Wichita. I was scheduled to leave for Clark Air Base in the Philippines on February 8. Rachel had five weeks to plan our wedding, followed by a one-week honeymoon. The wedding was announced, and invitations printed and mailed. Rachel organized the reception and found a wedding dress at Filene's that had just been returned the day before. We met with the minister at the Episcopal church, and I bought tickets for the honeymoon. I'm sure everyone thought the rush was due to a pregnancy. (She wouldn't become pregnant for another seven years.) My college roommate was best man.

After the reception, we returned to the marriage suite in Copley Plaza to change into our traveling clothes. My roommate and his wife accompanied us. Our suitcases were open on the floor. "You're taking those on your honeymoon?" My roommate pointed to several nursing textbooks in Rachel's suitcase.

"I have exams when I return." Rachel was halfway through her last year in the five-year nursing program at Boston College. "My professors said I could delay them, but I'd only have to take them later."

The nursing books were never opened.

After our honeymoon, I left home three days later. Rachel returned to college. I was married now, and four years later I discovered the effect my marriage played in Mom's outlook on life.

CHAPTER 21

"I WANT TO BE PART OF YOUR FUTURE"

I suspect something is wrong when Rachel doesn't respond to "I'm home," but I put it down to her either not hearing me or being too busy to answer. I look in the kitchen, the living room; I call down the cellar steps, and finally find her in our bedroom folding clothes. She doesn't turn around when I enter the room. "I'm home." I lean over to kiss her, but she shrugs me off.

"What's happened?"

"Listen to the message on the phone."

"Who called?"

"Just listen to it."

In the kitchen I press the button to replay the messages, but first I have to listen to all the old messages that haven't been deleted: wrong numbers, reminders for doctor visits, unintelligible messages, or calls we expect are solicitations for donations. Eventually I reach today's calls. The final message is from my headhunter.

"Mark, I had an interesting call from a company in northern Massachusetts. You have most of the skills they're looking for and I set up a phone interview for Thursday."

I feel like I'm standing under a bucket of freezing water; I can only close my eyes, steel my muscles, and hope it ends soon.

"I gave them your home number, but if you'd rather they contact you at work, call me tomorrow with the number. This sounds like a position you'd be interested in. Call me."

While I listen to the message, Rachel comes downstairs and stands in the hallway. When the message ends, a potent silence fills the house.

"When did you plan to tell me you're looking for a job in Massachusetts? The day before you fly out to start the job? Or do you plan to commute each week and fly home for occasional weekends?"

This isn't the way I'd planned to tell her about my decision. I wanted to clearly and logically explain my decision to avoid a flat-out no, avoid a reluctance to move near my parents, or avoid a resistance to move halfway across the country.

"Well?"

"In fact, I was planning to tell you tonight. I didn't want to say anything until there was a possible job worth moving back east for."

"That's a crock. It has little to do with a job. Instead, it's how you see your future: here or back home? But did you even stop and think how *my* life would change? To give up my close friends in the neighborhood? To uproot myself and start over again after twenty years living here? Why did you think I'd agree with your plans?"

"I'll have to uproot myself too."

"It's not like you have any close friends."

That was a low blow. "It's not going to be a walk in the park for me either."

"It's all about you because you're pissed off about losing the promotion. That's a reason to make a huge change in our lives? And it will cost money to move… oh, I forgot… Aunt Alice came to the rescue."

"We can deduct the moving costs off our taxes."

"Mark, get a grip. That's not the point. What about finding a place to live, selling this place, getting a mortgage and insurance? All the to-dos involved in a major upheaval. And you know who will end up doing them."

"Who?"

"Who do you think? Me. You'll be off starting your new job and won't have time to run around to take care of the problems."

"Most companies will give me time to get settled."

Rachel says nothing.

"I need to support Leslie—"

"That's the first valid statement you've made. Do you think I don't understand you wanting to support your family?" She sits on a kitchen chair. "I had a feeling you were planning to make a change like this. I'm not totally surprised. Don't think I'm cold-hearted or selfish. I feel for Leslie and your mother. But have you thought about how you plan to react to your father on a regular basis?" She holds out her hands. "I want to be part of your future no matter where we live, but I expect you to keep me in the loop. I'm not a casual acquaintance who has no skin in this game. I've said my piece." Her eyes bore into mine. "I want you to promise to keep me informed."

"I will."

"Give me a kiss."

I lean down and raise her up so I can hug and kiss her.

"By the way"—her tone is edged with sarcasm—"your dinner is in Massachusetts. I'll be upstairs."

She's halfway to the second floor when she says, "It's a good thing you've never had a mistress. You have no skill hiding your tracks. A blind man could follow your trail. I've told you before I'd find out what you're up to."

She's right. I'd make a terrible spy. I'd be caught my first day on the job. Fortunately, I've never been seriously tempted to stray from the straight and narrow.

The many consequential changes in my life involved a physical move: applying to one college and then moving away from home for the first time; deciding to spend a year studying abroad and then boarding a student ship for Europe; deciding to enter graduate school and then travelling to Chicago away from my parents; and now changing jobs and moving back hundreds of miles to Boston.

In each case I had no problem making the decision, but I always had second thoughts at the last moment when it came time to carry out the change. The one change that was the most frightening of all was my decision to avoid the draft after college.

I graduated in 1968. The Tet Offensive in January had shocked Americans who'd been told for years by politicians and generals and the president that there was "light at the end of the tunnel."

During spring vacation, I spent an afternoon at the naval recruitment center to interview for the officers' training program, as did a significant portion of male college seniors in the Boston area. The applicants sat in a row of chairs circling the office walls. A sailor called us one at a time for the interview. The rest of us moved to the next seat.

With thousands of men trying to avoid the draft and the Army, the recruiters were sadistically selective. The line of musical chairs moved quickly. Each interview lasted just under two minutes. During the two hours I was there, only one young man was escorted to another office for a more comprehensive face-to-face. We were contestants on a military version of *Queen for a Day*. My interview took one minute and twenty-five seconds.

Back on campus, panic and hysteria reigned among the male senior population. I was scheduled to attend a playwriting program in New York City in the fall. My summer job was selling men's pajamas, bathing suits, and underwear at Jordan Marsh. At any moment, the selective service could draft me into the Army for two years. Once I received my letter, I couldn't enlist in any other branch of the military.

By the end of the summer, the uncertainty drove me to turn down my acceptance to the playwriting program and join the Air Force. Four years in the USAF was better than two in the Army to avoid the risk of dying in Vietnam. Enlisting in the military was like going to prison, but at least the service had medals and more attractive uniforms.

During the week before induction, I was visited by (1) my college roommate: "Can't you put off enlisting? Nixon has a plan to end the war."; (2) a cousin already in the Air Force: "It's like working a regular job. You'll forget you're in the military."; and (3) Rachel, who gave me a copy of the complete poems by Robert Frost. We had an unspoken promise that we would marry, but she must have wondered when that might happen. Her roommate told me she wouldn't wait four years.

Dad gave me the most encouragement and support. The moment stands out in my mind because it was unexpected, and for the first time he treated me as a grown man, proud I'd chosen to serve my country and not flee to Canada.

Although he was a lieutenant during WWII and a captain in the Army Reserves during the Korean War, I was enlisting as a lowly airman. We both understood this was safer than enlisting as a second lieutenant, a soldier with the shortest life expectancy in Vietnam. Nevertheless, I saw myself as a failure by joining as an enlisted man. Perhaps Dad recognized this, and his awareness prompted a comment one evening during dinner.

"You're smart to sign up as an enlisted man. When enlisted men ask for leave, they get it. Officers serve at the whim of the commanding officer. We didn't always get the time we wanted." No doubt he remembered his own experience on Whidbey Island when he asked for leave for his honeymoon. Even in 1968, all AF personnel had to ask their CO's permission to marry. "If the Army wanted you to be married," my father said, "they'd have issued you a wife."

His support made all the difference and helped me to be more optimistic. His words stand out as an indelible moment in my life. I wish there had been more of them. As the family dispenser of encouragement and praise, Mom wouldn't have known to tell me this. Dad rose to the occasion, and his words were a gift I've never forgotten.

Two days later, I took the Oath of Enlistment at the fifty-eight-acre military complex in South Boston and flew to Texas for basic training. Relieved that a decision had been made, I experienced a cleansing rebirth, much as I did after confessing my theft and my cheating in grammar school. My enlistment delayed decisions about everything: marriage, graduate school, career, living on my own—all put on hold. How many times in your life can you press the reset button, escape into the future, leaving your past behind, and reinvent yourself? Two or three times if you're lucky. Those moments are to be treasured.

CHAPTER 22

"THE BIG SHOT BEING A SCOUTMASTER'S SON"

Rachel and I start emptying the attic. We're determined to locate all the belongings Jenn stored temporarily in our basement and attic—college texts, photographs, dorm furniture, sports equipment, and clothes. She claimed she didn't need them, but now that she's married and back from Ireland with a house of her own, we've warned her that she has a choice when she comes for the holidays: take it or donate it. Merry Christmas.

The holiday deadline is a great motivator, and the attic seems like the easiest place to start. I haven't looked up here since I trapped the squirrels last spring that had made the attic their winter residence. Lowering the steps from the ceiling into the hall, I'm showered with a hail of roofing nails, scraps of tar paper, and broken pieces of roofing. "What the hell?" I mutter. Then I remember that when we had the roof redone last summer, we hadn't bothered to spread drop cloths over our belongings. With Rachel at the supermarket, I have time to take the sheet covering the hall rug and dump the debris in the trash can.

I climb up and turn on the light. The air is damp and cold, and I doubt that anything made of paper or cardboard will be in any condition to save. As I'd feared, the entire floor and every horizontal space is coated with roofing material. I haul the dry vac into the attic. With the noise of the vacuum and the satisfying clatter of material sucked up into the can, I don't hear Rachel coming home. I'm unaware of her until I see her head sticking above the floor.

"You scared me," I say. "Your head looked like it was waiting on the floor."

"What are you doing?"

"Vacuuming up some dirt." Then I notice Roger Dietrich, a neighborhood friend who lives on a street parallel to ours. "Hey, Rog."

"I met him walking past our driveway when I came home and we got talking," Rachel says, laughing. "He's probably wishing he'd taken another way home. I told him we were cleaning out the attic and you needed a hand getting a few things down."

"That'll teach you, Roger. Rachel always has a reason to snag an innocent bystander minding his own business."

"No problem." Roger rubs his hands together. "Glad to help."

"He doesn't have his sons this weekend, so I invited him for dinner."

"I didn't know you're moving," Roger says. "Rachel says you're going back east."

"My parents need help. My Dad has health problems, and my mother will need to go into a nursing home soon."

"That's tough."

"And my sister Leslie has her hands full keeping— Careful of your head standing up."

Roger crouches under the low roof. "What needs to be done? I love cleaning out other people's houses. I don't have a guilty conscience when I chuck things out."

Roger and I drag boxes across the floor and hand them down to Rachel. We unpack some of the heavier boxes to make them lighter. Rachel maintains a running commentary about disposal options: Jon's stuff, Jenn's stuff, trash, thrift shop, possible things neighbors might need.

"Roger," she calls up, "don't hesitate to take anything we're not moving."

We leave the largest things last. I pull over a large trunk whose lock is broken. "What trunk is that?" Rachel asks.

"It's probably the one Dad took to Oregon. The stickers display landmarks on the West Coast."

"Is it clean?"

"There's nothing inside."

"This trunk looks like one my grandfather had when he came to this country." Roger turns it to see its side. "Everything he, my grandmother, and three kids owned were packed in his trunk."

"We don't need it," I say. "Could you use it when your scout troop goes camping?"

"You're sure you don't want it? I'll take it and show it to my sister."

I find a bureau with three drawers of toys. "We saved these for our grandkids." Rachel shrugs. "Whenever that happens. Well, Jenn can take them now."

Roger also takes a bed frame and nightstand Rachel hasn't used in twenty years. I hold up a remnant of the rug we once had in the upstairs hall. "This can get the heave-ho."

"I can use it. There's enough to carpet the stairs to our loft. What are you doing with that insulation?"

"All yours."

Rachel pokes her head up. "I'm getting dinner ready. Half an hour, okay?"

Roger and I carry down the last items. We fill three trash bags and drag them out to the curb, and then we move the items Roger will take and load them in my car.

Rachel comes to the door. "Dinner will be ready in five."

"Okay." I close the trunk of the car. "We'll need the time to clean up."

"Wash your faces while you're at it."

Back in the house, I offer a beer to Roger. "I'm glad we didn't have to do that in the middle of summer."

"Although moving in winter is no joke," Rachel says, serving steak tips and rice.

We sit at the kitchen table. I'm suddenly exhausted and wish Rachel hadn't been so quick to invite Roger to dinner. Hopefully, he won't get too comfortable and decide he'll spend the evening drinking beer. I try to keep up my end of the conversation but remind myself that Roger is twenty years younger with more energy and Rachel has the most to say.

"Rachel said your decision to move was sudden?"

"My sister has been the principle caregiver all these years, and it's too much for her."

"And you already have a new job. Rachel told me you got the offer two days ago."

"I'm relieved I found one before moving. I'd gone as far as I could at my last job. And I'm enjoying the time off. I tell the kids I'm practicing for retirement."

"Surely you're not that close."

"I still have a good twelve years to go."

Roger laughs. "Not that you're counting."

"I was nervous at first Mark would have a problem finding a new job. I've read that once you're in your fifties, employers start to think you're obsolete."

"They consider you too expensive," I add.

"Still, without the kids you're almost semi-retired. In my case Matthew has basketball practice during the week and games on Sunday. Eric has basketball practice two evenings and his away games on Saturday. And if that's not enough, Eric wants to take ski lessons. Matthew has joined my scout troop."

"My brothers were both Eagle Scouts," Rachel says. "And Mark's dad was an assistant scout leader for years. I didn't know scouts were that popular these days."

"Our church has a troop, but its membership is decreasing. Matthew is trying to get his friends to join, and I've got a new assistant starting next month who has some good ideas on boosting membership. It takes up a lot of my time—as my ex will tell you—but I think some boys benefit a great deal from the program."

"Mark's father used to take him to troop events when he was four or five years old—"

"I enjoyed the attention and thought I was quite the big shot being a scoutmaster's son. Eventually I joined when I was in seventh grade. Tried it for a year but it wasn't for me."

"Was your father disappointed when you dropped out of the troop?"

"He was probably more disappointed when I was *in* the troop. I wasn't the gung-ho type and never earned many badges. By the way, I've got an old scout handbook around here somewhere. I'm sure it'll turn up as we pack everything for the move."

I drive Roger home soon after. "Don't forget to show me the handbook if you find it. Rachel, thanks so much for dinner."

"We should thank *you* for all your help."

"Let me know when I can help with the cellar."

"That'll be great. And bring your appetite."

Dad maintained his interest in scouting most of his life and, after the war, he volunteered as an assistant scoutmaster in his boyhood troop. When I was four or five, he took me with him when the troop went on camping trips. There's a photograph of me with a grin on my face standing on a picnic table with Dad beside me. Without that picture to remind me, I'd have no recollection of those trips.

When I was in seventh grade, on the spur of the moment and against my better judgment, I told Dad I wanted to join the scouts. I'd decided to make an effort to show my interest in something he enjoyed. He was surprised but pleased.

The next spring, I prepared for my first camping trip: packing my clothes in a backpack along with my scout manual, a flashlight, mess kit, and poncho in case of rain. Dad bought a waterproof ground cloth to place under my sleeping bag. He drove me and two other scouts to the trailhead in New Hampshire to meet the rest of the troop. After parking the car, Dad helped the three of us put on our backpacks. We leaned against the car for support while he tightened the straps and tied our sleeping bags on top. A full canteen, a compass, and a Swiss army knife hung from clips on my belt, creating a metallic undertone of anticipation.

When Dad finished cinching the straps, I stepped away from the car. Before I could react, the weight of the backpack pulled me flat onto my back with a crash, the breath knocked out of me. I was like a beetle, flipped over, its legs wriggling in the air. The other scouts couldn't stop laughing at my futile attempts to stand. They didn't help me up, afraid the weight of their own packs would shift, and they'd also end up on the ground. I burned with humiliation. Today I laugh at my backward flip, but at the time I was helpless, almost in tears, and furious with my father.

Dad helped me up. I leaned forward far enough to support the pack on my back until I gained my balance. I dreaded the hike to the campsite, when at any second I risked stumbling over a tree root or rock. But, for the moment, I was thankful I was no longer the center of attention. Nevertheless, the fear that I might fall on the trail only fed my anger. I couldn't forgive my father. Why didn't he wait until I was ready before letting me go?

That weekend I earned my cooking badge. Dad suggested I prepare spaghetti with meat sauce for dinner. I'd cooked this meal at home and could easily make it over a campfire for three other scouts and myself. I collected twigs and branches to start a fire and filled the cooking pot with water. I chopped an onion and green pepper to brown in the skillet, adding the hamburger five minutes later. After draining the fat, I poured diced tomatoes and tomato sauce into the frying pan and moved it to simmer at the back of the fire. When the water boiled, I dumped in a box of spaghetti.

All this time, a younger scout, kneeling beside the campfire, watched everything I did. He acted impressed, but he was also hungry. He collected more wood to keep the water boiling. With time to relax until the spaghetti was ready, I looked up, surprised to find dark clouds crowding across the lake. The pine trees, swaying in the wind, creaked and showered us with needles. I picked a few out of the sauce and covered the pan.

Another scout sauntered over. "That stuff smells good." He stood hunched over, his hands in his pockets. Another guest for dinner. "It's going to rain, you know."

The boy tending the fire held out his hand. "Yup. It's already started."

The skies opened. The rain hissed on the embers, sending up clouds of steam. I grabbed the skillet and carried it under the tarp Dad had suspended over the picnic table. I ran back to the campfire and tested a strand of spaghetti. "Another couple of minutes."

The tarp snapped in the wind like a sail threatening to rip and fly away. The support poles bent, pulling at the ropes around the stakes anchored in the ground. Except for our group, the campsite was deserted, with most of the scouts sheltering in their tents. Three older boys, bare-chested, with towels over their heads, ran up from the lake with life preservers and paddles. Smelling the food, they changed direction and headed toward us. I served them plates of sauce, and Dad carried over the pot of spaghetti.

The rain pummeled the tarp bulging above our heads. We took turns poking the center of the bulge with a paddle and cheered when the water cascaded onto the grass. The day turned raw, and by the end of the meal, we shivered in our wet uniforms. Dad put the dishes into the spaghetti pot to soak.

Before I could follow the other scouts and dry off, Dad grabbed my arm. "You did an excellent job, Mark."

I laughed with surprise, realizing that indeed I had. I caught up with the scouts splashing across the field to the lodge for the evening program and found a place to sit beside the fire, whose warmth enveloped me. No longer shivering, I relaxed, feeling competent and confident. I had succeeded in the eyes of my father. I also rose in the esteem of the other scouts when their friends talked about the fantastic dinner they'd eaten. My beetle flip of the previous day was forgotten.

Later that evening, the scoutmaster approached me. "Heard you cooked an excellent spaghetti dinner this evening."

"Yes, sir."

"I've signed the paper for your cooking badge. Congratulations."

And with his words, I felt part of the troop for the first time. It is also one of my fondest memories of my father.

CHAPTER 23

"DON'T DO MUCH EXCEPT RELAX"

Dad calls me on my cell phone at our new home. Mom fell on the way to her bedroom. Since he hasn't the strength to lift her, he asks if I'd drive over and help him get her to bed. I'm in the middle of dinner but promise to leave right away.

"Why didn't he use the Life Alert button?" Rachel asks.

"He says she's not hurt, and they'll take her to the hospital which she doesn't need."

"But it's okay to call you?" Rachel is annoyed; we had plans to watch a movie together.

"I won't be long. I'll be back before the movie starts."

"I hope this doesn't become a habit."

Rachel is concerned that having given Dad my cell-phone number, I will be on call 24/7. I know this is a risk, but in a way I'm happy to know he'll call me when there's trouble.

The swirl of snow makes driving difficult. The windshield wiper streaks the window at eye level, requiring me to look over or below it. I understand

Dad's dilemma. When the EMTs come and help Mom up, they won't risk leaving her in the apartment in case she later discovers she's hurt.

Forty minutes later, I reach the apartment. I use my spare key rather than ring the bell. I don't want to disturb Dad if he's sitting on the floor holding Mom's hand. Instead, looking from the entry hall, I see him in his recliner.

"Where's Mom?" Is the emergency over and I've made the trip for no reason?

He points down the hall where Mom lies on the floor covered with a blanket. Her head rests on a pillow, her eyes closed. For a horrible moment I think she's dead and Dad didn't tell me because he didn't want me to be upset while driving.

"Is that you, Mark?"

"Are you in pain?" I kneel beside her. "Does your neck hurt?"

"I'm fine." She acts as if she's been forced to lie there against her will. "I tripped on the rug—"

Dad interrupts. "Because you refuse to use your walker. This is what happens."

"I'm sorry I'm late." I take her hand. "Did you think you'd have to spend the night on the floor?"

"I'd have fallen asleep if your father had turned off the hall light shining in my eyes."

We lift Mom and help her into the bathroom. Her nightgown is damp and smells of urine. I return with a clean one from her bureau, hand it to Dad, and close the door. While I'm waiting, I lie back on Mom's bed and close my eyes. I hear water running into the walk-in tub. When the bathroom door opens, I jump up and help maneuver her into bed. Dad counts out her pills while I fetch a glass of water.

"Better than sleeping on the floor," she says, yawning. I wish her goodnight.

Dad turns off her light and joins me in the living room. "Thanks for coming over." He's relieved, but his face shows how worried he'd been.

"No big deal." I wonder how often he'll call me in the future. I can't run over once or twice a week to raise the HMS *Queen Katherine.* One of these days, a fall will be serious.

I call Leslie the next day and say we must hire a home health aide for the evenings. "Dad can't help her if there's a problem getting her to bed."

When Leslie and I visit the next Saturday, Mom is taking a nap—the perfect opportunity to discuss our idea with Dad. But when we suggest an aide, he acts surprised. "We're not at that point yet."

Leslie will brook no excuses. "We will be if Mom starts falling on a regular basis."

Dad waves his hand dismissively. "The other night only happened because she didn't use her walker." He shakes his head, annoyed. "She's trying to prove she doesn't need it."

Leslie tries to be calm. "She'll fracture her hip—"

Dad throws up his arms. "She won't listen to me—"

"You need to insist. And walk behind her in case she loses her balance. Dad, you can't expect Mark to be available every time you call—"

"The home aide will take the burden off you," I interrupt, before Leslie or Dad lose their tempers. I don't want him to think I'm unwilling to help. "You'll be more relaxed."

"I don't do much *except* relax."

The doorbell rings.

"That's the grocery store." He opens the door.

"Good evening, Mr. Aherne." The delivery man is in his twenties. He carries two boxes into the kitchen. Leslie clears the kitchen table to unload the food.

Dad waves several coupons in the air. "Don't forget these."

The delivery man takes the coupons. "These will come off your next order." They walk to the door where Dad hands him a dollar.

"Oh, thanks." The man politely acts surprised. "You have a good evening now."

Back in the kitchen, Dad checks each item off the list. "What do you know? Nothing's missing!"

Leslie picks up the conversation where we'd left off. "The aide will give Mom a bath and help her into bed. She'll be more relaxed and will sleep better—"

"Who wants coffee?" Dad asks, pretending he hasn't heard her. "I ordered half-and-half. The other carton turned bad. Coffee isn't the same with the skim milk your mother uses."

I take three mugs down from the cabinet.

"Get another one, will you? Your mother likes coffee when she wakes up."

Leslie sits at the kitchen table and stares at the traffic on Mass Avenue, waiting until we're settled with our coffee. She won't give up until Dad agrees.

"Seriously," she begins, leaning toward him, her elbows on the table. "It's not safe for the two of you to be alone all the time."

"Besides the young mother who comes when Dad's out, is there anyone else in the building you can call for help?" I speak before remembering that most of his neighbors are in their seventies and eighties. If one of them tries to help, my father will likely have two people on the floor.

We finish our coffee. Leslie washes up while I rip apart the boxes and bag the trash for the bins.

By the end of the visit, Dad says he'll *think* about an aide.

Better than a definite no. Keep chipping away.

Leslie kisses Dad. "Tell Mom we're sorry we missed her."

I hug and kiss him too, half expecting him to rebuke me. "We love you guys," I tell him.

The pressure of his hug tells me how much he misses human contact. I'm heartsick to feel a spark of relief when I'm out of his arms. A childhood memory is hard to forget.

When I step into the hall, Dad reminds me to carry the pile of newspapers down for recycling. "Thanks for stopping by." He closes the door.

Leslie unlocks her car. "That settles it. I'm getting a home health aide in there before I go on vacation if it's the last thing I do. How's Rachel coping with the move?"

"We're not rushing. We unpack one or two boxes a day. She has a couple of interviews next week. And I start my job on Monday. Come out and see the house tomorrow. Then we'll go out for dinner. By the way, did I give you my cell-phone number?"

Dad agrees to *try* a home health aide. After three days of calling, Leslie finds a woman who's available four evenings a week. I talk with her on the phone. She sounds friendly, and I tell her I'll be at the apartment on Monday after dinner to welcome her and introduce her to my parents. Leslie starts her vacation on Saturday at a ski resort in New Hampshire. She's satisfied with the progress she's made.

And Mom? Getting out of bed early Sunday morning, she trips and falls again. Dad uses his Life Alert button, an ambulance arrives, and Mom is off to the hospital. I call the health aide to tell her not to come for at least a week. "I'll call you and keep you informed." I expect she'll get another job instead of waiting around until Mom comes home.

Then I call Leslie at her ski lodge. "Mom's at Symmes."

"Oh God! What now?"

"The usual. She fell."

"Did she hurt herself?"

"No, but it was four in the morning. Dad pushed the button. Thank God for that."

"I'll come this morning and drive back tonight—"

"Don't ruin your vacation. Dad says there's nothing you can do now anyway. Call her tonight. I'll be there after work. Mom's having some tests, and she's groggy from being awake half—"

"What tests? Is something wrong with her? I mean, more than falling."

"The doctor says they're routine. Like bringing your car in for an oil change. They'll run a twenty-four-point inspection."

"At least they have good insurance. I'll call Dad tonight. Is he staying in her room?"

"He followed the EMTs in his car. He's home now taking a nap and will drive himself back this afternoon."

Mom remains in the hospital for three days. The doctor says she'll be sent to a nursing home for rehabilitation to strengthen her legs and improve her balance. Mom is ineligible for Medicaid benefits because our parents' savings and income are too high. She'll be charged an amount far higher than what Medicaid would pay the facility. Mom's the golden goose who brings a sparkle to the eyes of nursing home administrators. In these circumstances, Dad has no trouble finding a vacancy within ten miles of their apartment.

Only later do I recognize a fundamental conflict of interest in the system. How much rehabilitation will the staff invest in Mom if helping her get stronger means she'll return home, taking her golden eggs with her?

CHAPTER 24

"Why Do I Have to Make Breakfast?"

I visit Mom the Saturday she enters the nursing home. The facility is off a main street in Melrose down a narrow road called Nursing Home Lane. A dozen small houses painted in pastel colors line the street. The houses are poorly maintained: chipping paint, sagging front porches, missing front steps. An unfortunate metaphor for the facility at the end of the street. The nursing home, painted dark green with cream trim, dwarfs the houses it overlooks. Behind the building, a small parking lot is crowded with weekend visitors.

The receptionist gives me Mom's room number, and I take the elevator to the second floor. Her room is opposite the back door to the parking lot. When I enter, the only person I find is Mom's roommate, sitting in a wheelchair, looking out the window. Hearing me, she wheels the chair around and squints at me. I nod and smile. She looks away. Apparently, I'm not interesting enough for a second glance. She grunts when I say, "Hello." Dressed in her nightgown, she wears a flat, wool hat a dockhand might wear.

A half-empty suitcase lies on Mom's bed. The second drawer of her bureau is open, filled with jerseys and sweaters.

"There you are." Leslie enters behind me. "When did you get here?"

"Just now. Where's Mom?"

"She and Dad are with the rehab specialist. She's watching Mom walk and perform simple tasks before deciding on a plan."

"I hope they get her more active. She sat around the apartment too much."

"That's Dad's fault. He's never pushed her to do anything. No patience." Leslie finishes unpacking the suitcase and closes the bureau drawer. "Easier to do everything himself."

"I blame the pills. They scatter her thoughts. She can't concentrate."

"Frankly, she's lazy. It will be a job getting her moving again. Maybe they'll figure out what the problem is. They better, considering Dad's forking over five thousand dollars a month."

"Good God." I knew it was expensive but had no idea it was that much.

"You didn't know?" Leslie is amused at my naïveté. "Imagine the cost when we'll need one."

She pushes the suitcase under the bed with her foot. "Before they get back, will you carry in your old bookcase from Dad's car? I have more of Mom's clothes to carry in."

"I'm good at that. I've had lots of practice moving and unpacking things."

We go to the back door. "Park behind the building and use this door." Leslie pushes a series of buttons. "Saves taking the elevator." The door unlocks with a snap.

"What's the code?"

"9-7-5-3-1. The only barrier between the grannies and freedom."

Crossing the parking lot, she explains the latest controversy. "Mom's roommate is Mrs. Gaskell, who has the bed by the window. When Mom walked over to look outside, Gaskell told her to stay on her side of the room." Leslie unlocks the trunk of Dad's car. "You know Mom. Tell her to stay away and she'll be rubber-necking out the window all day long."

"What happened?"

"I wasn't there, but Dad said the floor nurse spoke to both of them. She told Mom that the area by the window is part of Gaskell's sitting area for visitors. And she told Gaskell that Mom can look out the window when Gaskell doesn't have visitors." Leslie shakes her head. "There'll always be one issue or another."

She brushes her hands on her jeans. "Okay, carry in the bookcase, and I'll meet you back inside."

I lift the bookcase out of Dad's car. "Do I use the same code to get back in?"

"No code to get in. You just can't get out."

When Leslie and I return, our parents are walking down the corridor. We wait for them outside the room. I give Mom a kiss and help her to her chair. "Getting settled in?" I ask. She looks annoyed and jerks her head in her roommate's direction.

Dad speaks before Mom has time to put her thoughts into words. "We had a good session with Emily, the rehab director."

"What did she have you do?" I address Mom, hoping to steer her onto this new topic.

"Walk." Mom sits in the only chair available for her visitors. "Whew, I'm worn out."

"That's all you did?" I wait for more details.

Dad speaks up. "They have a kitchen in rehab. The director asked her to pretend she's making breakfast."

"Why do I have to make breakfast? They'll bring me breakfast in the dining room."

"They want to see how they can help you," Leslie says.

"To make sure you can cook something to eat when you get home," I add.

Mom sighs with an impatient puff of air. "I told her Charles gets my breakfast at home."

"Oh boy." Leslie groans through her teeth.

"Kat, are you warm enough? Do you need a sweater?"

She waves away Dad's offer.

"Let me explain where I've stored everything." Leslie shows Mom what's in the closet and the layout of the bureau. After Dad and I adjust the shelves in the bookcase, we move it between the bureau and the bedside table. I arrange photographs on the top shelf.

An aide pokes her head in to tell us that dinner will be served in five minutes.

"Dinner already?" I look at my watch.

"Dinner's at five." The aide smiles at Mom. "Ready, Kathleen?"

"I'm Katherine."

"I'm sorry, Katherine. I'll be back in five minutes to walk with you and get you settled at your table."

"I need a wheelchair."

"I'll bring a walker." The aide leaves the room.

Mom throws up her hands as if to say, *See what I mean?*

"Mom, you've got to build up strength in your legs," Leslie says.

From Dad's expression, I can tell he's had this discussion with Mom many times.

Despite the rocky start, Mom thrives in the nursing home. Within three months, her roommate problem is resolved: Gaskell dies. Mom promptly claims her space beside the window before the dead woman's bed has had a chance to cool.

She makes several friends on her floor and spends most of the day with them. I especially like Kay. She looks younger than Mom, has bright-red hair, and always wears a scarf around her neck. She doesn't use a walker, and I hope that seeing her, Mom will work harder to gain the strength and balance to walk without one.

Mom wholeheartedly enjoys the intrigues and feuds between residents. For many years, my parents rarely invited friends to their home, and their lives became uneventful and lonely. Now, surrounded by other patients, she takes an interest in what's happening around her. These friends, along with Dad's daily visits, keep Mom from focusing on her physical problems. During the first months, she rarely speaks about going home.

When I visit, I often wonder if she's more interested in her friends than in me. She responds to news about her grandkids but never follows up with a question about them. Instead, she'll wait for me to toss another morsel of news. I ask her about Dad: What is he up to? Do you sit together outside in the sunroom or take part in a group activity? Her answers state the facts, unadorned with details. She then returns to the conversations around her. Occasionally she tells me she's making progress. If she mentions going home, she never asks when that might happen. Meanwhile, Dad is more relaxed now that he no longer has to care for her twenty-four hours a day.

One day after a dentist appointment in Arlington, I walk to my car parked on Mass Avenue. After starting it up, I wait for the traffic to stop for the light. To my surprise, I see my parents in the car next to mine. They don't notice me. What are they doing here? I hesitate to blow my horn, not wanting to alarm Dad. The light changes, and I follow them, curious about where they're going.

We continue down Mass Avenue, past the library, the firehouse, and the parking lot in front of Walgreens. At Lake Street, Dad takes a right toward Spy Pond. He pulls into the lot next to the playground. I park beside them. Mom is halfway out of the front seat when she recognizes me.

I roll down the window, laughing. "Surprise! I followed you from Arlington Center."

They're delighted to see me, especially Dad, who acts relieved at the change in routine. His expression makes my effort worthwhile.

"What brings you to Arlington?"

"I take Mom out once or twice a week. We had lunch at the new restaurant where the Suffolk Five used to be."

"We sat in the vault," Mom says.

This is the first time I've seen her outside the nursing home. She appears more alert, and her speech is more understandable. Having friends around her all day seems to have had a positive effect.

"Less noise in the vault than in the main dining room. Everything echoes." Dad presses his ear. "I couldn't adjust my hearing aid in the main room."

We steer Mom to a bench where the grass meets the sand. Her feet don't reach the ground. The ducks resting nearby mutter at the inconvenience and waddle to the water. With a soft plop, they swim a few feet offshore where the other ducks are floating.

"Charles, you should have brought some bread—oh, you did!" Mom takes the bag from him.

"The bread fell behind the microwave. It's stale, but the ducks won't complain."

"I haven't been here in I don't know how many years." Mom tears the bread into pieces. "Your father and I used to come here after high school." She throws a handful at the ducks, but without the strength, most falls at her feet. "I didn't do that very well, did I?"

I pick up the pieces. At the edge of the water, I toss them among the ducks. They fight for the food, stirring up the water, quacking angrily when outwitted. Several ducks dive underwater to retrieve the bread sinking to the bottom.

"I played baseball where those restrooms are," Dad says. "They weren't there in those days."

"When we started dating, I always came and watched him."

"Was he any good?" I ask as if I don't know the answer.

"Oh yes. Everyone wanted him on their team."

Another apple that fell far from the tree. I was always chosen last for a team at recess.

I look across the lake. When I was a teenager, the town cut down the hundred-year-old willow trees on the opposite bank to widen Route 2. After construction, the cars were no longer a soft rumble hidden behind a tangle of branches. Instead, they roared by, picking up speed under the

Pleasant Street bridge to climb the hill. The pond, still beautiful, is no longer an oasis amid a hectic civilization—another loss in their lifetime. And mine too. A reminder of my advancing years.

Dad points to a group of drakes congregating a short distance from the females. The iridescent colors of their feathers shift in the sunlight filtering through the leaves. "They look like a men's club, quacking and preening, pretending they're bachelors again."

When I was in high school, I once came down to the lake with friends after a dance. Brian Wilkes drove his parents' car, and we cruised up and down behind the vehicles facing the water. "Everybody's down here watching the submarine races," he joked. When he saw a license plate he recognized, he maneuvered his car to illuminate the fogged-up windows with his high beams. Then he'd stick a light on the roof. It flashed red and blue, giving the occupants a scare. Two people can untangle themselves and arrange their clothes fast when necessary. How we laughed.

"At the end of the game, your mother and I cut through those backyards over there to Pleasant Street."

"We climbed Grey Street. That was tough," says Mom. "At the top, we still had two more blocks."

Their words evoke a vision of my standing on my grandmother's porch, with Mom and Dad approaching on the sidewalk. I lean on the railing, watching them from the end of the porch. They're holding hands, and Mom is tired. I try hard to imagine them as two high-school kids, but can't picture their hairstyles, the clothes they wore in the thirties, or what they talked about.

Is Dad aware that Grandma would disapprove if she knew her daughter was dating a Catholic? I see them stop two houses away and part. Ahh, so he has been told. Dad stands at the corner and waits until she's on the porch before he walks away.

Mom opens the front door only feet away from me. "I'm home," she shouts. She seems real enough to touch, and yet I can't believe she's a teenager. At that moment, my dream vanishes, and I see them once more as my elderly parents imagining a moment in their youth.

CHAPTER 25

"Next Time You'll Remember the Vault Opens At Nine"

Besides visiting Mom on weekends, I sometimes leave work early and drop by once a week on my way home. Delayed by rush-hour traffic, I arrive around six thirty and park in the back lot. I'm surprised at the difficulty of finding a space during the week considering residents don't own cars and fewer people visit on weekday evenings. Often, I'm the only visitor on Mom's floor. It's a mystery.

By the time I arrive, the residents have finished dinner. The staff has cleared and washed the dining-room tables, vacuumed the rug, and locked the doors. This precaution became necessary after eighty-eight-year-old Mrs. Petterson wandered into the darkened room and snagged a wheel of her walker on a table leg. Impatient and unwilling to call for help, she wrenched the walker free but lost her balance, avoiding a broken hip only by holding on to the walker for dear life. It softened her fall before rolling away. With the dining room off limits in the evening, residents either return to their rooms or sit in chairs lining the corridor, chatting with friends until bedtime.

Mom isn't in her room, so I continue down the hallway, its lights dimmed for the night. Passing each room, I say hello to those residents I've met. I want to be friendly, although some stare at me without recognition.

I find Mom and her friend Kay in the communal area near the nurses' station, holding court with other members of the Hen Club, as they call themselves. Hard of hearing, they lean toward each other, but sitting in a single line prevents more than three women from taking part in any one conversation. A chorus of "What did she say?" prompts a retelling of the story up and down the line, like a game of telephone. God knows what's said to the person at the end of the line. Male residents avoid this gauntlet like the plague.

When she sees me, Kay cackles and announces, "The rooster is here, girls. Eggs tomorrow." Everyone turns to look, and I'm blushing red as bright as a rooster's wattle. They titter, enjoying the disruption to their routine, and make room for me beside Mom.

Mom is always happy to see me. Having a visitor in the evening confers a special status on a resident, surpassed only by an evening visit from a grandchild. "My son," Mom introduces me each time I arrive.

I kiss her and ask how she's feeling and if there's anything she needs. That's Kay's cue: "Yeah, you can tell us the code to get out of here." This comment elicits no laughter and isn't meant to.

Tonight, Mom is animated, full of laughter, trading jokes, a keen observer of the passing parade. She tells me about Dad's visit that afternoon and the progress of her rehab; I tell her what Rachel and the grandchildren are up to. When I bring new snapshots of the kids, they're passed up and down the row.

Leslie expects a call after every visit. Is she clean and healthy? Are her clothes washed and pressed? Do you think she's eating enough?

I notice an old woman passing us with her walker, acting agitated and looking in every direction. Kay mutters something to my mother, who then turns to me. "That's Mrs. Petterson. She was a bank manager at the Suffolk Franklin—in Park Square, I think—before it merged."

Mrs. Petterson continues down the corridor. Her wheels squeak on the linoleum, until she bumps over the edge of the rug in the reception area.

Mom glances over my shoulder. "Uh-oh. She's heading back this way."

I turn around to look before she can warn me not to draw attention to myself.

"Too late! She's found you."

Mrs. Petterson stops and taps my arm. "Is the vault locked for the night?"

She must be mistaking me for someone from the office where residents' valuables are locked in a safe. "Someone can help you in admitting." I smile and turn back to Mom.

She tugs at my sleeve. "I'm speaking about the bank vault."

That's when I realize she believes I'm her employee. "I th-think it's locked," I stammer, trying to be serious when I want to laugh.

"You *think* it's locked?" Her voice rises with indignation. "That's unacceptable. You must make sure."

The women sitting along the wall look off into space. Mom gestures for me to leave; I stand obediently and tell Mrs. Petterson I'll check and return. Then I walk around the corner to the nurses' station.

I remember acting in college when another actor playing the role of a powerful man forgot his lines. He jumped ahead six pages to the scene where he orders me off the stage. He quickly recovered his place in the script, but given my character's lowly status, I had no recourse but to obey him. That wouldn't have been a problem except I had a major speech to deliver in four pages. I spent the next few minutes deciding how to slip back onstage in time to say my lines. I always wondered if the audience guessed something had gone wrong.

"Can I help you?" Helen, the evening nurse, looks up and smiles expectantly.

"I'm only here to check that the vault is locked."

"Ah, you've met Mrs. Petterson."

"Now what do I do?"

Helen laughs. "I guess you'd best check the vault."

To kill time, I enter a sitting room and scan the romance paperbacks on a bookcase.

"Psst." Helen pokes her head around the corner. "You'd better get back before you're in trouble for taking too long."

I return to my seat. "The vault is securely locked. It won't open until ten o'clock tomorrow."

"Ten o'clock?" Her disapproval surprises me. "The bank opens at nine! What if a customer wants to withdraw more money than we have in the tills?"

"Oh, sorry." My tone of voice is one of sincere regret. Her piercing stare almost convinces me that I have, in fact, made a terrible mistake.

"Go back and change the timer. The password is in my top drawer. You've been here long enough to know better."

I return to the nurses' station. Helen looks up from the drug cart. "Aha, Mrs. Petterson's employee is back again."

"I set the vault to open at the wrong time. She's going to fire me!"

"I hope you remember where to find the password."

"God, I can't remember. Where is it?" I've been sucked into her fantasy and almost forget there is no password and no vault to reset.

Helen reaches over and pats my back. "We appreciate your help. It's difficult settling her down once she starts worrying about the vault."

I take off my glasses and rub my eyes. My stomach growls. I haven't eaten since noon.

"You can go back now." Helen shoos me away. "Adjusting the timer doesn't take long."

"She must have been a bitch to work for."

Helen nods. "She had to be in those days to rise as high as she did."

Returning to my seat, I say to Mrs. Petterson, "The timer has been reset to nine."

Satisfied, she pushes off with her walker, clattering down the corridor. At her bedroom door, she catches a wheel on the doorjamb. She yanks the walker away and enters her room.

The ladies around me laugh softly. Kay leans over. "You're lucky you still have a job. Next time you'll remember the vault opens at nine."

"My boy's a smart one," Mom says proudly. "He'll remember."

CHAPTER 26

"Children are the Cruelest Critics"

When Mom entered the nursing home, we hoped the rehabilitation would make a positive change in her life. Whenever I visit, I ask about her progress and encourage her to keep plugging away. Mom expects to be discharged and return home. She'll say, "I think I'm getting better. I should be able to go home soon." I say nothing definite and never speculate as to when this might happen. Leslie also avoids the subject. We can't make any promises about when she'll leave, not knowing what criteria determines her fitness to go home. Dad can sign her out of the facility at any time, but I've never been there with Dad when she's discussed going home.

Dad is happier with Mom in the nursing home. He was fearful for her safety when alone with him. In an emergency, he hadn't the strength to help her. As much as I want to see Mom leave the facility, I'm sympathetic with his concern. Dad, Leslie, and I agree that, considering her present infirmities, remaining in the nursing home is the best resolution, although none of us has the courage to tell her. We remain silent or change the subject when she prefaces a sentence with "Once I get home…" or "When I leave here…"

It's not long before the rehab director tells Dad that Mom is complaining about her exercises. She makes the minimum effort during her sessions and won't accept that she must push herself if she wants to improve. "She says the exercises hurt her legs," the rehab director explains to Dad, "and she wants to be left alone."

Dad requests that her schedule be changed to the afternoon when he attends the sessions. He encourages her to work harder, but this only makes her more irritable. Finally, he stops going. He asks the staff to continue her exercises. I suspect they don't do so for long. The physical therapist must be frustrated and consider it a waste of her time. I can't blame her. Who wouldn't want to spend more time with those residents who go the extra mile? Once she decides against doing something, Mom is stubborn and paranoid.

When we visit, we insist that Mom use her walker. We proceed slowly forward. *Creeping* is the way Leslie puts it. I stay beside the walker, ready to support her if she stumbles. My own sense of balance isn't reliable and walking slowly aggravates *my* instability. I want to scream with impatience, but she'll never improve if we give in to her. But time after time, we arrive to find her in a wheelchair. We realize that she isn't trying to walk on her own anymore. As the months pass, she stops talking about going home, as if she's lost hope.

I wonder how many of her friends leave the facility. Some residents with significant disabilities can't leave and others leave escorted by Death, but there must be several in Mom's situation. Do any of them go home? But then I remember Mom's condition. She can't walk without danger of falling, use the bathroom alone, wash herself in the tub, and on and on. This is not a recipe that demonstrates independence.

I expect it's a vicious cycle: little by little she gives up pushing herself to walk, which limits her mobility, which in turn reduces her hope of leaving. Perhaps she willingly gives up the frustration and pain of rehabilitation in return for sacrificing her expectation of going home. Will there be a day when she understands with devastating clarity that she will never leave? Her room here is "home" and will be until she dies. Her future possibilities are diminishing. There will be fewer and fewer surprises; her life will become the numbing routine of the nursing home, ticking off the hours she has left.

There's nothing wrong with Mom's arms, which surprises me. I expected her to sit passively in her wheelchair waiting for an aide or a candy striper to push her where she wants to go. This is not the case. Mom masters the technique of wheeling herself down the hall to the TV room or a meal in the dining room. She takes mischievous delight rolling along in front of us, forcing us to walk faster and faster to keep up. But as with most elderly people using walkers or wheelchairs, her peripheral vision is unreliable. She never turns right or left at a corner without catching a wheel on the baseboard. She purses her lips with defiance, and like an octogenarian driving a car in Florida, she backs up and pulls into traffic without looking. Every wheelchair should have a beeping signal when operating in reverse.

I understand she's proving to us that she's independent and still has control over her life. I grin watching her maneuver among the tables and other wheelchairs in the dining room. Her weaving is surprisingly successful, but there's a comical element in her determination, which saddens me.

At family get-togethers, we adults regale ourselves with the misadventures of our parents. Children are the cruelest critics. Our parents are a reminder that we'll become like them whether we want to or not. In the face of that depressing situation, humor helps us accept the future.

Mom's wheelchair independence deteriorates over time. Coming in to visit after lunch, we find an aide wheeling her back to her room. We make no comment. Eventually, she asks us to wheel her around the facility when we visit.

In warm weather, I wheel Mom across the dining room, through the French doors, and onto the patio. The fresh air is invigorating after the stuffy odor of pills and elderly bodies. I help Mom into her coat, and we sit in the sun with our faces shaded by an umbrella and watch the birds at the feeders.

To help pass the time, I wheel Mom through the parking lot. The wheelchair pulls on my arms as I steer her down the ramp. I enjoy walking on the main street past the clapboard and quarried stone mansions, each with its own architectural oddities. Once single-family homes, they have been converted into offices for doctors, lawyers, and CPAs.

On the way back, I stop at Dunkin' Donuts to buy an iced coffee for Mom and a mocha for me. She can manage to drink the coffee herself if the cover is tight and she uses a bent straw that prevents having to tilt the cup.

Pushing her back to the nursing home, I enjoy a satisfied feeling. *You're a good son, Mark, taking your mother for a walk and buying her a treat,* but at the same time, I'm plotting to leave as soon as she's safe in her room.

This reminds me of taking my daughter, Jenn, for a walk in her stroller. We'd flag down the ice-cream truck as it rolled along the street, tilting perilously at corners, and replaying the same circus tune. *You're a good father, Mark, taking your daughter for a walk and buying her an ice-cream cone.* But all the time hoping that, once home, she'd take a nap, and I'd have two hours of peace to read.

Steering the wheelchair back to the nursing home, I'm overwhelmed with a sense of loss—sorrow for my mother's physical and mental decline but also regret that the days when my daughter and son were young are over. Sometimes my thoughts are unbearable, and I trot along the sidewalk, speeding toward the ramp, trying to outrun my despair. I don't want to frighten my mother with the speed, but I need to exhaust myself, to shout and laugh. Life is a trickle of water evaporating in the heat of the day.

When the weather grows colder, Dad continues driving her to a restaurant. Instead of going to the park after lunch, he takes her back to the apartment. When I tell Leslie this, she's upset. "I don't want to spoil Mom's outings, but one of these days she'll refuse to go back to the nursing home, and what will we do then? Dad has to think of unexpected results."

December 1999 is a strange month positioned at the end of the century with Y2K looming like the end of the world. Everyone is talking about how society might fail. Rumors of nightmarish scenarios are passed along as if fact: computing interest on loans and financial investments will fail, flying in a plane at midnight on New Year's Eve will be dangerous, nuclear power plants will fail and risk meltdown, government computer systems will be unable to process social-security checks. Everything computerized is susceptible to failure.

Working in IT, I tell friends that computer systems have been modified and tested throughout the year. I try to convince them that any problems will be minor and easily fixed. Nothing major will go wrong. But not even I am totally convinced because I can't know if every organization has tested their programs as rigorously as banks and financial institutions have done.

In the middle of all this is the usual tension surrounding Christmas: mailing cards out on time, decorating in and outside the house, and deciding what the kids want for presents. In the end, Rachel and I decide that gift cards and certificates will be most appreciated. We also open an account for each of them and deposit some of the money I inherited from my uncle, of whom they have no memory.

Jenn and Jon thought about what could be done to make the holiday as special as possible for their grandmother. Leslie planned a Christmas Eve party and told Dad to take Mom out of the nursing home and to stay overnight at her house. No one wants her to be alone at any time during the holiday.

Rachel and I arrive at Leslie's early to help her prepare for the party. The children will come later after visiting friends. They have so many to see and can't waste a moment of their time at home.

I help Leslie set the dining-room table for ten. "What time do you expect Dad?"

"He'll leave with Mom before dinner is served. The staff has live music in the rec room with singing and dancing that Mom doesn't want to miss."

"Dancing?"

"One of the nurses told me many residents get up and dance. They'll choose a patient in a wheelchair and roll them around in time to the music. These women don't brood over memories of past Christmases. They're too busy enjoying themselves. When the performers start singing carols, the MC projects the words on the wall, and everyone sings along.

Mom and Dad show up at six. He comes to the door and asks me to help move Mom into the house. I put on my coat while he wheels her down the driveway to the front door. The frigid wind whips our scarfs behind us, and snow from the roof showers us with ice crystals. The cold air must be refreshing for Mom after sitting all day in the overheated nursing home. The heat is like a drug that saps the energy from everyone inside.

With no ramp bypassing the front steps, Dad and I stand on either side of the chair and lift it up three steps to the front-door landing. Once we're in the house, Rachel closes the door.

"Merry Christmas." She leans over Mom to give her a kiss. "It's cold out there."

Leslie comes in with a tray of mugs with warm cider and glasses of eggnog. "Let's get you out of that coat, and then you can have something to drink."

"Where are the kids?" Mom asks.

"They'll be here soon. They're spending the afternoon with friends," I tell her. "At least we'll have a chance to talk quietly before they arrive."

"Your tree is beautiful, Leslie. So many presents."

"And I saw a few with your name on them." I wheel Mom up for a closer look.

"Are you going to be Santa and give out the presents? Leslie, remember how Mark always wanted to be Santa?"

"I remember Mark wanted to be as far apart from your brother as possible."

That Christmas Day when we ate at my uncle's house surrounds me. I can see where each person sat in the living room, while I knelt beside the fireplace pulling the presents out from under the tree. How old was I? And then I remember telling Aunt Alice I had started high school that fall.

The children arrive, and all thoughts of that long-ago Christmas vanish.

CHAPTER 27

"WHAT DO YOU WANT TO BE WHEN YOU GROW UP?"

My family always celebrated Christmas dinner at the Concord Inn, except the year Uncle Neal, my mother's brother, invited us to his house. I wasn't happy when Mom told me. Uncle Neal, a heavy, boisterous man, always lunged at me whenever I walked by. He laughed, thinking it funny, but he'd done this since I was young, and it still made me nervous. I kept my distance.

On Christmas morning, after opening family presents at home, we picked up Aunt Ellen and Grandma Bess, before driving to Weston. Neither of them had ever learned to drive.

My grandmother, whose large bosom fascinated my fourteen-year-old libido, always dressed in black with a multi-strand of pearls around her neck. "They're fake," she admitted when once I asked if they were valuable. In the car, she snapped open her purse and took out a cigarette. She tapped it on the back of her hand, then lit it. After her first puff, she popped open the ashtray in the door handle. Leslie rolled down her window a crack.

"The Baptists came caroling last night," she said.

Aunt Ellen looked up from poking around in her pocketbook. "Who came?"

"THE BAPTISTS!"

"What did they want?" Aunt Ellen asked.

"THEY WERE CAROLING."

Mom turned from the front seat to show she was listening.

Grandma continued her story. "When I heard singing, I thought I'd left the radio on. I went into the living room to shut it off when I noticed people on the front porch looking in my windows. I opened the door, and there was Frank Darby, the pastor from the Baptist Church. And *there I was* with a cocktail in one hand and a cigarette in the other."

We all laughed, although I didn't know why it was funny.

"Why stare through my windows on Christmas Eve? They might see something they shouldn't."

"They came because you live alone," Mom explained. "They wanted to share the Christmas spirit."

"I don't go to their church." Grandma was indignant. "It seems a bit high-handed to me. They probably wanted a donation."

"I live alone, and they didn't come by *my* house." Aunt Ellen couldn't understand why see hadn't seen them. "I would have enjoyed hearing them."

"*You* live on the second floor," her sister said. "They can't look through your windows!"

At my uncle's house, I went to the kitchen to wish Aunt Alice a Merry Christmas.

"My goodness. I think you've grown a foot since I saw you last." She leaned toward me for a kiss, but she didn't want my lips touching her cheeks. "How old are you now?"

"Fourteen last month."

"You'll be off to college before we know it."

"I only started high school this year."

She waved her hand dismissively. "High school will fly by in a flash! I've made ham, cheese potatoes, and peas. All your favorites."

I returned to the living room to look at the presents under the tree. "Are all the presents ready, Santa?" my uncle roared, trying to grab me as I passed him. Startled, I jumped back, almost knocking into my grandmother and stepping on her corns.

"Neal! Stop pestering him!" she scolded. "Your voice is enough to wake the dead."

"You don't mind, do you, Bub?"

Pretending I didn't hear him, I knelt by the tree. "Time for presents." I read the tag on the first package. "The first one's for Aunt Ellen."

"I'm first?" She smiled with pleasure. "You're a good Santa Claus."

"That present is from me, not Santa," Grandma said to her sister.

I examined the tag on another gift. "The next one's for Aunt Alice—"

"Hey, Alice, get in here," Neal shouted. "You got a present."

"And this present's for—"

"Mark, slow down," Mom said. "I want to see what everyone gets."

"This one's for Grandma."

"Finally." My grandmother smoothed her dress as I passed her the gift.

The next gift was for Leslie. She ripped the paper off and crumpled it into a ball. Aunt Alice had picked out some 45-rpm rock-and-roll records for her. Leslie smiled and oohed-and-aahed. "Thank you, Aunt Alice."

"I hope you don't have them already."

"Oh no. They're just what I wanted. How did you know?"

Aunt Alice beamed. "I asked the store manager."

When no one was watching, Leslie made a face at me.

At the dining-room table, Grandma turned to Dad. "Charles, take some pictures while Neal carves the ham."

My father excused himself and brought the camera from the living room. I sat between my great-aunt and grandmother, grinning, while Dad adjusted the focus. "Mark, stop grinning. You look like a halfwit. Okay. Ready now." The flashcube illuminated the room like a burst of lightning.

"Goodness." Aunt Ellen jerked beside me. "What happened?"

"One more please. Stop talking and smile." Another bright flash. Aunt Ellen gripped my arm. Purple spots floated in front of my eyes.

Alice held up her hand. "Mark, will you say grace?"

She asked me to say grace because none of the adults wanted to. I took a deep breath. "Thank you, God, for this food…"

Out of the corner of my eye, I looked around. Grandma was rubbing her lips together to even out her lipstick. Aunt Alice scanned the table for anything missing.

"We thank the Lord for all our presents…"

Mom's eyes were closed, her hands folded in front of her plate. Dad stared at the centerpiece of dried flowers.

"We thank Thee for bringing us all together…"

Leslie was picking the Greek olives out of her salad. Beside me and still gripping my arm, Aunt Ellen stared around the room in an agitated manner.

"… to celebrate Christmas—"

"We can't start without Walter," Aunt Ellen interrupted me. "He should be here by now!"

My mouth fell open, and I swallowed the "Amen."

Silence around the table. Neal stood with the knife halfway through the ham.

"He promised to be here." A tear ran down Aunt Ellen's cheek. "He promised."

"He'll be here soon." Aunt Alice stood up. She didn't act the least bit surprised.

Aunt Ellen reached down for her napkin to wipe her eyes, but she'd taken hold of the tablecloth. Her glass of water tipped over, silverware fell off the table, and one of the candles plopped into the dried flowers.

Everyone began talking at once. Dad reached over to pull the candle out of the centerpiece where a small flame peeked through the dried leaves.

"Oh, look." Mom emptied her glass of water into the flowers.

My grandmother pushed back her chair. "Ellen, stop this foolishness and eat your dinner!"

But Aunt Alice was on her feet, helping my great-aunt from her chair. "I'll take her upstairs. The spare room is made up."

Mom joined her at Aunt Ellen's side. I followed behind with a mixture of confusion and fascinated horror. She was frail and light. Even I could hold her up.

On the second floor, Aunt Alice ran ahead to pull back the spread. I heard the whir as she lowered the shades on the front windows.

At the bedroom door, Aunt Ellen became more agitated. "Don't take me in there. It's too dark."

"I'll turn a light on, dear." The bedside lamp cast a pink glow through its shade. The two women helped her into bed. Mom removed her shoes while Aunt Alice covered her with the spread.

Mom saw me standing in the doorway. "Go downstairs. There's nothing more to do here."

"Walter?" My great-aunt raised her head and stared straight at me. She struggled to free her hand from the bedspread. "Come here."

"She's always calling me Walter." Was this somehow my fault? Had she forgotten my name again?

I sat on the bed and held her hand. She looked at me for a long moment, then abruptly closed her eyes. Her breathing was shallow but regular.

"Should we call a doctor?" Aunt Alice whispered to my mother.

"She's overexcited. A little rest will do her good."

"But she needs something to eat. I'll bring up tea and toast." Aunt Alice went downstairs.

"Mom, it's all right. I'll stay with her."

She hesitated. "Promise you'll stay right here. Call me if she tries to get up. I'll have a bite to eat and be right back."

In the double bed, Aunt Ellen looked like a child who'd been tucked in for the night. Her rings pressed against the bones in my hand. I thought of her telling me the story about her train ride out west.

Dusk was filling the woods. Through the side window facing the backyard, I watched the pine trees sway in the wind, snow drifting down like a veil.

I got up from the bed. My great-aunt's body rose higher with my weight off the mattress. In the hallway, I leaned over the stair railing. The rattle of silverware on china, the low murmur of voices came from the dining room. Then below me, I heard Mom:

"… should go right after dinner, Charles. Mother will stay with her tonight."

I stepped back from the railing. I didn't want her to see me and think I'd broken my promise to watch Aunt Ellen. The hall floor creaked under my feet.

"… to a home. We can't put it off any longer." At first, I didn't recognize my uncle's voice. It wasn't the loud, joking voice I knew.

"… hate the thought of it, but you're right." Mom again. "We'll talk tomorrow. I'll send Mark down for his dinner."

I tiptoed back to the bedroom. When she entered the room, I stood by the bed.

"Is she still asleep?"

I nodded.

"Go down and have dinner."

"Will she be okay?"

"She'll be better when she wakes up. She hasn't slept well lately and gets confused."

"What home are you taking her to?"

"We're bringing her back to her own house. Grandma will stay with her for a few days."

"Grandma is angry with her."

"She's not angry. When people are worried, they sound angry but they're not."

Downstairs, Aunt Alice filled my plate with ham, potato, peas, and squash. Over the ham, she poured a sweet sauce with raisins. The squash had brown sugar mixed in it.

Uncle Neal sat at the table and watched me eat. "What do you want to be when you grow up?"

"I just started high school."

"Study science. That's the subject these days. Can't let the Commies beat us in space."

I looked down at my plate, hoping my expression didn't reveal how little I cared for science.

"They'll beat us to the moon. We should have bombed them when we had the chance."

"Really, Neal!" Grandma and her son argued over dessert while I ate in silence. I thought of Aunt Ellen lying asleep upstairs like a toy someone had forgotten to wind up.

Soon after dinner, we left for home. Standing in the light snowfall outside my uncle's house, I smelled the pine trees. Dad and Uncle Neal helped Aunt Ellen into the car. She had recovered and insisted she was capable of walking by herself. Even I knew that wouldn't last long. Tears filled my eyes. More than Christmas had ended.

The goodbyes were hurried: "Call tomorrow and let me know how she is... Thanks for having us... Hope this snow doesn't keep up much longer." I hoped the snow would fall all night.

In the distance, a church clock struck the hour. My mother looked at her watch. "Charles, it's eight o'clock!" The church bells played "Silent Night," the notes drifting down lighter than snow. Staring up at the sky, I wondered how many miles the flakes fell.

On the ride home, I listened to the rhythm of the windshield wipers scraping away the ice. When another automobile passed, its headlights flashed across the interior of our car. Aunt Ellen had fallen asleep. On my other side, Grandma twisted a ring around her finger. She looked through the windows as if anything out there would be more interesting than what was happening inside. Leslie was sleeping against her shoulder. The tires skimmed the road. Each vibration shivered through me. I wished the ride would go on forever.

CHAPTER 28

"Something Is Wrong"

I often find Mom dozing in her wheelchair. She responds when I kiss her and is happy to see me, but once I start talking, I wonder if she understands what I tell her or if she'll remember anything I've said after I leave. I sit beside her, massaging her hand. She looks up if I vary my tone or the cadence of my speech. Perhaps she suspects I've changed the subject. I often think she enjoys the rhythm of my voice but pays no attention to the words.

When I've exhausted the family news, I talk about the birds fluttering at the feeders and splashing in the birdbath or comment on what's happening around us. To be honest, how much can you say about a group of elderly women sleeping in their wheelchairs or talking with the staff or with no one in particular? Once, a patient leaned forward to talk with a friend. When she saw me watching, she cupped her hand to hide her mouth. Was she talking about me?

This Saturday, I arrive at the nursing home at four. I search for Dad's car as I circle the lot, hunting for a place to park. There are fewer places because of the snow heaped into piles by the snowplows. I'm disappointed when I don't see his car. I don't find my sister's car either, but Leslie visits

Mom on her way home from work, so I don't expect to see hers. Without Dad or Leslie there, the hour will stretch on forever. I consider putting off my visit until tomorrow but feel guilty even thinking it. If Dad or Leslie is there when I arrive, I notice their look of relief. They too struggle to entertain Mom. We forget that sitting with Mom and touching her is what's most important.

When I don't find Mom in the recreation area, I check the room she shares with Mrs. Battersby, her latest roommate, who is often in bed. In the late afternoon, the sun shines through the trees, providing a soft glow in their room. The odor of pills and dry skin is never disguised by the air freshener hanging on the wall. Mom's bed is hidden behind a screen. When I cross the room, her roommate blinks at me.

When I first met Mrs. Battersby, I thought she was flirting with me. Only later did I realize her eyes twitch uncontrollably. If Mom isn't in the room, I stop a moment to say hello and ask about her grandchildren. Her daughter brings them to visit every weekend. She is animated when showing me the latest pictures they've drawn. Their artwork covers the wall beside her bed. A family tree hangs above her bureau with a photo of each relative.

Behind the screen, I find Mom in bed asleep. I place a chair beside her bed. I'll wait until she wakes up, although I regret not bringing a book. There's no newspaper or magazine on her bedside table.

When I look back at Mom, her eyes are open. I smile and lean over to kiss her. Her eyes, usually shiny and watchful, are dull, and I wonder if she's not feeling well.

"Hi, Mom. Did I wake you?"

She frowns and shakes her head.

"It's beautiful out today. I always feel optimistic when we move the clocks forward." In winter weather, I often wheel her out to the sunporch by the large windows. But finding her in bed, I don't want to disturb her. Besides, one of the aides will come shortly to get her ready for dinner.

"Are you sick?"

Again, she shakes her head. She often won't tell me, so I'll ask the nurse before I leave.

"Was Dad here this afternoon?" My conversation begins with several yes or no questions to prime the pump.

She looks up at the ceiling, frowning, trying to focus her mind. "Dad?" Her voice is barely audible, as if she's conserving energy. "I can't remember." There's wonder in her voice, as if she doesn't understand why she can't remember. I'll call Dad when I get home to make sure there's nothing wrong with him or his car.

"Rachel got a promotion and a raise at work last week." I count down the family news: the five things you need to know to start your day, as they say on the news. Mom no longer asks about her grandchildren—a continuing irritant for Rachel. I've learned to add specific details about them to refresh her memory.

"Leslie's daughter, Elaine, is interning once a week with a real estate company. She hopes it'll lead to a job after graduation."

Mom doesn't respond. I can't tell if she's smiling or not.

"And Jon will finish his sophomore year in a few months. Rachel is happy he's closer."

Finding something to do, I check her radio to ensure it's tuned correctly. When she was no longer interested in watching TV, Dad set up a radio beside her bed. Mom complained the station kept changing when she turned it on. Dad soon realized the tremor in her fingers inadvertently moved the dial. He covered the tuner with tape so she couldn't knock it off her favorite station.

"Would you like me to turn on your radio?"

She twists her head as if checking to make sure the radio hasn't wandered off while she wasn't looking. She shrugs.

"I'll leave it off. Almost time for dinner anyway."

I see a pair of nylons hanging from a bureau drawer. One has a run starting from the toe, usually caused when the aide puts it on, and it snags on a sharp toenail.

"When's the podiatrist coming?" The nursing staff isn't allowed to cut a resident's nails, but why? Are they afraid a blood clot could be dislodged? A cynic might suspect the podiatrists' association had a law passed to protect their nursing home boondoggle.

"Let me check your toenails."

When she doesn't answer, I pull the sheet up at the end of the bed. She draws her feet back so only her toes are showing. I once opened a trunk in our basement to find four baby mice, their heads tucked into the foot of one of Jenn's baby shoes. They thought they were safely hidden, except their tails stretched back to the heel.

When I reach down and hold her foot, her leg jerks from my touch.

"Sorry. I didn't mean to tickle you. I only want to check your nails."

She lets me draw her foot from under the sheet. Her nylon is torn and twisted around her little toe. How can she bear the discomfort? My little toe is so sensitive, I shudder when its nail snags on a sock.

I take the nylons off. Her toenails have begun to curl over her toes. Dad has forgotten to schedule the podiatrist.

"Let me get the clippers."

In the bathroom, I dampen a washcloth with warm water and soap and gently wash her feet. The smell is the worst part of the job, but lavender soap takes care of that. I cautiously cut each nail. Some are thicker and require pressure. I steel myself for her cry of pain, but she doesn't react. I brush the nails onto the floor and push them under the bed. "That'll do you for a while." I return the clippers and washcloth.

I can't think of anything to talk about. I listen to the cars on the main street. There's a pause for twenty seconds when the light turns red. On green, the cars accelerate once again.

Someone shovels snow while listening to a hockey game. The roar of the crowd echoes off the sides of his neighbor's house. Some people play their radios at a volume that's impossible to escape.

"Rachel and I are off to the Cape next week for a few days. We're house-sitting for friends. It's a small cottage, but cozy in winter." I add, as if being exact makes a difference, "Nothing fancy."

"Where?"

"South Yarmouth. The owners are friends from college. I don't think you've met them."

Now the sun is shining in my face. I cross the room and lower the venetian blinds. I close my eyes, and the bars of light turn green and float across my lids. Returning to my chair, I find Mom's eyes are closed as if she thinks I've left. I squeeze her hand.

A flash of alarm in her eyes and she focuses on my face. She twists her hand away.

"I haven't gone. I'm still here."

She's agitated and pulls her hands under the blanket. If she had the strength, I believe she'd pull the covers over her head.

Something is wrong. "I'll be back in a moment."

At the nurses' station, Mrs. Webster, shift supervisor on weekends, is updating the whiteboard on the wall. "Yes?" She turns around. "Oh, how are you, Mr. Aherne?"

"It's my mother. She's been withdrawn since I arrived, but now she's extremely agitated. Did the doctor reevaluate her medications?" After Rachel reviewed Mom's prescriptions, Leslie passed on her questions to the doctor.

"Let me see." She pulls Mom's records from the cart. I'm surprised at how thick her file is. She clicks her tongue as she scans them. "The doctor increased her Aricept. That should improve her attention and clarity, but it takes a couple of weeks to have an effect."

She turns to the previous page. "Your sister talked with the doctor about this?" She looks up. "He lowered the Ativan. We're monitoring her to make sure this change doesn't increase her agitation."

"I think it has. Would you come and check on her?"

Closing the folder, she smiles. "I'll have one of the aides look in."

When I return to her room, Mom's favorite aide is helping her into her wheelchair. He lifts her feet onto the footrests. Born in Martinique, he speaks with a soothing, light French accent. He smiles when he sees me, his teeth flashing white against his black skin. "For the dinner, I'm making her ready, but I'll take her later if you are to visit."

"Thanks. I won't be staying much longer."

He leaves the room.

"He's my favorite."

"I know. He takes good care of you."

To my relief, Mom is less anxious. Her eyes are brighter, and she smiles. "You look like you've had a scare."

I can't help laughing. "That's the pot calling the kettle black. *I* was worried about *you*." What will Nurse Webster think if she comes to check? It's like bringing my car to a mechanic with a loud rattle and finding it runs for him without a problem.

"I'm fine. I had a good nap, but"—and she lowers her voice—"I'm not looking forward to what they're serving for dinner."

We talk for a few minutes. She's more animated and engaged, almost a different person.

The aide returns to take her to dinner.

"I have to leave now." I kiss her on the cheek. "Say hello to Nurse Webster for me."

"Thanks for coming. I'm sorry I was asleep most of the time."

In the car, I rest my forehead on the steering wheel, relieved to be away but also afraid that I'm failing my mother. I wish the three of us could afford to move her to a better facility, but now that she's on Medicaid, finding space in a new place won't be easy. I sympathize with elderly people who buy lottery tickets with money they can't spare to enjoy a few days of hope. Perhaps I'll stop on my way home and splurge on a few myself.

I tell Rachel about the visit and Mom's agitation. "The doc's adjusted her medications. It'll take a couple of weeks to see if it helps."

"I can't interfere, you know that. You saw how the nursing home reacted at the annual review when they learned I'm a nurse. I'm trouble, and they wish I'd stop asking questions and just disappear."

I remember that day, but at the time I was more worried about Dad. He left the family meeting wondering if he'd made the right decision to keep Mom there. He was losing confidence in the staff. I told Rachel in the future not to question Mom's care when my father is present. "We'd be lost without your advice."

"I'll visit her the next time you go and see how she's doing."

I'm relieved. "Thanks. I rely on your medical know-how."

"I'll stay under their radar," she adds. "They don't want to know me."

Upstairs, I lie on our bed exhausted. Rachel's last words run over and over in my head. I try to relax, but the refrain is constant. *They don't want to know me.*

I jump out of bed. "Oh my God."

Rachel meets me at the bottom of the stairs, frightened by my shouting. "What happened?"

I sink down on the steps. "When I arrived today, I sensed something was wrong with Mom."

"What?"

"When I first came in, she was in bed. When she woke, she didn't know who I was!"

CHAPTER 29

"WHAT OTHER MAN?"

Visiting Mom becomes more and more distressing. I now visit only on the weekends. Talking with her is like lobbing a tennis ball of conversation over the net that Mom is unable to return. I could be an automated server and say anything. By the end of the visit, I lapse into silence. I'm impatient with Mom, as if she's deliberately being difficult, and then I'm disgusted at my impatience. After kissing her goodbye, I vacate the court, leaving the balls where they lie.

I'm heartbroken when I watch her because nothing can be done. Her mind is failing. She's no longer the mother I've known all my life. I fight against the fear this could be me in thirty years. Leslie worries about this too. She's told me, "If I ever get this bad, shoot me." It's a macabre joke, but it helps distance us from our own dread.

I hold Mom's hand. It's like a bird's claw, all bone and knuckles, the dark veins lying beneath the skin thin as tracing paper. When I arrive, I doubt she knows who I am. In the past, I'd say, "How about a kiss for your only son," and she'd locate me in her memory. That no longer works. She frowns when I tell her I'm her son. Is she wondering why this stranger is making such a ridiculous statement? I don't press the point. Doing so confuses her.

She accepts me as someone who visits occasionally, someone who sits beside her and holds her hand. I tell her stories about the past, hoping a detail will strike a chord. I think she copies my facial expressions to prove she's paying attention.

After two hours, when I tell her I'm leaving, she turns toward me, smiling like she's surprised I've arrived. I kiss her and rub her back and leave when an aide places her dinner tray in front of her. The meal is a distraction that will sweep me from her mind. Outside in the fresh air and sunshine, I'm light-hearted—and light-headed—relieved I won't have to visit for another week. How has Dad come here day after day for almost two years?

Why do I consider this visit such a burden? She's my mother whether she remembers me or not. Can't I cheerfully spend a couple of hours with her and provide human interaction? Some children care for an ailing parent in their home for years with little help and little complaint. I'm incapable of that. Too selfish and self-absorbed? I'm embarrassed to admit I find visiting more of a burden since she no longer recognizes me. Do I require a medal for my weekly presence from someone who's raised me, sacrificing many of her own dreams? At some point, do we only pretend to act the part of the caring child? What a terrible son I am.

As a teenager, I read how Eskimos treated an elderly parent who became sick and would never recover. The nomadic family wouldn't survive if they fed someone unable to contribute during the yearly migration in search of food. The family left the parent behind to freeze to death.

Reading this shocked me. I imagined myself left behind, listening to the sledge on snow, the crunch of boots, the panting of dogs. All the sounds of one's family fading into silence.

Was it as heartless as it sounds? Freezing to death must have been a blessing to those exhausted beyond endurance or in unbearable pain who welcomed falling into a peaceful sleep, ending it all. We will all meet death and be left behind.

I plan my visits for weekend afternoons. Dad won't have doctors' appointments, so I count on his being there. His face lights up when he sees that he'll have company. We talk with each other, explaining something to my mother to maintain the falsehood she is part of the conversation. Mom watches us speaking as if waiting for one of us to make sense. She never cared for films with subtitles, so our conversation must be like a never-ending foreign film with actors who talk, talk, talk in a language she can't understand.

Today, by coincidence, Leslie is visiting at the same time. This happens occasionally. We relax at these impromptu family reunions that take on a carefree atmosphere as we pretend we're still a family of four. Leslie often brings soft cookies and fruit that don't require a set of teeth to eat. Once she brought ginger candy—Mom's favorite. She asked the store to cut it short, so Mom could suck them without having to bite off a piece. The downside of bringing food is the need to watch her, prepared to act quickly if she chokes.

Leslie and I take turns buying coffee at Dunkin' Donuts. We're honest enough to admit to each other the trip offers a chance to escape for half an hour. This afternoon, it's my turn. I write the orders on a napkin. I can't remember the details of everyone's order even when mumbling them over and over all the way to the store. This puzzles me because in school I memorized hundreds of lines when acting in plays.

When I return with the coffee, Mom is no longer sitting with Dad and Leslie. I unpack the coffee, cream, and sugar. "Is Mom in the bathroom?"

Dad, staring out the windows, says nothing. Leslie gestures toward the center of the room where Mom sits at another table beside a male patient. I don't remember seeing him in the hallway. Slouched in his wheelchair, he's dressed in gym pants and a sweatshirt. His hair is uncombed or, if once combed, has since been pulled in all directions. I see his face in profile and notice he hasn't shaved. One hand holds a stuffed animal in his lap; the other holds my mother's hand.

I turn to Leslie, frowning in confusion, and whisper, "What the hell?" She puts a finger on her lips then mouths, *Later.*

I pass around the coffee, leaving Mom's cup in the cardboard tray in the middle of the table. Her coffee is more eloquent than Mom would be had she remained with us.

Leslie resumes her conversation with Dad about her son Palmer winning a local photography contest. "The picture will be printed in next year's calendar distributed by our town's rec department. His photograph shows two squirrels sitting in a birdbath grooming each other while two red cardinals perch on an overhanging branch, waiting their turn."

Without turning away from the window, Dad says, "I'll send a card to congratulate him."

"He'll appreciate that." Leslie adds more half-and-half to her coffee. "Since he won, I've had to stop his bragging. His reincarnation as Ansel Adams gets old fast."

She reaches out to touch Dad's arm. "Drink your coffee before it gets cold."

He swings around to pick up his coffee. His expression reveals nothing about how he feels. He's never been one to show emotion. Arguing with Mom in the past, he'd act like nothing bothered him, driving her to distraction because she could never hide how she felt.

With relief, I hear the rattle of dinner carts bumping off the elevator and the soft whir of their wheels on linoleum. Three of us stand as if someone yelled, "Ten-hut!"

Leslie takes Mom's coffee to her and places it in front of her. With her free hand Mom reaches out for the cup at the edge of the table, but her tremor causes it to shake. "Mom, sip." Leslie steadies the cup. "Use the straw."

I tap Mom's shoulder, hoping she drops the man's hand and turns to me. "Bye, Mom. See you soon." I kiss the top of her head. She looks up without any change in her demeanor. I kiss her cheek. She remains holding the man's hand. His stuffed animal is a black cat. He appears grubby and unclean. I want to send him rolling across the dining room. His touching my mother is repulsive.

Leslie bends down to kiss Mom. "See you Tuesday. I love you."

Mom mumbles something like "I love you too," but I can't be sure. She turns back to the man.

Dad has left the room without saying goodbye. When our visits overlap, we always have a car-side chat where we talk freely, but Leslie and I find him unlocking his car door. It's obvious he doesn't want to discuss what's happened.

Leslie calls to him, "Dad, I'll see you Wednesday for dinner. Decide where you want to go."

He attempts to smile to show he looks forward to dinner, but it's obvious he's upset. When he backs out of his parking spot, I signal with my hand to help him avoid a collision with a parked car. The scrapes and dents on the side of his car alarm me.

As we watch him drive down the street, Leslie shakes her head. "We should send out a town alert and warn other cars to stay off the road for half an hour. Elderly driver: failing eyesight, poor depth perception, stiff neck prevents looking in any direction."

I'm laughing. "He's not that bad."

"Not yet, but I don't want him hitting someone when he puts his car into reverse by mistake."

With Dad out of sight, we walk back to Leslie's car. "What's the deal with Mom?"

"Today's the third time Mom's done this that I know of. When I saw it the first time, I was alone with her. For no reason, she wheeled her chair around and made a beeline for that man. I was speechless."

"When did this start?"

"I've asked Dad, but he ignores the question. The second time I was with Dad. He was embarrassed but not surprised." Her voice rises in frustration. "How does he put up with it? If I were him, I'd put on my coat and leave."

"He's never said anything to you?" This is unusual. Leslie has always been closer to him. "How does she know this man? I've never seen her talking to him."

"They don't talk. They just sit and hold hands."

"Dad must feel abandoned."

Leslie crosses her arms. "He was abandoned long before this. You remember her in the apartment. She rarely took part in conversations and showed little interest in what was going on. The psychological distance between the two of them took a long time for him to accept. This is just one more step along the way."

I remember Rachel saying, "*Your father's alone when he visits her and alone when he goes back to the apartment.*"

"He's used to it by now." The circumstances sadden Leslie. "He's ashamed when anyone sees her leave him."

"It's not his fault."

"He's past thinking objectively. He feels like a chump."

"But why this man? He's nothing like Dad. It's like he hypnotized her or something."

"The social worker says this behavior isn't uncommon." Leslie stares off into space, her lips a thin, hard line. "When I asked her how Mom could be attracted to this man, she said she may see something that reminds her of Dad long ago. There's no way to know. The social worker spoke with Dad. She thinks he's come to terms with it. But going off with another man? Dad knows their relationship is over. How can a husband ever accept that?"

When Leslie looks back at me, I'm shocked to find tears streaking her cheeks.

I put my arm around her. "Sometimes I wonder if after a long life together, it's better if a loved one passes without warning. You're haunted by what you never said, and you can't pretend there's still a chance to say goodbye. You can only grieve and accept it. In Dad's case, Mom is still here, except the person he knew is dead. There's nothing he can say or do. Every day her presence reminds him of what they used to have—"

Leslie is sobbing again. Her tears wet my shirt. With a sinking heart, I realize she must be thinking of her husband's death. In an instant, a heart attack took him, and he was gone, leaving her alone at forty-two with two young children. She must think about him every day. How could she not? Has she found any peace knowing she'll never experience what Dad is going through?

Of course not. How can I even consider such a thing? One always wants to experience a full lifetime with a loved one, even if there's a risk that the end may be heartbreaking. I can't know how someone feels in either situation. I pray I'll die before Rachel. As much as I fear death, I fear her death more. Wanting to die first is a selfish but comforting thought, due in no small part to my growing suspicion that Mom's infirmities might someday be mine.

"Mankind has cursed itself," I say. "All these medical advances repair our physical bodies and keep them running like antique cars. But our brains haven't evolved to keep up. Our bodies live, but inside we're dying."

I follow Leslie's car. At the end of the street, she turns right. I wait for the green arrow to turn left. I'll call her tomorrow and invite myself to dinner with our father.

We become used to Mom leaving us when she sees the other man. I'm amazed at the strength in her arms as she propels her wheelchair across the room, like she's afraid another patient might usurp her place. They never speak but are content holding hands.

Dad's learned it's useless trying to convince her to come back. He comes every day, but Mom rarely reacts to anything he says. He sits beside her, makes sure she swallows her medication, and notifies an aide when she needs to use the bathroom. His only thanks? Her wheeling away from him, spending more time beside the other man than with him.

How can he not take it to heart? Why does he come day after day when Mom seems oblivious to his presence? He promised to visit her every day. And he's keeping his word.

One evening two weeks later, Rachel looks up from her magazine. "By the way, how's your mother doing?"

"Not any better. Her spending time with the other man still upsets Dad."

She closes the magazine in surprise. "What other man?"

"I told you about him."

"You did not."

"I thought I had."

She tosses the magazine on the table. "Okay. Tell me again."

When I describe Mom's behavior, Rachel is upset. "Your father visits her every afternoon, and she leaves him?"

"Not right away." I want to defend Mom. "They sit together when Dad first arrives."

"Yeah, and then what?"

"This man is wheeled into the rec room, Mom sees him, and goes to him."

"What does she say to your father?" The whole situation is incomprehensible to Rachel.

"She doesn't say anything. She just leaves."

"Your poor father. Does he go over to bring her back?"

"He did at first."

"Have you or Leslie tried bringing her back?"

"Leslie did. She wheeled Mom back, talking to her and holding her hand, but when she let go of her, Mom rolled herself back across the room. Leslie started after her, but Dad shook his head. 'Leave her be.' Leslie said it broke her heart. She took Dad out to dinner to give him a chance to talk about it, but he wouldn't. He keeps everything in."

"Your father can't go on like this every day. Encourage him to take time off every week."

"I doubt he would. He feels guilty keeping her there. His visits are a kind of penance."

"That's his Catholic upbringing."

Later, when Rachel settles herself in bed and turns off her bedside lamp, she is noticeably quiet and still. From experience I know she has something to say and I wonder if I've done anything wrong. "Mark, are you still awake?"

I feel my body tense. This was often a prelude to her voicing a complaint about moving during our last days in Chicago. I'd listen and try to reassure her. Our talks often continued for over an hour but eventually helped her to accept my reasons for wanting to move.

Tonight is different. She talks more about Mom leaving Dad's side in the nursing home. "You need to help your father. Perhaps you can meet him there on weekends and provide support." When I say nothing, she asks, "Don't you agree?"

"Yes."

"I know she has dementia, but this must be the final stab in the back. To be a husband watching your life partner taken from you by mental illness is a horrible experience. It must be like those times in the past when the baby of an unwed mother was taken away from her in the mistaken belief this was in the best interest of the child."

We don't discuss it much longer, for which I'm grateful since I'm barely awake at this point. But I was awake long enough to hear Rachel's last words about loss. When I awake at 2:30, her words roam endlessly through my mind like a band of thieves pulling open drawers and rifling through papers until they find one written before Mom was born. A note that foreshadowed her entire life.

CHAPTER 30

"NOTHING IS COLDER THAN THE GRAVE"

Home from college for Christmas vacation. Day three and looking forward to returning to school. I'm like a guest obliged to entertain his hosts as a thank you for their invitation. Rachel and her family were visiting her cousins in New Jersey. I passed the time getting a head start on my reading for next semester.

That evening, the telephone rang during dinner. Dad answered it in the hall. "Hello?" and "Give us a call," he said before hanging up. "That was Uncle Neal. The doctor is at the nursing home. He doesn't expect Aunt Ellen to live through the night."

No one said a word. Leslie's chin quivered, and her face was pale.

I remained silent, knowing my throat would choke up. I tried not to think of Aunt Ellen as she was the last time I'd visited her with Mom in the nursing home. Instead, I remembered her telling me stories when I was a child: sailing across the ocean with a friend from work, dancing with her beaus as a debutante, and visiting me when I was a baby.

"I would cover my face with a scarf," she told me. "When I took it off, you laughed and laughed. Your mother said you wouldn't fall asleep if I stayed, but you screamed when I tried to leave. You sat on my lap, playing with the shiny locket around my neck, mesmerized by the light reflected on the walls. Cuddled against me, you closed your eyes and fell asleep."

We remained at the dinner table, quietly talking. Maybe Mom was telling Leslie her own stories about Aunt Ellen as a way to comfort my sister and herself.

"Mom, I remember when Aunt Ellen visited us when I was in my playpen."

"In your playpen? What happened?"

"You wanted me to take a nap, but I screamed when Aunt Ellen tried to leave."

"You screamed all the time in your playpen. That was just a story she told you. You can't remember anything that far back."

She was wrong. I could clearly see Aunt Ellen coming in the front door and lifting me out of my playpen. I reach out to touch the locket she always wore. A memory that distinct must have happened. Why would I make it up?

While Leslie and I washed the dishes, the telephone rang again. "Hello?" Dad listened a moment. "Tell us the details when the arrangements are final." He hung up. "Aunt Ellen died ten minutes ago."

I didn't care if crying was childish. Who cares if I was a freshman in college? She was an important part of my childhood, and now she was gone. But ever since that Christmas dinner four years ago, she hadn't been the great-aunt I'd known most of my life. Grandma was right when she said her death would be a blessing.

After Aunt Ellen's funeral and the New Year holiday was over, our family drove to the White Mountains to ski. Three of us skied; Mom camped out in the chalet with her book. We planned to stay three days but had to cut the trip short.

Mom's brother called the hotel to tell us Aunt Ellen's lawyer had scheduled the reading of her will the next day. The attorney asked Mom, Leslie, and me to attend. Since she had no money, Uncle Neal didn't see a reason for him to attend but had promised to extend the lawyer's invitation. "He probably wasn't asked to attend," Mom said.

We packed the car the next morning and drove to the lawyer's office in Central Square. The traffic was heavy, but at the last moment Dad found an empty space on the street.

"Why is it empty?" Always suspicious of good luck, Mom peered through the windshield at the parking signs along the curb. "It's confusing. They contradict one another."

"I'm not moving. I'll wait in the coffee shop over there in case a cop comes along."

The lawyer's office occupied a three-story brick building, once an elegant private home. The receptionist rang Mr. Brookner's office. He descended in the elevator.

"I'm pleased to meet you, Mrs. Aherne." He shook Mom's hand. "Regrettably, I never had the pleasure of meeting Miss Wisdom. She made her will with my former partner, Mr. Erickson, over ten years ago. When he died, I inherited her affairs, you might say." He led us to the elevator. "First, allow me to express our firm's sympathy on Miss Wisdom's passing."

He spoke with precision, as if spooning each word out of his mouth. Despite his white hair, he looked athletic—not at all dusty and threadbare, like a lawyer in a Dickens novel. That was a letdown. Meeting a lawyer sounded exciting, but there was nothing mysterious here.

He ushered us through a tiny reception area into his office where five chairs surrounded a table. "Please be seated." He noticed the extra chair. "I expected your husband."

"He's out in the car."

"I see." He moved the fifth chair back, careful to prevent it from touching the wall. "Would anyone like a beverage before we start? Coffee, tea, water?"

Mom said she was fine. I also declined. Leslie said she'd like an orangeade.

"Give me a moment to ask Miss Nicholson if we have that beverage." He left the room.

Leslie turned to me. "Why didn't you ask for one?"

I shrugged. Orangeade had no class. Sherry was more appropriate for the surroundings.

"I'm sure Leslie will let you have a sip of hers."

"No way. He had a chance to get his own." If we'd been alone, my sister would have stuck her tongue out. How juvenile.

"One ice-cold orangeade coming up." Mr. Brookner acted delighted he'd succeeded in providing this token of hospitality. He poured the soda into a glass and handed it to Leslie. "Here's a coaster." He wiped his hands on his handkerchief.

"Now if you're all comfortable, we can begin. This shouldn't take long, but as the deceased's representative, I like to do this in person. I'm a great believer in tradition."

While he talked, I examined the office. The bookshelves were filled with books from floor to ceiling. Each set of books, perfectly aligned, had the same colored binding. Boring. I wondered how often he read them.

"Miss Wisdom was farsighted. There's no need to probate her will. I understand the family distributed her possessions among relatives when her home was sold."

"My brother took care of the details."

"Of course." Mr. Brookner opened a folder and removed several pages stapled together. "I'll skip the boilerplate and go straight to the bequests. She left two in the names of your children." He handed two envelopes to Mom. "You're the trustee until Mark and Leslie reach the age of twenty-one."

"That's five years away," Leslie grumbled.

"It'll be here faster than you think." Mom spoke sharply. Leslie's behavior would be discussed later.

"She opened the brokerage accounts with ten thousand dollars. They're worth substantially more now."

"We never expected she had any money."

"There's one other bequest. She left this locket to Mark."

He opened a velvet bag and took out the locket she'd always worn around her neck.

Mr. Brookner returned it to the velvet bag, which he then handed to me. "With that settled, perhaps your children will return to the waiting room."

Leslie and I got up, and Mr. Brookner opened the door to the outer room. As he closed it, he spoke to Mom. "This provision may come as a surprise—" The door clicked shut.

Angry, Leslie sat with her arms crossed. "Why did we miss a day of skiing for this?"

"Give me a break. Aren't you happy to get the money?"

"Yeah, when I'm twenty-one. In a thousand years from now— Rats! I forgot my drink."

I slipped the locket out of its bag and turned it over. *My Family* was engraved on the front. I pressed a tiny latch on the side, and it snapped open, revealing two sepia photographs. Before I could examine them, we heard a muffled cry from the office. Then silence. Leslie and I looked at each other.

"I guess Aunt Ellen had more money than Mom thought," she said.

The door opened. Mr. Brookner's lawyerly composure was rattled. "Mark, ask your father to come up right away."

Mom was sobbing in the room behind him.

"What's wrong?" Leslie asked.

"Go now, Mark. Leslie, come in and stay with your mother."

I found Dad in the coffee shop. "Something's happened to Mom."

His face went white. Leaving his coffee behind, he followed me. "Is she hurt?"

"I don't think so. Leslie and I were in another room."

Back in the office, Mr. Brookner shook my father's hand. "Mr. Aherne, I'm afraid your wife has had a shock. She's calmer now. She didn't expect to hear what was in the will."

Dad pushed by the lawyer and went into the office. I crowded in behind him.

"Charles, I can't believe this is happening."

"Believe what? Did she have money after all?"

"There's no money, but that isn't the point. Aunt Ellen is—was—my mother!"

My father frowned. "She was? Then who was your father?"

Calling the revelation an earthquake was no overstatement. Just as things got interesting, I had to return to college.

I called Leslie the next day. She said Mom was still in shock and rarely left her bedroom. "She stays in bed most of the time. Dr. Madison prescribed some pills to help her sleep. Dad's wonderful. He's taken time off from work."

What did they talk about? Leslie said she didn't know.

I buried myself studying for exams and forgot about the will until the weekend when Leslie called me on the dorm phone. "Mom's better, although she still has periods when she loses her composure. She's started drinking more. The slightest comment sets her off. Sometimes she unloads on Dad as if he had something to do with it. You're lucky you're not around. In case you can't tell, I'm going crazy."

Given Mom's state of mind, Dad didn't want her calling Grandma until she could talk coherently about what she'd learned. He told Leslie Grandma had a lot to explain. As a freshman, I found the news surprising but not a big deal.

For a long time, we still used the names Aunt Ellen and Grandma, even though these were incorrect. From force of habit, we saw the family as it was and not the way it would be for the rest of our lives. Looking back thirty-five years, I now understand what a terrible shock Mom experienced. She must have spent hours reevaluating every family event, every conversation, every facial expression, trying to orient herself in a world where, in an instant, every landmark shifted.

At the time, I sympathized more with Aunt Ellen. She always acted like a second grandmother. When I was a child, I'd catch her calling me her grandson. Realizing her mistake, she'd quickly change the subject. Aunt Ellen was jealous when Grandma Bess invited Leslie and me to stay at her house. She'd call us on the phone and try to convince us to walk over and visit her. She lived in a prison with no chance for parole.

Leslie called two days later. "Dad took Mom to see Grandma. I wish I'd been a fly on that wall."

"What did Grandma say?"

"Dad thought she'd have a heart attack. She couldn't believe Aunt Ellen spilled her guts. She claimed Aunt Ellen wanted to protect Mom. Unwed mothers were the lowest of the low, and they thought Mom's future would be ruined if people found out."

"How's Mom doing now?"

"Better. Out of the blue, she'll say, 'I should have put two and two together. How could I have been so blind?' She accepts what happened but can't understand why Grandma never accepted her. Poor Mom."

Leslie talked for almost an hour. I wanted to remind her I had *beaucoup* studying to do, but Leslie needed someone to talk with. Before hanging up, she asked if I'd come home the next weekend. "I need a break. All I do is go to school, cook dinner, do my homework, and listen to Mom. There better not be any more surprises like this."

I agreed to come home after my last exam on Thursday.

"Thanks, Mark! You're not mad, are you?"

"Of course not. Don't worry. I need a break from this place too."

After my last exam, I took a taxi downtown in time to catch the bus home. Dad drove into Boston to pick me up. I wished Leslie had come with him because it was awkward talking to Dad about personal topics when they skirted the subject of sex. But I needn't have worried. "The damn traffic in Boston is ridiculous," was all he said. I agreed and waited for him to say something about Mom.

Halfway home, I broke the silence. "How's Mom doing?"

"Much better. She's had some good news considering everything that's happened over the last three weeks. Grandma admitted Walter was Mom's father."

"Granddad?" I whistled. I hadn't seen that coming. "That was simple. Her father *was* her father."

"This was good news. Mom assumed no one knew who her father was. You know how much she loved him. Walter didn't want to give up the daughter he'd always wanted. I don't think he gave Grandma any choice in the matter. She agreed to pretend to be the mother."

We arrived home. Mom acted normal. She was glad to see me, and when we hugged, she laughed a little. "How do you like having a new grandmother?" But she said little after that.

I picked up the rest of the story from Leslie. "Mom thinks Grandma didn't want sex after Uncle Neal was born. After thirteen years, Granddad's eye wandered."

"Maybe he saw Aunt Ellen off and on for years," I said. "A regular Peyton Place."

Before going to bed, I took the locket from my bureau drawer and looked at the pictures. Now I understood why Mom's baby picture was next to a photo of Granddad. Each sister suffered: one with a husband who cheated on her and perhaps never genuinely loved her; the other with a baby an intolerant society thought best to take away from her. I understood Mom's pain and could even believe I knew how she felt. But I couldn't forget Aunt Ellen's lifelong loneliness watching her child grow up from a distance. No wonder she took her revenge by revealing the truth after her death. It's been said, "Revenge is a dish best served cold." And nothing is colder than the grave.

CHAPTER 31

"She Won't Remember I Missed the Weekend"

I work in the garden on Sundays, only stopping for a drink of water from the cooler. Once I start, I want to keep going. If I take a break, I realize how exhausted I am and find it hard to get back into the rhythm of weeding.

At 2:45, Rachel calls from the back door, "Mark, are you planning to visit your mother today?"

I'm bagging the clippings from the juniper bushes along the back fence. I shout to her, "Yes. I'm coming inside in a minute."

On the deck, I sink into a lawn chair and remove my work boots. In the shade, my sweat is clammy and my T-shirt sticks to my back. My arms itch from the juniper branches. Through the open French doors, I hear the cooking show Rachel is watching on cable. She hits *mute.* "I didn't mean to interrupt you. I'm not forcing you to go."

"I was ready to stop. Do you want to go with me?" Rachel hasn't seen her recently.

Rachel twists her mouth and shakes her head. "But I'll go with you next time. By the way, have you eaten anything since breakfast?"

"Not yet."

"I'll make something for you to eat on the way— Oh, don't bring that filthy T-shirt into the house."

"It stinks too." I roll the T-shirt into a ball to toss at her.

"Don't you dare."

I laugh and start climbing the stairs.

"You can't work all day without eating. I'll be taking you to the hospital if you don't—" The TV drowns out the rest of her sentence.

The tepid shower relaxes me. I don't have the energy to trek to the nursing home. All I want is a nap. I build up a froth of suds, accidentally flicking soap in both eyes. I pull down my lower lids to help flush my eyes. God, it stings like hell! Clenching my eyes tight against the pain, I turn off the shower and grope for my towel on the floor. My feet slip on the soap scum and my knee bangs on the edge of the tub. Squinting out of one eye is painful, and now I'm limping.

In the bedroom, I turn on the fan and let the air dry my body. I lie back on the bed, burying my face in the cold washcloth. My eyeballs feel like they've been scraped raw. The sunlight through the window turns the inside of my eyelids a bright orange. I can't go to the nursing home now. I'm tired, my eyes are swollen, and a rash from brushing against the juniper bushes itches along both arms. Plus, my knee is throbbing.

I try to convince myself to make the effort. I'll relax when I return home. Or I can visit Mom tomorrow after work. She won't remember I missed the weekend. The fan makes me cold, and I draw the sheet up to my neck. The sound of lawnmowers and children playing in the street make me drowsy. I let go and sink into a delicious unconsciousness…

CHAPTER 32

"THE GREATEST GIFT YOU CAN GIVE"

I arrive at the hospital straight from work. I'm surprised to learn at reception that Mom is still in the emergency room. At the ER entrance, EMTs and hospital staff unload an ambulance. I step aside for a stretcher carrying a middle-aged man in a business suit. A nurse runs beside the stretcher holding a compress against his chest where blood soaks through his shirt. He must be a victim of the accident on the highway.

The ER is hectic: staff shout orders, phones ring, and bedside monitors beep insistently. No one asks me what I want, and I look for Mom. Leslie waves from the back where she's standing with Dad.

Leslie gives me a kiss. "What's all that confusion?"

"Pile-up on 128. Not my side of the highway. The police closed two lanes." I give my father a hug. "How are you?"

"Thanks for coming."

His words surprise me. Did he think I might not come?

"Sorry I wasn't here sooner." I'm convinced Mom's condition isn't as serious as they think. She's been rushed to the ER many times.

I turn to Leslie. "What happened this morning?"

"She was unresponsive when they woke her for breakfast, so they called an ambulance."

"Why is she not in a room?"

"They're backlogged discharging patients." Leslie has no tolerance for inefficiency.

"Just like the military." Dad leans on his cane. "Hurry up and wait."

He looks like he hasn't slept. His face is puffy. His cardigan hangs from his thin shoulders.

"Dad, let me get you a chair."

"I'm fine. I've been sitting all morning."

"Mom seemed better in the ambulance," Leslie continues. "That's what the EMT told the ER nurse. She said Mom was conscious when she came in but confused."

I try to look past them into the cubicle. "I'll peek in for a minute and say hello."

Dad nods and steps aside. "She may not respond."

Leslie closes the curtain behind me, hoping to block out some noise. When she said Mom was confused, I expect to find her thrashing about, but she lies peacefully, her eyes closed.

"Mom?" I wait. "It's Mark."

Her eyelids flutter, but she exhibits no other sign of recognition. I hold her left hand. She's not wearing her engagement ring. I assume Leslie removed it for safekeeping.

"How are you feeling? Do you want anything?"

She doesn't answer. She must be asleep because she'd respond if she heard my voice. I hope she'll recognize me when she wakes.

I pull back the curtain. Leslie looks up. "Any reaction?"

I shake my head. "Still asleep."

A nurse brushes by to check Mom's vitals. I wonder if we're in the way. Tough luck if we are.

Looking up from the monitor, the nurse speaks to Dad. "The doctor's ordered a higher dose of morphine when needed. There'll be a room soon."

I lower my voice to speak to Leslie. "Why is she on morphine?"

Leslie takes a deep breath. "This is the end."

"What do you mean 'the end'?" I frown as if it's a bad joke.

Leslie assumes I know. "The doctor doesn't expect her to last the night."

I step back from Leslie, shocked by her negativity. Mom's been admitted before with a dire prognosis but pulled through every time. She always said she had nine lives. "Why on earth does the doctor say that?"

"Her kidneys have failed. There's no chance of recovery."

"There must be *something* he can do." I look from Leslie to Dad.

He shrugs. Empty of emotion, unable to act, he's a bystander waiting for someone to tell him what to do.

My chin quivers. This can't be true. I saw her only a week ago, and she seemed the same as always.

"I'll be right back." My throat aches, and my tongue fumbles the words. I walk to the front of the ER. My eyes filling with tears, I push through the swinging doors and find myself on the platform used to unload supplies. Sobs burst from me.

I'd planned to see her two days ago but cancelled after working in the garden. How can I forgive myself for not seeing her? I might have noticed a change. I could have alerted the nursing staff she needed more fluids. Instead, I threw away my last chance to see her, to tell her I loved her, maybe even to save her. And why? My eyes stung and I wanted a nap!

With my head thrown back, I open my mouth and roar in anguish. Three or four times. And then I'm quiet and start breathing again, gulping in the air. Each beat of my heart echoes in my forehead. I hope I'm not getting a migraine.

Wiping my cheeks, I see an orderly in blue scrubs smoking a cigarette. He stares at me like I'm an alien stepping out of a spaceship. I ignore him. I'm not the first person he's seen acting like this.

The staff is wheeling a patient out of Mom's room when we arrive upstairs. After helping an aide settle Mom on the bed, the nurse moves the morphine drip from the stretcher to an IV stand. She draws the curtain around the empty bed when two cleaners enter the room.

The women speak quietly in Spanish, but even so, we listen, saying nothing. The curtain billows around the woman stripping the bed. The other woman cleans the bathroom. She flushes the toilet, runs water in the sink. Once the bed's made, the cleaner looks around the curtain. "We're finished. You want the curtain pulled back?"

Dad shakes his head. "It's okay the way it is."

When they leave the room, the women resume talking in a normal tone of voice.

Leslie breaks the silence. "Mark, I'll take Dad down for something to eat. We never had lunch. Then you can go to supper."

She turns to Dad. "Let's find the cafeteria." He isn't listening. She touches him on the shoulder. "You haven't eaten anything all day."

He scowls as if she's being unreasonable. "I had two packs of peanut-butter crackers. And a Coke."

"You need something more substantial than that."

He brushes her suggestion aside. "Not hungry. Don't feel like eating."

"You don't want to cook when you get home, do you?" Leslie holds his arm to steady him when he stands. "You can keep me company."

He pauses to gain his balance. "Gotta make sure my legs are ready to go."

"Take all the time you need." Leslie puts her arm around his back. "Would you like a walker?"

Dad gives me a withering look. "Over my dead body."

I'm surprised at how casually he speaks of death. I suppose for a moment he's forgotten Mom lying in the bed.

"I don't want anything to eat. My stomach's been acting up..." Their voices fade as they walk down the corridor.

I stand at the window watching the sun balance on the horizon. It'll be dark by six thirty. Several cars use their headlights.

I sit in a chair by the bed and hold Mom's hand, which is all bones and fingernails. She lies with her head tilted back, her neck exposed. Breathing in with a rasping sound, she pauses and then expels the air with a sound like clearing her throat. She's wearing the bathrobe Rachel gave her last Christmas. Her cheekbones are sharp in her thin face, and her lips twitch as if she's trying to form a word. I lean closer. "Mom, what do you want to say?"

As much as I try to reconcile myself to her dying, I cannot believe it. Physically frail, her mind drifting out of reach, she's been unable to regain any quality of life. In her living will, she requested that no heroic attempt be made to resuscitate her if she stops breathing. I must let her go; it's her time to die. As soon as I think this, I'm ashamed. I almost expect Mom to lift her head off the pillow and say, "I've changed my mind. I'm not going to die."

In that instance, I remember her sitting in the living room, knitting a sweater, the needles clicking independently of her fingers. Her hair is dark brown, her skin smooth and clear. I haven't thought of her as a young mother for the longest time. "By the way," she asks, looking up, her hands still, the needles no longer clicking, "who are you?"

My false memory collapses. I'm lightheaded as if turned upside down and shaken free of all sensation. What's wrong with me? I'm experiencing a gaping emptiness in this sterile, nondescript room, sitting beside my mother, who stands on the edge of an ocean of silence.

I've lived over fifty-seven years, but I've never been in the presence of someone close to death. I'm surprised by the staff's nonchalance. Another day at work. No one seems to care that something momentous is happening—the ending of life. What do I expect? Mom isn't an urgent case requiring constant attention from the staff. She isn't a dying child with grieving parents needing comfort. She's lived her life, and her time to die is approaching.

I wonder if, at this exact moment, she's reliving, in flashes, the events of her life. Is this possible with morphine dulling her senses, or is the will to exist so strong nothing can suppress those indelible memories in the brain?

I imagine her soul is free of her body, leaving it behind without regret, her brain running down like a forgotten clock, memories evaporating one by one. Even her tremors are gone. Her hands lie quietly by her side.

I sit up, alert. Her tremors are gone! I lean over, listening for her breath. Did she die without my noticing? Then, with relief, I feel her breath against my cheek.

"Mom," I whisper, "we're all here with you. We'll never leave you alone." I massage her hand, and her fingers flutter. "Leslie and Dad are having dinner, but they'll be back soon."

Now I have questions I want to ask her. What was your marriage like with Dad? Did you have happiness in childhood? And the most important question: Did you have a good life?

I freeze. Did I utter those last words aloud? I shouldn't speak as if her life is over. She may not realize she's dying. Maybe she's fighting with all her strength to stay alive. Is a pale flame of life enough to fuel the will to fight?

"Uncle Mark."

I turn in surprise. Elaine, Leslie's daughter. She looks more mature than her nineteen years, coming straight from her part-time job, dressed in the latest style. Her boss speculates in real estate. I wish her skirt wasn't so short, but maybe its length is part of the speculation.

"I didn't mean to startle you."

"I was in another world. I didn't expect anyone." I stand to hug her. "Your mother and grandfather are in the cafeteria."

"I don't want to interrupt you. I'll go find them." She turns to leave.

"Please stay. I'd like the company, and your grandmother will want to hear your voice."

"She's not in any pain?"

I shake my head. "She's quiet. I don't know how aware she is, but I believe she hears our voices."

"I feel bad for Granddad," Elaine whispers. "How's he doing?"

"It hasn't hit him yet. He's expected it for a long time, but it's always hard to accept."

Elaine puts her arm around me. We look down at Mom. "She was a wonderful grandmother. I'll always remember her."

"Here. Take my chair. I need to use the washroom."

I'm afraid if I stay in the room, I might cry again, and I don't want to embarrass Elaine. Or myself. "I'll be back in a few minutes."

Closing the bathroom door, I hear Elaine speaking to Mom. "Grandma, it's me, Elaine..."

I turn on the fan for more privacy then rinse my eyes and face. I lower the seat cover and sit on the toilet, leaning forward, my head in my hands, thankful for a moment alone to collect my thoughts.

Mom was always closer to Leslie's kids, for which Rachel never forgave her. When Jennifer was three, we asked my parents to babysit while we were away for the day. They agreed, but the night before, Dad called to say they wouldn't be coming. "Jennifer is too much for us to handle alone. She's wild and won't listen to us."

When I told Rachel, she was livid. "How can they not want to be with their granddaughter? Their attitude is unnatural. They have no patience to play with her. They'll be sorry when she grows up and doesn't care about them."

A knock on the bathroom door. "Uncle Mark, someone's here."

I flush the toilet and run water in the sink. When I come out, Elaine points to the door.

"Excuse me." A middle-aged, heavyset woman in street clothes stands in the doorway. She must be the wife of the patient transferred earlier, wondering where her husband has gone. Then I see she's pushing a cart with punch and cookies. "I'm with the Ladies' Auxiliary. I'm sorry about your mother. Our prayers are with you." She rolls the cart against the wall outside the room. "I've come by with refreshments. Is there anything else I can do?"

"No. You're very kind. We're trying to get used to the idea she's dying."

"Is it unexpected?"

"Yes... and no. She's been failing for a long time."

"Here's the Auxiliary's number. Don't hesitate to call if there's anything we can do to help. Enjoy the cookies and punch." She returns to the nurses' station.

Elaine takes a cookie. "Do they always do this?"

"I think putting a table outside a door is a signal to the staff that someone is dying. They don't want loud talking or laughter to disturb the family."

"Kinda thoughtful, all the same." Elaine finishes her cookie and pours a cup of punch, which she hands to me.

Leslie and Dad open the doors at the end of the corridor. Their voices turn to whispers as they near the room.

"Dad, look who's here. It's Elaine."

Dad isn't aware of her until she comes over to kiss him. His face brightens. "Hi, Elaine." All his attention turns to her. Elaine helps him into his chair by the bed.

Leslie signals to Elaine. "Let's give Grandpa some time alone with Grandma." The three of us leave the room. "He's expected this for over a year, but now he can't take it in."

We stand in the hallway eating cookies. Everything is unreal: cookies and death.

"I'll take the first shift tonight," Leslie says to me. "Can you nap and be back at two?"

"Sure. I'll eat, and then try to sleep—"

"You can take the first shift if you'd rather."

Before I can answer, Dad calls from the room, "Leslie?"

Leslie motions that she'll be right back.

"I'm tired now," he says. "Can Elaine drive me home?"

"Are you sure you're ready to go?" Leslie is surprised he wants to leave so soon.

"Yes. I'd like to go home now. I'll come back in the morning."

Has Dad forgotten what's happening? I want to remind him that Mom could die before morning. "We'll call you if there's any change.

"You can tell me when you come by to pick me up in the morning."

Leslie glances at me, disturbed by his attitude. Dad appears unaware of the situation.

Elaine helps him put on his coat.

"Let me make sure they get off okay," Leslie whispers to me, her eyes wide to express her confusion. "Then you can take off."

Supporting himself on Elaine's arm, Dad turns toward the bed. He looks older than I've ever seen him. He raises his hand to his mouth to send Mom a kiss. "Goodnight, Katherine. See you tomorrow." He continues to stare at her—the girl he met in high school, the bride he married during the war, the woman he's lived with for over sixty years. He takes two steps toward the bed. When he whispers, it sounds like he's saying, "This is the end," but I can't be certain. He adjusts his coat and picks up his hat and cane. Leslie takes his other arm.

Watching them walk down the corridor, I wonder if I heard him correctly. Does he know he'll never see her again? Is he acknowledging tonight is the end of their life together? Or does he mean this is the end for him too, left to face his death without her?

I'm alone in the room again. "We'll always be here with you," I whisper in her ear. "Do you understand?" I'm desperate for any sign that she hears me one last time before she's gone forever. Her eyes are open, but there's no expression.

"Do you know what came into my mind on the elevator today when we came up to the room? There was an elderly man wearing aftershave. The smell was familiar. It reminded me of the week before I left for my junior year in Europe. Remember? You took me to the drugstore to buy toiletries, and the saleswoman convinced me to buy aftershave. It was Aqua Velva. That was the smell." I'm always surprised at the bank of memories our sense of smell builds during our life.

"You talked about coming to England for a visit, but Dad wouldn't bring you. You could have traveled by yourself; instead, you told your friends I'd be too busy studying to take you around as a tourist. You wanted to visit so much, but I said nothing. I'm sorry I never encouraged you."

I sit back, empty, the memory gone. Mom wanted to do so many things but never had the courage to stand up for herself. At our death, are we punished with regret for what we wished we'd done?

The thought of dying with regrets is one of my fears. How cruel it would be to have a good life but forget all that and remember only what one never had. I console myself with the hope that at death, regrets become insignificant. The only lasting fact is we lived and had a spark of consciousness during the brief time when mankind existed in the universe. Yet once gone, our existence means nothing.

"Remember camping one summer—we went to a talk about stars at the rangers' station? Leslie saw everything through the telescope right away. You and I had no luck. But when, at last, we saw the planet come into view, it was like discovering the mystery of the universe."

I hear a series of beeps, loud and long. I frown at the monitor beside Mom's bed. What's wrong with it? This is the worst time for a malfunction! A nurse rushes into the room.

"Why is it buzzing?"

She doesn't answer. She presses a finger against Mom's neck, staring at the ceiling to concentrate on taking her pulse. Then she calls for the doctor from a phone on the wall.

I can't move. My fingers tingle and become cold. A numbness stretches up my arms. I wonder why my hands are floating above the bed, but when I look down, I find them lying on the blanket.

The doctor also feels for a pulse. "I'm so sorry." He acts like he's apologizing. "Your mother has passed." The nurse turns off the monitor.

I reach for Mom's hand. The skin is warm. She could be alive for all I can tell. The doctor reaches over and closes her eyes. A single tear in the corner of her left eye slides down her cheek.

The nurse places Mom's hands together on her stomach, then wheels the monitor to the corner. "I'll give you time alone with her." She adjusts the curtain to give me more privacy.

Grief wells up inside, and I can't hold it back. I start sobbing from an overpowering hopelessness. I remember the day when Mom answered the telephone and learned her father had died. She flung herself across the bed, crying inconsolably. I was three and followed her into the bedroom, sipping Coke from a bottle through a straw, wondering what happened. I'd never seen a grown-up cry. Putting the Coke bottle down, I climbed on the bed and patted her back. "Don't fry, Mommy. Don't fry." I grieve now for my loss of her and for her loss of life.

The wheel has turned full circle, and now I'm the one who is inconsolable. She had a hard life. But she loved Leslie and me. She did the best she could. And we had good times with her. I wish she could live her life again, but this time with everything happy.

I blow my nose. How sentimental. No one can live a life of perfect happiness. We all have terrors, disappointments, and betrayals, moments of regret, and paths we foolishly didn't take.

With her eyes closed, I imagine she's looking inside herself. Without her dentures, her cheeks are sunken. Her eyes, with large black circles around them, seem smaller than usual. Her nose is more prominent, sharper, almost like a beak. With her white hair in disarray, I can't help thinking that she's like a bird, broken and dead on the side of the road.

"How's she doing?" Leslie is back.

"She's gone." My tears come again, but thankfully not the sobbing. "It was peaceful. It happened quietly."

"When?"

"Five minutes ago. I didn't realize she'd died until the nurse came in."

"I shouldn't have left." Leslie's hands are fists but hang at her side. "On the way down in the elevator, I told myself, 'Go back. GO BACK!' I should have been—" She starts to weep silently. "I should have been here with her." She covers her face with her hands. Leslie's grief overwhelms me.

Mom is gone and with her a significant part of my life. Now I'm the only one who will remember what we did together, what we said to each other. *Come back*, I want to shout. *Please come back*. I cover my mouth to keep the words in, but instead the darkness comes out in a wail, starting low and increasing in volume. I don't want to stop it. Leslie closes the door. But I'm done. That moment released the pressure in my chest. I breathe more deeply than I have since coming up to the room. "I'm sorry."

"About what?"

Mom appears smaller under the blankets, as if in death she's shrinking. "She had a hard life with many fears and demons to fight. She deserved better. I should have been a better son."

"Mark, you're upset now, but you know that's not true. You were a good son. She was so proud of you, I was jealous. She had a difficult life, but she also had a good life. Dad stayed by her side all the way to the end. We must think of him now. Help him get stronger. Give him something to live for. He went to the nursing home every day. His life will seem empty now."

The nurse returns. "You can stay as long as you want. Let us know when you leave."

"Mom cried at the end," I tell Leslie. "I saw a tear."

The nurse turns from dimming the overhead light. "That's not a sad tear. It's a happy one, because you were here, talking to her, helping her meet the end. She felt her hand in yours, she heard your voice, and then she left. She was happy, and this was how she could tell you. Your presence is the greatest gift you can give anyone."

Leslie and I stay another ten minutes. Before leaving the room, we each hug Mom. Leslie touches her cheek.

At the nurses' station, I tell them we're leaving, and then, arm in arm, we go to the garage.

"I'll call and tell Dad tomorrow." Tears fill her eyes. "Let's meet at noon at the apartment and take him out to lunch."

CHAPTER 33

"Sue the Nursing Home"

Leslie is taken aback when she calls Dad the next morning. He begins the conversation as he usually does by asking what she's up to and how the kids are doing. He continues to list the chores he'll do today. Has he forgotten that when he left the hospital, Mom was dying? Or does he assume the worst and just can't deal with her death?

"Dad," she interrupts, "Mom died last night."

Silence.

"Dad?"

"I'm here. What time?"

"Around ten thirty. It was peaceful."

"That's the way it should be. I'm glad she didn't struggle at the end."

Leslie waits to see if he'll say anything more. Nothing.

"Mark and I want to come by today around noon. We'll take you out for lunch."

"Noon?"

"Later if you'd like. We don't want to rush you."

"Noon's good."

"Are you all right for now?"

"I'm making breakfast. See you at noon."

Leslie calls me after Dad hangs up. She's confused and upset. "I don't know what I expected. I thought he might break down, but instead he sounded numb."

"He's been living alone for years. It would be different if Mom had still been living with him at the end."

"Except now he has nowhere to go in the afternoons. Wouldn't he have some emotion?" she asks.

"Maybe he's upset but doesn't want to show it. I never saw Dad cry about anything."

"Pick me up around eleven. If lunch goes well, we should stop at the funeral home."

I call work and tell them I'll be out the rest of the week. Then I take a shower. Letting the hot water pummel my back, I think about what Leslie told me. It's natural she's shocked at Dad's apparent lack of emotion. She must be reliving her own husband's death.

Rachel and I were shocked when we heard about Sean's first heart attack. Although serious, the operation was a success and his prognosis good if he followed his doctor's orders. Sean could be stubborn about following anyone's orders, but the seriousness of his condition put the fear of God in him. We all thought the crisis was over. Six months later Dad called to tell me that he'd had a second heart attack. I asked if he was still in surgery. "No, you don't understand. He's dead!"

I'll never forget that moment. Besides feeling heartbroken for my sister, I was thankful that Rachel hadn't been the one to die.

After my shower, I sit on the edge of the bed. I'm dry-eyed but depressed. And afraid. Afraid of the future.

What I'd told Leslie about never seeing Dad cry wasn't strictly true. Once when arriving home from high school, I heard Dad crying in his bedroom with the door closed. Mom met me at the door and whispered, "Dad got a phone call with bad news." Mr. Crawford, best man at his wedding, the man who'd sold us our dog, had died while hunting. He was climbing over a stone wall when his shotgun discharged into his face. He'd been hunting alone. They searched for two days before finding him.

I wondered how an experienced hunter could be so careless with his shotgun. Poor Dad. Always careful to hide any emotion, he'd been brought to tears by the death of his best friend.

Leslie waits for me in the apartment's parking lot. "I hope this goes well." She's on edge, unsettled by Dad's reaction.

I knock once to alert him that we've arrived, but before I can unlock the door, it opens. Dad's wearing his coat, with hat and gloves in his hand. He blocks the doorway, preventing us from entering. Is he afraid we'll become emotional remembering Mom in the apartment?

"Where are we off to?" He closes and locks the door.

"How about your favorite spot? The place with the sirloin tips you—"

I chime in. "I've been thinking about their burgers all morning."

Leslie drives with me in back and Dad in front. He looks out the window as if seeing the town for the first time. "It's a treat when someone else drives. I can enjoy the scenery."

I'm in awe of his ability to suppress reality when he can't deal with the emotional fallout.

We've beaten the lunch crowd, and the hostess takes us immediately to the back of the restaurant. Leslie looks around. "How about that table by the window?"

The hostess changes direction, seats us, and hands out the menus. "Enjoy your lunch."

Leslie is indignant. "The place is empty, and she tries to stick us next to the kitchen."

We place our orders as soon as the waitress arrives. "We're easy to please," Dad says.

"Sounds like you've been here before. I'll be back with rolls and water."

Leslie watches her while she enters our meals into the computer. "She looks familiar. I think her mother was in my class in high school. Do you remember her, Mark? Ann-Marie Ottermann?"

I shrug. "Unless she was in the drama club, I wouldn't have a clue who she is."

"You're no fun." Leslie is exasperated. I wonder if I should pretend to remember her. "Don't you remember anyone from high school?"

"I remember Rachel."

The waitress returns with a basket of warm rolls. "Can I get you folks anything else before lunch?"

"My daughter is curious," Dad says. "She thinks she knew your mother in high school."

The waitress smiles. "You went to Lynnfield High? Both my parents went there."

"No, I went to Arlington High." Leslie is confused. "I'm sorry. I thought you were the daughter of a classmate, Ann-Marie Ottermann. You could be her twin."

"Oh, no. Ann-Marie is my grandmother." The manager signals to her from across the room. She nods to acknowledge him then turns back to Leslie. "Her maiden name was Ottermann." The waitress leaves to speak with her manager.

Leslie slumps in her seat. "Damn! That makes me feel old."

I laugh. "Don't ask the question if you can't handle the answer."

"Both generations must have had kids before they were twenty, for heaven's sake."

During lunch, Dad announces his plans to sue the nursing home.

"You what?" His news is surprising.

"Dr. Madison called me before you arrived. He was sorry to hear about Mom. He said dehydration caused her kidneys to fail." Dad spreads his hands on the table as if his conclusion is self-evident. "The staff was negligent."

Leslie is skeptical. "Won't that be hard to prove?"

"And expensive," I add. "You'll have to pay a retainer unless it's an open-and-shut case."

"I've already requested the nursing home to send me a copy of her records."

"What did they say when you told them Mom had died?" Leslie asks.

"I didn't talk with the nurses. I called Patient Records. The man said it will take a couple of days to copy them."

Leslie asks how much the copying will cost.

"Dr. Madison said there's no cost. I have a right to a copy."

Leslie leans forward. "Did he put you up to this?"

"No. I said I had questions, but he needs a copy of her records before saying anything."

From the restaurant, we drive to the funeral home to initiate arrangements for Mom's memorial service. Both she and Dad prepaid for their cremations. We sit on a sofa in one of the viewing rooms, waiting for the funeral director to finish talking with another family.

"We'd just started dating. Walking back to her house from the baseball park, I held her hand for the first time. Her hand fluttered in mine, and I remember thinking, 'She must really like me.' Later I learned the truth." Dad smiles. "Ah, the blindness of love."

Dad calls three days before Mom's service to tell me her records are ready to pick up. He doesn't want to pay the postage. "I'm packing Mom's belongings tomorrow," I remind him. "I'll get them then."

I park at the building's front door. The ombudsman left the records at the receptionist's desk. Then I drive around to the back. From habit I look for Dad's car until I remember he'll never be here again. Inside, the hallway is empty. No staff. No residents. Walking to Mom's room, I have the sensation that the nursing home, seeing me on the premises, evacuated the floor.

When I enter Mom's room, I find her roommate in bed. Mrs. Battersby beckons to me. Her eyes are clouded, and I wonder how she always recognizes me. She takes my hand and pulls me closer. "I miss your mother. I was sad when they told me she'd died." She has little hairs above her cracked lips. "How's your father? He's a good husband. Never missed a day." Two tears run down her cheeks, and she pats my hand. "God bless."

"How are you doing?"

Mrs. Battersby sighs. "I'm ready to die. I've been ready for a long time. God doesn't want me yet." She shows no anger or fear, only bewilderment at God taking His time. "Maybe I'll see your mother soon. We might even share a room in heaven."

"I hope so. She'll be happy to see you." I bend over and kiss her forehead.

She reaches up to touch my cheek. "I'll tell her how much you love her."

Mom's space is not yet reassigned. I clear off her bureau and remove the pictures from the wall. Her suitcases are not in her closet. I look under the bed but find only a pair of dusty slippers. Then I remember—the staff stores the suitcases in the basement.

At the nurses' station, I don't recognize the nurse. "I'm looking for Katherine Aherne's suitcases."

"I'll have one of the aides bring them to her room." The nurse doesn't look up from organizing the patients' pills. I wait for her to say something, like how sorry she is about Mom's death, but she says nothing more.

Back in Mom's room, I pile her dresses on the bed with her two coats and the contents of her bureau. I unplug her radio and carry it over to Mrs. Battersby. "Would you like this?"

She nods. I plug it in and place it on her bedside table, then I pace the room, waiting for her suitcases. The room is overheated and I'm sweating. While looking out the window at the parking lot, I remember the day she didn't recognize me. It seems so long ago.

A trolley rolls down the corridor, and an aide arrives with two suitcases. After packing her clothes, I take a last look around the room and wave goodbye to Mrs. Battersby.

I'd planned to drive to Dad's apartment and drop off Mom's belongings and records, but I don't have the energy. Seeing her roommate and the nurse, and emptying the bureau and closet is more than I can handle in one day. I want to drive home and crawl into bed. The sun is setting, and the blessed darkness gathering in the corners of the world is all I want.

Mom is cremated two days later. Her ashes will be kept in an urn at the funeral home until the ground thaws. We hold a memorial service a week later. Since I'm speaking at the morning service, I'm preoccupied with performance anxiety. At a signal from the minister, Dad, Leslie, and I follow her into the nave.

The minister welcomes the congregation and says a prayer of invocation. As soon as she says, "Amen," the organist plays a chord to begin a musical selection. The thrilling sound electrifies me, tears well up, and at that moment I accept the fact Mom is gone.

After my remarks, Dad pats my hand. "Good job."

The Ladies' Auxiliary serves a collation in the church parlor after the service.

I don't remember what I was to do after Mom's death until it's too late. I'm watching a medical drama on TV. A brain surgeon is performing an operation. "Oh, hell."

Rachel comes in from the kitchen. "What happened? Something on TV?"

"I forgot to ask the hospital to do a brain biopsy on Mom."

"She's already cremated. Too late now."

Long before they moved into the apartment, Mom began having trouble remembering events that happened only a few days before. It wasn't serious yet, but since her biological mother had dementia, Dr. Madison suggested she see a specialist for evaluation. Dad asked me to accompany them. We told Mom the visit was to discuss how she could improve her memory. We didn't want to use any loaded words that might alarm her.

At the hospital, I waited while Dad helped Mom out of the car. After parking, I joined them in the doctor's office. The woman who did the testing was escorting Mom into another room. "We'll be back in about an hour."

The doctor told us to be seated and closed the office door. He was young and thin with the scrubbed, spic-and-span face of an athlete. I bet he ran a marathon every Saturday, and two on Sundays. He got right to the point.

"Today's test will serve as a baseline for future testing. I'll estimate the extent of the disease, but there's no test that's definitive. I could order a CT scan, but I think the procedure would upset your wife. Research is making progress, but it will be years before there are drugs to prevent further damage.

"Since the disease may be passed on to her children, I encourage you to request a biopsy of Katherine's brain to identify the disease your wife has. If in the future her children have a problem, medication may be available to target that specific kind of brain disease."

Dad had a question. "The biopsy you mentioned, is this done on an outpatient basis?"

The doctor, to his credit, maintained his professional poise. "Oh, no, this would be done after Katherine's death."

CHAPTER 34

"DAD HAS WHAT?"

O nce a week, we take Dad to his favorite restaurant. Tonight, he dresses up to impress the waitress. We always sit in the same booth because they pretend to flirt with each other. The waitress greets him by name. "Charles, you're all dolled up tonight. Do you have a date after dinner?"

"I might have. What time do you get off?"

During dinner, I tell Dad that his suit against the nursing home could take two or three years to make its way through the courts. "The back and forth among the lawyers will be a constant reminder of the nursing home and Mom's death." Did he want the anger and regret to overshadow the remaining years of his life?

"Sometimes you must do what's right," is his answer.

"I'll support you, but I don't want to see you aggravated when it doesn't go your way."

"That's what you said when I contested my ticket."

"What ticket?" Leslie asks. "When was—"

The waitress arrives with dinner, leaving Leslie hanging. "Enjoy your meal, folks."

"What's this about a ticket?"

Dad launches into the story of the minor accident he'd had leaving the crowded supermarket parking lot two months ago. "Another car passed behind me. I looked in the rear-view mirror. No one was there, so I backed out, and *bam!* I hit a car. The damn fool was in my way."

I'll admit Dad has a point. The other driver *was* a damn fool. Instead of waiting for Dad to leave, he started backing up to prevent anyone behind him from stealing Dad's space.

"It was dark and raining," Dad continued, "and I wasn't about to get out of my car. The cop said I was at fault. I explained that the other driver had reversed out of the blue. The cop gave me a ticket and said if I didn't like it, I could take it up with the judge."

"He shouldn't have spoken that way. How old was the other driver?"

"Old enough to know better."

Dad had stewed about this injustice for almost a week before I stopped by to visit. He was determined to fight the ticket. "It wasn't my fault. It was dark and raining and—"

I appeal to Leslie. "All I said was I didn't think the weather would carry much weight with the judge."

"—he got in my way. I'm not paying an insurance surcharge for the next *six* years!"

"I reminded Dad about what happened to Mom. Bring attention to your age, and the Registry might make you retake the driving test."

Leslie's hopeful expression says Dad's failing the test would solve our concern about his driving.

Dad had made up his mind, and I gave up. That was the last I'd heard about the ticket. Now, as he tells Leslie the story, I learn he had to reschedule his appearance in traffic court twice because of doctor appointments.

"When I called the third time, a nice lady answered the phone. I explained I wanted to contest a ticket, and she asked how old I was. "Eighty-six."

"'Oh, dear,' she said. 'You don't have to come in. We'll take care of it here for you.' And they did." Dad pulls an envelope from his pocket and flaps it triumphantly in front of me. "Case dismissed without prejudice."

I imagine he's told the story to all his neighbors: "My son said I couldn't win…" I wonder how long he's waited to tell me.

"All I'm saying is if I can beat this ticket, who says I can't beat the nursing home?"

The waitress stops by with the check. "Have a good evening, folks."

I hand her my credit card.

Leslie looks from one of us to the other. "Dad, I think you're comparing apples to oranges but"—she pauses—"we'll see what happens."

When I pay the bill, Dad cranes his neck to check the credit-card slip. "Make sure you leave her a good tip."

"I always do."

We return to his apartment. Leslie puts aside a bedside table from Mom's bedroom that Dad promised to Elaine for her new apartment.

"You're sure you don't mind, Dad? You might find a need for it," Leslie says.

"Elaine's welcome to it. I have more tables than things to put on them."

Before we leave, he takes us into his bedroom where he keeps a file cabinet. "All my financial information is here." He picks up several papers stapled together from the top of the cabinet. "Here's a summary explaining what's in each folder. I don't have much to leave you, but at least you can take your families out to dinner. My treat." He grins.

Leslie protests. "Don't worry about us. You spend every nickel you've got on yourself."

"Rachel and I tell our kids not to expect us to leave them anything. We're spending our last dime on the taxi to the funeral home."

Dad replaces the papers on the cabinet. "Everything is left to you two. You decide if you want to give anything to the kids."

We walk back to the living room.

"It's a relief to get everything down on paper. It was weighing on my mind."

Leslie and I soon leave. She'll call Dad tomorrow. "To schedule our next dinner."

He stands at the apartment door to see us out. "Thanks for the grub, guys."

Walking to our cars, Leslie says, "I'm happy he has everything organized, but I hate talking about it. I hope he isn't giving up." She stops abruptly. "He doesn't have a medical problem you're not telling me about?"

"No, there's been no change *I'm* aware of."

"I don't want you to keep anything from me. Promise?"

"I promise."

We reach her car. "We should try once again to convince him to go to the senior center now that the weather is warm."

"We didn't have any luck the last time we tried."

"But now everything's changed. He's alone all day. A couple of friends might give him a new lease on life."

Leslie is distracted looking for her keys.

"Don't you agree? I can only guess what he's feeling: a widower, in poor health, alone. There might be a support group at the center—"

"Are you nuts? Can I be a fly on the wall when you suggest to Dad that he unburden himself to a group of strangers?"

I laugh. "Okay, that won't happen, but he needs to find someone to talk to, someone he can go out to dinner with, do something with."

Leslie raises her left eyebrow the way she does when she wonders what I'm getting at. "Did Mom tell you what she thought?"

"Depends on what you're talking about."

"Mom told me something about a month before she died. Dad wasn't there when I arrived, so I was alone with her. I was surprised that he'd gone, but since she was angry and agitated, I assumed they'd argued about something. She seemed more lucid than she'd been for weeks. I asked her what the problem was. Guess what she said?"

I've no patience for this kind of game. "How would I know what went on in her mind?"

Leslie lowers her voice as if someone is listening from behind a car. "She was angry because Dad was having sex with his boyfriend!"

"He was *what?*" My mouth hangs open.

"Honest to God, that's what she said. She told me Dad goes off for dinner and sex with his boyfriend and doesn't tell her."

"How does she know if he doesn't tell her? Did he say something?" I shake my head in disbelief. "Mom had some weird ideas at the end, but this is off the charts. Dad's so straitlaced... He's eighty-six, for heaven's sake. C'mon. This is crazy."

"I asked her what she'd said. I thought I hadn't heard correctly, but she repeated the same thing in the exact same words, then clammed up when I began asking more questions. She was peeved I didn't believe her."

"She never said anything like that to me."

"It's another one of her delusions." Leslie sounds like she hasn't quite convinced herself. "If he has a boyfriend, then good for him. At least he's having fun. He deserves a little joy."

Driving home, I think about what Leslie has told me. She wasn't happy when I laughed. I shouldn't joke about Mom's off-the-wall fantasies, but this one takes the cake. Sadly, it was Mom being Mom.

Thinking it over, I conclude Mom was projecting her own loneliness, desires, and regrets onto Dad. Did it have something to do with the man she sat beside? These hidden impulses rise to the surface in old age, undisguised as if dissembling is too much work at their time of life. As if worrying about what other people think is no longer important.

The next morning while shaving, I'm grinning at myself in the mirror when Rachel comes in to return the hairdryer. "Is it something about my hair?" She turns around to inspect it in the mirror. She adjusts the collar of her blouse then examines my reflection. "What's so funny?"

"It's nothing about you. It's something Leslie told me."

"When you took your father out for dinner?"

I swish the razor in the water then hit the plunger. "After we dropped him off." The water leaves behind whiskers and shaving-cream scum.

"Make sure you rinse the sink." She hangs up the hairdryer. "And check that drain again. It takes forever to empty and drives me crazy."

"I'll use that chemical stuff and let it sit all day."

"If it's still slow tonight, use the snake."

"You mean what the lady said to her gynecologist—"

"Very funny." Rachel is on her way downstairs.

"Wait," I call to her. "Let me tell you what Leslie said."

"Tell me at breakfast. I'm in a rush today."

By the time I shower and dress in my casual-Friday clothes, I hear, "Don't forget the drain," and the front door closing behind her.

This evening Rachel and I don't eat dinner in front of the TV. Instead, we sit at the kitchen table eating like civilized people. And talking.

"Didn't you want to tell me something Leslie said the other day?"

I begin laughing, anticipating Rachel's reaction. My giddiness is a combination of stress from work and lack of sleep. I try to stop, but every time I think about Leslie's story, I start again, like stumbling down a sidewalk unable to get my feet under me to stop accelerating.

Rachel gets up from the table to clear the dishes. "Honestly, Mark. You worry me sometimes. I have a sense what you're about to tell me isn't the least bit funny."

Her rebuke sobers me up. "Sorry. I'm overtired. Mom told Leslie Dad has a boyfriend."

Rachel stares at me as if I'm a lunatic. "Boyfriend? Leslie said boyfriend?"

"Leslie told me Mom said he went off with his *boy*friend for dinner and sex."

"What?"

"And Leslie said Mom was angry because he didn't tell her."

"Then how did she know? Leslie must have misunderstood. Your mother didn't speak clearly."

"She insisted that Mom was quite clear."

"You don't think there's any truth in what she said." When I don't answer, she adds, "Or do you?"

"What? No. Are you kidding? He's eighty-six years old."

"He might have a friend. Why not? But I agree it's likely your mother's imagination took over. She probably misunderstood something he said."

"That's a doozy of a misunderstanding. But really, when would he have had the time? He spent most of the day sitting with her in the nursing home."

"Who says it's happening now? Your mother wasn't living in the present. The past was more real."

"You think she was talking about something that happened twenty or thirty years ago?"

"I agree the story sounds crazy, but something caused her to mention it. What were she and Leslie talking about at the time?"

"Nothing to do with that. Mom brought it up out of the blue."

"*Something* triggered it. Probably one of her friends at the rehab center said something."

Two hours later, Rachel and I are in bed discussing her plans to visit her college roommate in New York. After a long silence, I assume Rachel's fallen asleep, her breathing quiet and regular. I roll over, plump my pillow, and prepare to drift off.

But it's no use. I keep replaying what Mom told Leslie. We'll never know. It's certainly not something I plan to discuss with my father.

CHAPTER 35

"I Didn't Want You to Go Through What I Had"

Dad calls me at work. "Can you stop by and pick up a prescription for me?"

After hanging up, I phone Rachel to tell her I'll be home late. "That's ridiculous," she says. "The pharmacy delivers prescriptions for a couple of bucks."

"He also asked me to pick up some groceries. He's been under the weather lately."

My wife's right. I'm a little annoyed by his last-minute request. Dad forgets that collecting and delivering a prescription adds forty-five minutes to my ride home, but sometimes he needs someone to shop for him, and he looks forward to having a visit. I'll go and be happy to do so. It's the least I can do.

In the evening, I'm late, caught in rush-hour traffic on the parkway. I stop at the supermarket across from Dad's apartment and run in to buy the Lean Cuisine and Stouffer's dinners he eats most evenings. "Cheaper than buying everything separate," he says. Not that Dad can't cook. He prepared all meals on family camping trips and, later, all meals once Mom stopped cooking.

Sometimes, he'll buy a piece of fresh fish and cook it with frozen vegetables. I hate visiting the apartment when he's frying fish. The smell sickens me. I'm reminded of my revulsion at nine years old when taking a fish off the hook and listening to it flopping to death in the bottom of the boat.

Once, I cut my thumb on a gill. It stung like a paper cut, but I wasn't upset until I saw how deep the cut was. A few seconds passed before a red thread on my skin welled into drops. I wanted to put the cut in my mouth, but the fish stink was all over my hands.

I never wanted to catch the fish in the first place. I'd have been happier sitting in the boat bored out of my mind. At least then I wouldn't have smelly fingers and a cut bleeding on my jeans. No wonder I hate the smell of fish.

Dad knows exactly what he wants from the supermarket and I breeze through the store, collecting the few items he needs. I'm amazed at the number of ways to package poultry. The photo of the chicken and gravy on one box looks tasty, and I'm hungry. I throw in a meal for myself.

After the grocery, a quick stop at the pharmacy. Not the convenient one in the supermarket, but the drugstore two miles away where my parents shopped all their lives and where, as a child, I bought cigarettes with a note from my mother. A mom-and-pop store, the building from the turn of the century, with a wooden floor worn down by generations of customers.

The pharmacist looks familiar; he was probably a senior when I started high school. He finds two prescriptions. Do I want them both? *No,* I want to say. *Let me make an extra trip tomorrow.* Instead, I smile and thank him for saving me a trip.

I'm shocked at the cost of Dad's medicine. Last March I helped him with his taxes. He had every receipt sorted by pharmacy and date. I expected nothing less than this painstaking precision from an engineer. Leslie and I learned not to ask him for help with math homework because his explanations were always long and detailed.

At his apartment, I don't ring the bell. Dad would have to get up from his recliner to answer it, and there's no need to risk a fall. To avoid startling him, I rattle my key in the lock as if I have trouble inserting it. He must think I'm going blind. "Hi. It's only me."

"Hello, Mark," he calls from the living room. He clears his throat, probably not having spoken since we talked this morning. "Did you find everything?"

"I didn't see your brand of cauliflower." I place the bags on the counter. "The boy stocking the freezer hadn't a clue. I got this instead."

Dad comes out to the kitchen to supervise. "What's the cheese sauce on it?" He picks up the package, tilts it toward the light, and looks over his glasses. "This is fine. I sometimes buy this when the store brand is out. Just as good. Not as cheap, but tasty."

"The pharmacist gave me two prescriptions."

Dad frowns and looks out the window. "Two?"

Uh-oh, I anticipate another trip to the pharmacy.

"Oh, that's right," he says, but I doubt he remembers what the other pills are. I should help him prepare two weeks of medicine in his pill tray.

Taking the pharmacy bag, he sits at the table.

I open the refrigerator. "Do you want anything?"

"Say what?"

"Do you want something to drink?"

"No, I've got my water bottle." It's an empty, blue milk of magnesia bottle he's washed out and keeps in his pocket like a flask. He unscrews the cap, takes a swig, and holds it in his mouth until he puts the cap back on, then swallows. He enjoys shocking people who think he's taking a nip of gin.

"What's going on at the high school? The parking lot is full."

The apartment overlooks the high school across the street. Twenty years ago, the town tore down the greenhouse and floral shop abutting the school property. They enlarged the parking lot from the street to the brook flowing along the edge of the athletic fields.

"They're putting on a play." Dad is preoccupied with rearranging the soup cans, labels facing out. We all have our quirks. I drive Rachel crazy creating designs with a handful of colored M&Ms. "I thought I'd go, but I'm not one for Shakespeare."

I ask him the name of the play. He concentrates, snapping his fingers as he tries to remember. "I read an ad for it the other day." He rummages through the town's weekly paper on the kitchen counter. "Here it is: *A Midsummer's Night's Dream.*"

"That's the play I was in my junior year. Remember?" Mom, of course, attended both performances, but I can't recall if Dad came to the Friday or Saturday performance. I hope it was Saturday. The memory of Friday's show still makes me wince with embarrassment.

I played the role of Oberon. In the whirl of activity—the rush of learning lines and daily rehearsals—I neglected to ask how the director might list Oberon in the program's cast of characters, so it was a shock when I glanced at the program just before going on stage Friday night. I was listed not as Oberon, Ruler of the Wood Sprites or Oberon, Leader of the Forest Dwellers. No. I was Oberon, King of the Fairies.

There I was backstage, dressed in pink tights and a dark-purple cape with loops around my little fingers, and wearing a jeweled crown more suited for the Queen of England. I went cold at the thought of what the jocks would say Monday morning. But I didn't have time to worry about them. Ready to go on stage, I was almost comatose with stage fright. I repeated my entrance line over and over like a mantra:

"Ill met by moonlight, proud Titania… Ill met by moonlight, proud Titania… Ill met…"

Then I heard my cue: "Here comes Oberon."

On stage, dazzled by the brilliant spotlights, I saw the insides of my eyeballs. Everything except the play melted away. Suddenly, I soared from abject terror to a state of euphoria. I gloried in my new power and the attention of the audience.

The next day, I walked downtown and bought black tights. That night, after make-up, I hid backstage and transformed myself. I applied extra mascara around my eyes and smudged on a charcoal beard. I taped twigs to my fingers and ditched the purple cape and crown backstage. Lastly, I spiked my hair with Dad's pomade. Titania shit a brick when she met me on stage. I wasn't a fairy. I was a motherfuckin' fairy!

Dad rubs his chin. "Was that the play where you looked like a pirate?"

Thank God, Dad attended Saturday night!

"I only went because you were in it."

We return to the living room. "Mrs. Robey always said you were the best Oberon she ever saw." A neighbor told my parents this every time she saw me visiting them.

"Do you remember when I was in a show at the church?" my father asks.

"That's right! The minstrel shows." I remember Dad practicing the complicated footwork for a routine in which all the minstrels sat in a row tapping their feet. Dad rehearsed for hours, shuffling his feet, shaking and banging the tambourine on his knees and elbow. With his other hand, he lifted the white straw hat and twirled it around his finger. At the finale, each minstrel flipped his hat backward onto his head. To their consternation, straw hats flew in every direction, but that was the fun of it.

Dad was a tenor and snagged a solo part. I loved watching him practice "My Mammy," making melodramatic faces as he sang. I memorized every word. Lying in bed, I heard him rehearsing in the living room, and I'd accompany him sotto voce. By the end of the song, I'd be out of bed, down on one knee, with my arms flung wide, singing in full voice.

I was eight when I attended the minstrel show at church. Walking through a side door with Aunt Ellen, I saw a man in blackface scurrying down the hallway. Thinking myself clever, I piped up in my shrill voice, "Look, Aunt Ellen, there's a nigger." My beloved great-aunt froze, then gave me such a scolding I remember my shame to this day.

"The show was lots of fun," I say, "but I only remember going once."

"The next year, the Jacksons joined the church. A black family in the congregation wasn't a big deal, although a few parishioners grumbled that they'd be better off down the street with the Baptists." Dad shakes his head. "The minister attended the first meeting of that year's show. He said, 'Hold on a minute. Let's think about this.' The shows ended."

"Reverend Lowden was the minister, wasn't he?" He had been good friends with my father and popular with Mom and the congregation. "Whatever happened to him?"

"He was caught fooling around with the organist in one of the pews."

"What happened to her?"

Dad pauses and pinches the crease in his slacks. "'Her' was a 'him.' They were gone before we knew anything." He stares at the wall behind the TV as if remembering the uproar at church. "Then the search committee hired that son of a bitch Watson, and we lost half our members. That was the end for your mother and me."

Something clicks, and he stares at me. "Speaking of sons of bitches, did my surgeon ever call you?" Dad asked his doctor to call me once his colonoscopy results came in. "I want to see if he tells you the same story."

Twenty years ago, he had a cancerous growth removed along with part of his colon. Since then every colonoscopy had found a dozen polyps to be removed, but no cancer.

"My doctor said everything's okay, but I'm suspicious. I have enough problems without any more blockage."

"Your surgeon called me at work this morning."

In fact, Dr. Deschamp told me, "Besides the expected crop of polyps, I found a cancerous tumor growing near the site of the tumor we removed. The new site is so close to the old incision, I'd have to remove that area as well. Your dad doesn't have the strength to undergo an operation, chemo would be hell, and radiation would kill his appetite. I didn't tell him it's malignant because there aren't any other options. The good news—"

There was good news? He hadn't said one thing I'd want to tell Dad.

"The good news is that the tumor is slow growing. One of his other health problems will kill him long before this will."

So I tell a white lie to my father. "Your surgeon's right. Nothing to worry about."

Dad watches me as if he's not convinced. Then he relaxes and slumps back in his chair. "By golly, I've got a few more years left in the old carcass." He pushes down on the arms of his chair to stand. "Time for my dinner. I don't want to keep you from yours." He walks into the kitchen, slowly unbending his body.

"I bought dinner for myself. Rachel isn't expecting me home for supper."

He opens the refrigerator. "Say what?"

"I bought a dinner for myself to eat here." I speak louder, trying not to shout.

Dad sticks his head around the corner, acting delighted at the thought of company. "Then I'll set another place at the table."

He disappears back into the kitchen, and I hear him open the silverware drawer. To my surprise, he whistles.

As much as I want to get home, I'm glad I'm staying. I dread saying goodbye and leaving him alone in the silent apartment. His loneliness is the image of old age that terrifies me the most. Yet his situation wasn't much better when Mom was alive.

I carry another plate to the table. Through the window, I watch the last ticketholders rushing to enter the school's theater. The building wasn't new when my parents were there in the thirties. When Rachel and I attended thirty years later, the main building seemed ancient, the steps to the second floor worn down from decades of students going to class. If *I* look at the building and think about how much time has passed, I wonder what my father thinks when he sees it from his kitchen.

The microwave buzzes. I take Dad's dinner out and put mine in.

"Get yourself a drink." He waves his hand in the general direction of the refrigerator. "I think your sister bought some juice the last time she shopped. Or there's a Diet Coke somewhere around here."

"Dad, you have Peapods. Let the supermarket deliver your groceries."

"Tried that. They only accept orders on the computer now. And I can't be bothered."

"I'll buy you a computer and show you how to use it." But already I sense his resistance.

He purses his lips and raises an eyebrow. "I can't play a goddamn DVD on the TV even when I follow your instructions. I'm too old to start learning about computers. It's just one more machine to break down, and I don't need the aggravation. Hell, I don't dare fiddle with the TV remote. Once I clicked the wrong button and I couldn't even watch TV."

I remember that. He called me at work, asking if I'd come by and fix his TV. In the meantime, he became impatient and telephoned Dietrich's Electronics two blocks away. He's bought his TVs there for half a century. The owner has long since died, but his son, my age, came to the apartment and solved the problem.

Dad called me back that afternoon. "Never mind coming. I took care of it myself. I got talking with the son and told him I'd known his father. Guess what? He didn't charge me. Some people still remember customer loyalty."

Throughout my childhood, I went shopping with my parents along Mass Avenue. My favorite was Shattuck's Hardware, with its creaking wooden floors and a half-dozen men behind the counters. No self-service. The salesmen used a ladder that rolled along tracks to reach the top shelves. After a customer paid, the money and sales slip were placed in a basket attached to a wire that circled the store, before disappearing through an opening in the wall. A moment later the basket reappeared with the receipt and any change and knew, to my amazement, where to stop.

Ding. My meal is ready. "Want me to make a salad?" I ask.

"I had one for lunch—oh, damn, I forgot to ask you to pick up some tomatoes. Well, that'll be my job tomorrow."

He's disinclined to talk during dinner, and we finish the meal in silence. I could talk about his grandchildren, but it saddens me when he mixes up their names or forgets which children are mine and which are Leslie's.

His confusion exasperates her. "Why can't he remember who's who?" She tries not to complain, but she's disappointed when he forgets to ask about them. Dad seems to have misplaced several years of his life, although a stranger might never suspect it.

I often wonder if, when his mind is far afield, he's searching for lost memories, surprised at losing his way. I hope he never realizes how many are missing. Years ago, I created a family tree for Mom. I make a mental note to print one for him.

After dinner, I'm in the mood for a cup of coffee, but Dad won't touch it after three in the afternoon. "If I wake up to pee, I can't fall asleep again."

We return to the living room, now only illuminated by the reflection of light over the kitchen counter. An ambulance shrieks down Mass Avenue and turns the corner toward Symmes Hospital.

"I'll review the DVD instructions with you before I go."

"I can get along without them. Plenty of movies on TV. The old ones are still the best. I watched *Robin Hood* the other night. Bette Davis is terrific as Maid Marian."

"Olivia de Havilland played the part of Maid Marian."

"She did? By the way, is she still alive?"

"She's in her late eighties. She was twenty-one, twenty-two when she played that part."

"Boy, she was my favorite. Her and Errol Flynn."

"I read somewhere that Flynn once asked her to sleep with him. She refused." I laugh. "Years later she told a friend that it was one of the biggest regrets of her life."

"That's old age for you: collecting diseases and regrets."

"What regrets do you have?" I wonder if he'll answer.

"Oh, you know the old saying: 'If I knew then what I know now…'"

There's a long silence, which I'm about to break when he adds, "Too many to mention." Another silence. "I probably wasn't meant to be married."

"I'm glad you did for my sake."

"I could have been a better father—"

"You don't own a monopoly on feeling that way. Sometimes I think you should have been Jon's father. He's more like you than I was. He loved baseball. I'd read in the bleachers during his games. But I *did* look up when he was at bat. We can only do the best we can."

"—and a better husband. I wasn't the easiest person to live with. If she were here, Mother would agree. Most of the things I liked to do were those I did alone." He pauses as if thinking about what Mom might have to say. "I hope you won't have as many regrets when you reach my age."

"There's something I always wanted to ask you about."

He looks at me as if he's reading my thoughts and is on guard.

"Do you remember the time when—I must have been about seven at the time—you told me that I was too old to kiss you before going to bed?"

He tilts his head like a bird suspecting that an unusual sound signals danger. He doesn't speak, and I wonder if he's trying to remember or just preparing to say *No.*

"When did I say that?"

I was seven, and I went to kiss you before going upstairs to bed like I'd done for years. You said those words, and I still remember them."

"And I said what?"

"That I was too old to kiss you before going to bed."

He looks to the side, then back to me, giving the barest shrug, a twitch of his shoulders.

"At the time, I was afraid you were becoming a sissy. And I didn't want you to grow up to be homosexual."

"Had I done something that day to make you think that?"

"I don't remember that specific occasion, but you weren't like other boys. You weren't interested in baseball. When I asked you to practice playing catch with me, you'd play for ten minutes and then say you were ready to quit."

"I know I wasn't the boy you hoped I'd be."

"You were smart in school, and I was proud of you, but you never had much interest in playing with other boys. I was worried about that. I knew that you'd be picked on by other boys."

"That did happen. It was embarrassing, but at least gym class was only three times a week."

"I thought if you joined the Boy Scouts you would meet other boys and become more interested in outdoor activity. If you went on the way you were heading, I knew you'd be called a fairy."

"I hate to ruin your memories of scouting, but that's where I learned to jerk off, and all of us in the tent knew that some boys were fooling around."

"It was the same way when I was in scouts. If you did anything like that, I knew you'd eventually become a homosexual." His mouth is dry, and he rubs his tongue between his lips. "I didn't want that for you. It's not easy. It's not an easy life."

"The reason I brought this up was what Mom said before she died."

He groans as if he knows it's something he doesn't want to hear.

"I know she wasn't always in tune with reality, but she was angry that day and said you'd left early because you were meeting a friend for dinner and… sex."

Had I gone too far? I was already trespassing on his private life.

"I loved your mother"—he pauses, taking a deep breath as if summoning the courage to dive off a high ledge—"but there was a part of me that was different. I didn't want you to go through what I had. I wasn't happy about it and, even though I was careful, your mother found out and confronted me. She didn't want a divorce. She thought I'd get over it, and I did for a time, but after a year I couldn't continue that way."

His admission makes sense to me. I'm not surprised by his words but by his willingness to tell me. It explains many moments in the past, and I know I will remember more over the next few days. I look over and see him crying silently, as if the anguish he suffered has overcome him. I go and sit beside him. At first we don't touch, but when I put my hand over his, he turns his hand to tightly hold on to mine.

"I didn't want you to suffer. I didn't want you to be miserable your whole life."

"I've had a good life." I take my hand out of his and put my arm around his shoulders.

How could I be angry with him? He hadn't acted maliciously but instead thought what he had done was best for me.

The ceiling is crisscrossed by light from street lamps shining through the swaying branches of trees far below us. We both feel more comfortable in the dark. We have both suffered in our own way, and I won't say anything to make it harder for him.

No longer crying, Dad reaches over for a tissue and wipes under his eyes. He breathes more calmly now, as if he is starting to finally let go of his past.

I too am relieved of a burden and know how his words have helped me.

"I hope you feel better now," I say.

"Not really. I tried to keep it secret, but I guess I didn't die soon enough."

"Don't say that. Leslie and I want you to live many more years. And don't think I was unhappy as a child. I had a wonderful childhood in my own way. I'm sorry I never tried to be the son you expected. Maybe if I had, you wouldn't have been worried about my future."

He sits bent forward with his head down. I pat his back to let him know that I won't say anything more. Except for one thing. "I'll never talk about this to Leslie."

He nods slowly without looking up.

"She'll never know." And one more thing. "I don't think of you any differently. I'll always remember you as a good parent I was lucky to have."

I take my hand off his back, and he slowly sits upright. He pats my hand, and I remember how he did the same thing after I spoke at Mom's funeral.

He turns on a table lamp and gestures toward Mom's desk. "I've finished cleaning it out. You're welcome to it and the china cabinet with the cups and saucers if you want them."

"Are you sure you want to give them away now?"

"I'm not hosting a tea party in the graveyard. I don't have the energy to dust them anymore. Let Rachel use them. There's another box of cups in the basement storage."

Rachel has admired those teacups ever since she first came to our house. Mom's teacup collection had been her pride and joy. Friends bought one for her wherever they traveled abroad.

"She'll be delighted to have them. Next time I'll bring boxes and pack them up."

A memory stirs then. "Dad, remember the day the painter broke the teacups?"

He looks up from scratching a crust of food off the arm of the sofa. "How's that?"

"The painter moved the china cabinet and the teacups fell out." I instantly regret my question; I don't want to upset him by mentioning something he might have forgotten.

The painter had realized too late that the cabinet wasn't attached to the desk. The other glass door unlatched, and a second wave of china tipped over the edge like a waterfall. Everything fell in slow motion.

The painter's face was frozen in disbelief. *Boy is he in trouble now,* I thought, thankful it wasn't my fault. At the same time, I was sorry for him, knowing how he felt.

I looked down at the pile of china. "*Here's* one that didn't break." I picked it up.

"You'll cut yourself." Mom grabbed the cup. She was unable to grasp what had happened. "Go to school."

Dad's eyes light up. "I remember now. We had Princess then. The smartest dog I ever had. When my sister and I were in bed at night—"

A cold numbness grips my chest. He's no longer thinking of my childhood but his own in East Arlington. He remembers the dog he'd had as a child and not Duchess. His tangled memories have many loose ends.

"—Princess would sleep on a blanket in the hall. Every couple of hours, she'd trot into each bedroom to make sure we were still there. If I was awake, I'd reach out and pat her head. Her tail thumped against the mattress. She'd finish checking the other rooms and come back and lick my face. She'd lie by my bed until I fell asleep."

He stops speaking. In the silence, I expect to see Princess appear in the hall. Maybe it's best to leave the present behind when there's nothing but death to look forward to. Better to live in a happier past when everyone you know is alive and you never think of being old.

I bow my head, not wanting to witness his confusion. Maybe he looks forward to seeing Princess again when he dies. Maybe she's what holds back his fear of death.

"It's hard when I wake up at four in the morning. I do a lot of thinking. But then the birds start scratching at the feeder outside the window." His eyes close, and he sits quietly, perhaps listening to the birds. "I'm tired now. I think I'll turn in." But he doesn't move, as if he hasn't the energy.

"Dad, let me help you get ready."

He jerks his head back and frowns. "You go home. I'm fine. I can take care of myself."

On the third try he stands. "I appreciate your coming, but you have your own life to live."

I put on my coat and follow him into the hall. "I'll call tomorrow and check in."

"Don't worry if I don't pick up. I may be out."

"Where are you going?" I'm alarmed at the thought of him driving his car.

"I have to get in my walk."

I embrace him, feeling his ribs and the bones in his spine. "I love you."

"Thanks again."

I kiss his cheek. "See you soon." I open the door.

He's turned away, already thinking of something else. When I close the door, the lock clicks home.

Driving home, I try not to think about what was said. It's impossible. And I think of the unhappiness we all carry around in our lives. I'm thankful I had a chance to understand a little of the humanity of my father. Some of life's unhappiness was lifted. A weight is gone, and I'm exhausted.

CHAPTER 36

"WE'LL HAVE TO PRY HIS FINGERS OFF"

When Mom was in the nursing home, Dad ate Christmas dinner with her and the other residents after that first year we'd taken her to Leslie's. The rest of our family visited them after dinner in one of the private meeting rooms near the reception center. We helped her open her gifts and, to make it a special occasion, served eggnog and pie—pumpkin, apple, and pecan. After cleaning up and bringing Mom back to her room, we left the rest of the pies for the nursing staff.

After her death, we assumed Dad would have Christmas dinner at our house with Leslie and her children. We assured him that one of us would drive him home as soon as he was tired. He agreed to come, but later said he was undecided, then finally declined. We promised to stop by in the afternoon. He said he looked forward to seeing us and coffee would be waiting.

On Christmas morning I think of him waking alone hearing church bells ring from the five steeples he could see from his kitchen window. He'll have no tree, no presents to open, no one to whom he can wish Merry

Christmas. He'll sit on the edge of his bed and take an inventory of his aches and pains. "Got to make sure I'm alive before I stand up." Perhaps he won't remember it's Christmas. The morning may sound to him like an ordinary Sunday with the church bells ringing.

Two days before Christmas, Jon drove in from upstate New York and helped Rachel decorate the tree. Jennifer and her husband, Declan, came down from Vermont on Christmas Eve. We sleep late in the morning, I play carols on the radio while we open gifts, and then we enjoy a leisurely brunch.

Calling Dad, we take turns wishing him a Merry Christmas. It's not a short call. We must often repeat what we say or talk louder. Sometimes he's hard to understand, but after asking "What?" too many times, we agree with him and hope it's the correct answer. I end the call by reminding him that he's invited for dinner.

"Thanks, but no." He'll be angry if I harp on his doing something he's decided not to do.

"Okay. We'll see you mid-afternoon."

Leslie and her children arrive for dinner. Over dessert, we discuss plans to visit Dad. Rachel and Declan elect to remain home and clean up. "With Leslie and the kids going," says Rachel, "there'll be more than enough confusion." Relieved of doing dishes, the rest of us don't try to change their minds.

Normally Rachel would come with us, but Dad didn't recognize her when she arrived for a visit on Thanksgiving. She saw the momentary confusion in his eyes and doesn't want to cause any unnecessary anxiety on Christmas. "I'll visit next week. Don't leave until I make up a couple of plates with leftovers. They'll be easy for him to heat."

We drive to his apartment in two cars. My niece, Elaine, drives the cousins in her mother's car. I imagine our children taking the opportunity to kibitz: "Guess what Mom wants us to do?" her kids might say. Our kids counter with a facetious remark about Rachel or me, or both of us.

Leslie gets into my car. "Dad didn't sound so hot on the phone this morning."

Before I can answer, she struggles to buckle her seat belt. "What's the matter with it?" She pulls the strap back and forth, trying to find the lock. It clicks and she leans back, sighing from the exertion. "By the way, I asked Dad about his suit against Mom's nursing home. Looks like he's given up on it. I don't think he's got the energy to be interested anymore. It's probably just as well."

Once we're on the highway, she turns to me. "We need to move Dad to assisted living. He can't care for himself alone in that apartment any longer."

"He'll never agree to move—"

"Then we must convince him." Leslie logically examines a problem and makes a rational decision. Only then does she consider the reality to implement her solution. I'm the exact opposite, so busy worrying about what people think of my ideas that I can't reach a reasonable resolution.

"What if the elevator breaks down again?" Leslie asks. "Last summer he'd have been trapped like a rat if I hadn't taken him in. Thank God for Elaine. And you too, with shopping." Unexpected problems dragged out the repair work for an unfathomable three weeks. Caring for Dad wore Leslie out despite her daughter's help.

She's right about the urgency to move him to assisted living. It won't be as easy as the last move. This time he has fewer belongings, but his room will be too small for little more than his bed, a bureau, his recliner, and a table for the TV. We'll sell or donate everything else, including Mom's clothes.

Her bedroom and closet remain just as they were while she was in the nursing home. When dementia set in and it was obvious she'd never come home, Dad didn't have the heart to change anything. Perhaps even now he senses her presence in her bedroom, and this helps him get through the day. Does he lie on her bed and hold a scarf or blouse to his face? All that will end when he moves one last time.

"Those places are damned expensive," Leslie says, "but with his pension and social security, we can swing it, if we both contribute to make ends meet."

"We'll have to lie about the cost," I warn her, "or he'll never agree to leave. Even then, we'll have to pry his fingers off the apartment doorknob on the way out."

We both can't help laughing. I offer a solution. "We'll forfeit his security deposit, take the apartment door off its hinges, and move it with him."

"I'll start looking." Leslie is like a bulldog with her eye on a bone. She'll line up five choices by the New Year, with a comparison of costs and amenities in a spreadsheet. I'm grateful she takes the initiative. If left up to me, I'd procrastinate, hoping everything would work out for the best.

I park the car and follow Leslie into the apartment building. I wonder what she expects I can contribute "to make ends meet." Not counting my inheritance, Rachel and I are wiped out paying for two college educations. We didn't qualify for financial help. I try not to be bitter, but if Rachel and I plan to retire in ten years, we'll barely have enough money saved for ourselves let alone Dad.

Leslie had it easier financially. Elaine, a high-school hockey star, won an athletic scholarship that overlooked her so-so grades. Palmer attends a university in the Midwest that awards scholarships to attract students from the two coasts.

The kids have arrived before us. I'm thankful to hear their laughter fill the living room. Their grandfather stands by his recliner, still bent from sitting. He always takes his time straightening up, afraid that moving too fast might break something.

His shirt is ironed and his slacks pressed. The laundry delivers his clothes once a week, and the son of the owner carries them up and hangs them in his closet. "And he won't accept a tip!" Dad still parts his hair in a way that reminds me of movie stars in the forties. He's shaved. Despite his neat appearance, his thinness alarms me. His shirt hangs from his shoulders as if on a hanger.

The grandchildren have kissed him and found places to sit. Leslie and I embrace him, and he sinks gratefully back into his chair.

"Rachel made up some dinners for you. I'll put them in the fridge."

He cups his hand around his ear. "Say what?"

Louder. "Rachel sent some dinners for you."

"Put them in the icebox."

Icebox? He hasn't seen one of those since the twenties. The refrigerator is filled with food. Has he been eating?

Jon is describing his new computer simulation game. My son is tall, with dark hair, athletic, and handsome. Luckily for him, he's only like me in height and hair color. His sister and cousins fidget listening to him. Dad is enjoying his grandson's explanation and pretends to understand him, but never having used a computer, he has no idea what Jon's talking about. I interrupt Jon by signaling him to wrap up his dissertation.

"Who wants to hand out Granddad's gifts?" I ask.

Palmer raises his hand. I pass the shopping bag to him.

"You're Santa Claus this year, are you? Your uncle liked to be Santa in the old days." Dad is pleased to be the center of attention.

Palmer smiles. He is quiet, artistic, always agreeable, unlike his father, a gregarious Irishman, who died when Palmer was six. My nephew tends to stand apart and observe people rather than join in. He's the family photographer.

Palmer hands Dad a gift. Leslie leans forward when he holds up two pairs of slacks. "Tell me if they're not the right size. I can exchange them."

Dad has trouble finding the tag. He puts on his glasses to read it. This takes a minute. "They're fine. I can cinch my belt until I put on more weight."

He opens the presents from the kids: two books about World War II, his favorite subject. One book tells the story of the British team that broke the German Ultra code; the other is about the war in the Pacific. I picked them up at the bookstore for the kids.

"Have you read them?" I ask. "They were published this year, so I think we're safe."

Dad has opened one book to read the flap. The room is silent, as if he's sampling a wine and the fate of the winery hangs in the balance. He raises the book and shakes it. "Looks good. The Germans thought their code was impenetrable and didn't use the full capacity of their Enigma machine."

He hefts the second hardcover in his other hand, pretending to bench-press them. "I'll get my exercise reading these. Thanks, guys."

The last package is from Rachel and me: an air purifier from Restoration Hardware. "This will help when the pollen starts to bother you. The machine is light enough to move to your bedroom at night."

Dad uses an inhaler during the allergy season, which for him lasts from spring through fall. On bad days, he's short of breath and can't leave his apartment. He rarely complains, but he's frustrated when an elevated level of pollen lasts more than two days. "That damn pollen wears me out."

"I'll set up the purifier next time I visit." I pray the controls are easier to understand than those on his DVD player.

Palmer is setting up his tripod. "Time for pictures."

Elaine rolls her eyes. Playing hockey has made her strong and healthy, but she's self-conscious and doesn't think of herself as pretty, despite what Leslie says. She has a job lined up after graduation.

Palmer moves an armchair opposite the picture window. "Grampy, you sit here."

Leslie helps Dad into the chair. From the expression on her face, I see she's also shocked at how thin he is. When she sees me watching her, she shakes her head.

"Uncle Mark, stand behind Grampy with Jon. Mom, sit here." Palmer pushes a hassock beside the chair with his foot. "Jenn, you kneel there. Elaine and I will stand on the other side of Uncle Mark."

He zooms in and out, trying to include us all in the frame, then draws the sheer curtains to soften the harsh afternoon light. "We have ten seconds before it takes the picture." He presses the time-release button and, scooting over to his place, knocks the tripod. "Damn."

We all laugh. Elaine pretends she's speaking to someone backstage. "Where's the professional photographer we hired?"

"Ha ha." Palmer is good-natured. He repositions the tripod, sets the timer, and tiptoes back beside his sister. The camera beeps, counting down the seconds. "Smile everyone."

After a blinding flash, he goes back to the camera. "Don't move. I'm taking another one. Don't forget to smile, Grampy."

Dad grins, showing all his teeth.

"You'll break the camera, Gramps," Jennifer jokes.

"When your grandmother sees this picture, she'll say I look like Death warmed over."

Palmer gasps in surprise, "What?" and almost upsets the camera. Jenn, trying to cover the awkward silence, only stutters, "S-s-stay in your p-p-places."

Palmer quickly recovers. "Okay, here we go."

The wait seems longer this time. No one moves, and our smiles become less and less natural. I imagine time is stopped. Everything will remain the same, nothing will change. Another blinding flash.

Photography over, Dad stands with Palmer's support. Leslie moves the armchair and hassock out of his way. Back in his recliner, Dad takes some envelopes from the end table. "It's not much." He says this every time he gives a check, but he's always generous with the kids.

He hands me the four envelopes, each with a name. "This one's for Jennifer." She steps forward to take it. "This is for you, Elaine."

While the girls thank him, I show the last two envelopes to Leslie standing beside me. With his distinct printing, Dad labeled one with Leslie's name, the other with mine. I glance at the table, hoping to see two envelopes for the boys. Dad appears far away, imagining something in his mind more real than we are.

"This is for Jon." I step closer to my son with a look that warns him to say nothing.

Leslie follows my lead. "And this is for you, Palmer." Intuitive as ever, he's already sensed something is amiss.

"Thanks, Grampy." Palmer speaks first, and Jon chimes in. The spell is broken.

Dad looks up and laughs. "Don't spend it all in one place." But his laugh sounds tired, and his face is drawn. I'm afraid the visit has worn him out. We won't stay for coffee.

"We better head back." I put on my coat. "They're predicting more snow before evening." I hate to leave, but the atmosphere is tense. The kids are relieved to be going home.

"Don't get up, Dad."

Ignoring Leslie, he stands. His knees creak. "Thanks for coming, everyone, and thanks again for my presents. I'll start one of the books tonight."

The kids kiss him in turn, exchanging glances with one another. The girls already know about the gift mix-up. On the way back, they'll discuss their grandfather's lapse in memory. I'll speak to them once we're home. No doubt Leslie will have plenty to say in the car. I only want to forget what's happened. And what it portends.

I'm last to embrace my father. "We love you." I kiss him on the cheek. "I'll call tomorrow to see if you need anything."

"Take the newspapers down when you go." Dad indicates a grocery bag by the door.

The elevator buzzes and its doors open. "Elevator's here," Jennifer calls from the hall.

"Jon, take these with you." I point to the papers.

He gestures as if to say, *What am I supposed to do with them?*

"Recycling is in the basement." I could have asked Palmer, but he's carrying the camera equipment.

"Bye, Dad. Merry Christmas. Don't forget the dinners in the fridge."

The elevator buzzes its impatience at my delay. Its doors slide open and close.

"Tell Rachel thanks."

"She sends her love."

I close the apartment door gently. I imagine the silence gathering around him like fog. My God, arrangements to move him from the apartment must be made soon.

Entering the elevator, I turn toward the doors as they close. They display the distorted reflection of everyone behind me.

I wish Dad was with us. I wish he was young, with my mother alive and laughing beside him, holding his arm. I wish I never had to make a decision about their lives.

As the elevator descends, no one says a word.

CHAPTER 37

"AM I PLUGGED IN AND READY TO GO?"

The day after Christmas, I'm back in the office. The week between Christmas and the New Year is quiet, allowing me to catch up on work. A hiatus from the incessant questions and problems.

My cell phone rings and makes me jump. It's Leslie. "Dad's in the hospital. The doc told him to call an ambulance and go straight to the emergency room."

I close my eyes. It's never-ending. "What happened?"

"Dad had trouble breathing last night. His heart rate was rapid, and his chest ached."

"He didn't act sick yesterday."

"You have to admit he was a little out of it."

"Tired, yeah, but not sick."

"The hospital admitted him for observation. I'll call you as soon as I hear from—oh, wait, this may be the Quack now." She hangs up.

I try to concentrate on work, but I'm distracted waiting for Leslie's call. I can't picture Dad *in* the hospital. He's always traipsing off to one doctor after another for tests—or so it seems—but he's not been *admitted* since his operation for colon cancer twenty years ago.

I continue working but am prepared to leave at any moment. After two hours, I call her, but her phone connects me to her secretary. "She's unavailable. Can I take a message?"

I remind her I'm Leslie's brother.

"Sorry, Mark, I didn't recognize your voice. She said to tell you she went to the hospital."

Then why didn't she call? Has something unexpected happened?

"I hope your father is better."

I thank her and hang up, then I leave a note on my computer screen saying I'm out for the rest of the day. I grab a report to read in case I'm stuck in the waiting room. At the elevators, I text Rachel not to expect me home for dinner.

The rush-hour traffic is unusually heavy at one o'clock. Getting onto Route 128 takes twenty minutes. Do people not work an entire day anymore? But it's not commuter traffic, I realize. Everyone has rushed out to return Christmas gifts.

I imagine Dad in the emergency room. He was fine yesterday except for looking tired. Maybe it's nothing serious and we'll take him home tomorrow.

The hospital parking lot is crowded. Valet parking reserves all the choice spaces, but I find a spot in overflow parking.

Reception checks my ID and tells me Dad is in a room. When I find it, he's not there and his name isn't on the door. At the nurses' station, I'm told there is no Aherne on the floor.

"But I was given this location downstairs."

The secretary checks her computer. "You're right. Admitting called to make sure the room is ready. He's on his way up. You can wait in there if you'd like."

The other bed is occupied, and I nod at the elderly man. He's watching TV but takes off his headphones and smiles, expecting I'm a doctor.

"My father will be here momentarily."

When the patient realizes I'm not here to visit him, his smile vanishes. He puts his headphones on and turns back to the TV screen flickering silently on the wall.

Outside, the darkening clouds look poised for a snowstorm. Many cars already have their headlights on. The room, in the newest wing of the hospital, has a magnificent view of the Boston skyline. Magnificent if one ignores the parking lot, the shopping mall down the street, and the interstate highway climbing between walls of granite.

The wall at the head of the bed looks like a modern art installation: hospital equipment hanging from hooks, colored cords looped into circles, and electrical sockets of every size and configuration waiting patiently. The room smells clean and fresh without the cloying odor of disinfectant. I turn on the lamp above the bed and angle it to shine on the chair. I remove the report from my briefcase and before reading I rest my eyes for a moment...

Leslie's voice wakes me. I look at the clock. I've been asleep for half an hour. I pull back the bed curtain when the orderly rolls the gurney through the doorway. Covered with a blanket, Dad lies without moving, his eyes closed.

Leslie comes in with his clothes in a green plastic bag. "There you are. I planned to call once we got a room." She shakes her head, rolling her eyes. "There was no need for two of us to wait around for his tests. I thought hospitals were emptied before the holidays."

The orderly maneuvers the gurney in the cramped space. A wheel knocks against a leg of the bed. Dad's eyes blink open and focus on me. "Hi, Mark." His voice sounds thick, and I clear my own throat without thinking. "Isn't this a nuisance?" But he's smiling and appears relaxed. I imagine he's enjoying not having to worry about taking care of himself for a day or two—a mini holiday. I'm also relieved.

The orderly turns on another light. "That's more like it."

"He did good calling the doctor." Leslie speaks to me then turns to Dad. "But you should have done it before Christmas. Or said something to us yesterday."

"I didn't want to spoil everyone's holiday."

"We'd have come to the hospital." Leslie rubs his shoulder. "You'd have been more comfortable."

A nurse enters the room and squirts sanitizer on her hands. She's young, pretty, and thin enough to blow away in a stiff breeze. The man in the other bed must have signaled to her because as she hurries by she says she'll see him "after I get your new roommate squared away." I get the impression he's one of the needier patients.

"My name is Janet." She leans over him. "Mr. Aherne, I'm your nurse for this shift."

"When does your shift end?"

"Why, Mr. Aherne, what are you suggesting?" Her laugh makes me smile.

"Nothing in my condition."

She lifts his wrist to check his pulse. "Our job is to get you back in tiptop shape."

"Well, good luck. I haven't been there in ten years!"

"Nonsense. Hmm, your pulse is a little rapid." Laughing again, she shakes her finger at him. "And don't you be saying it's because of me." She sticks an instrument in his ear. "Your temp is higher than we'd like. How do you feel, Mr. Aherne?"

"Run-down." He turns on his charm. "But doing better now you're here." Tomorrow all the nurses will be telling me how sweet my father is. He wasn't so sweet while I was growing up.

"How's your appetite?"

Dad rocks his hand back and forth. "Mezza-mezza."

"Do you live alone?"

He nods.

"It's hard to be enthusiastic when cooking for one. We'll fatten you up." She removes his blanket and lowers the gurney to the level of the mattress. "Any pain or tightness?"

"A heaviness in my chest."

"A sharp pain?"

"More a dull ache. Short of breath."

"Do you have an inhaler?"

"There's one in my bag, but I'm alright for now."

"Relax while we move you into bed. It'll only take a moment."

She's correct. Before I know it, she and the orderly lift-slide him onto the mattress. I'm surprised by her strength. The orderly raises the end of the bed and plumps the pillows behind Dad's head. Janet hangs the IV and attaches the leads from his chest to the cardiac monitor.

"Am I plugged in and ready to go?"

"We'll light you up like a Christmas tree." She checks the IV where it enters the back of his left hand. The sight of it makes me cringe. His skin looks like crêpe paper. She places a plastic clip on his middle finger. "You're good to go." She looks around with satisfaction. "I'll let you enjoy dinner, and then I'll be back to check your vitals." She leaves.

Only now do I recognize the sounds of trays pulled from racks down the hall. I hear the cheerful greetings of the dietary staff when they carry in a patient's dinner.

Leslie moves a chair closer to the bed and holds Dad's hand without the IV. "You look better now than you did when I saw you this morning."

"I'm always better once I'm in the doctor's office. I let him do the worrying."

"You're in good hands now. There's no need to worry."

Dad complains he's had more pressure in his chest over the last week. "I've been weak lately, but this morning I almost fainted. I had trouble breathing, and my inhaler didn't help."

"Maybe it's used up."

"It's brand new." He turns to me. "You picked it up the other day."

In fact, it's been three weeks.

"Don't hesitate to press your Life Alert when you need—"

Dad interrupts her. "I *did* press it. Those guys don't waste any time." Despite being ill, he enjoys the commotion he created. "I was packing some clothes for the hospital when they knocked on the door. They'd have knocked it down if I hadn't given a shout."

"I thought you called 911—" I start to say.

"Why should I? You've been paying for this button." He reaches up with the hand attached to the IV to the chain around his neck. "Might as well get your money's worth. It's strange not to talk with anyone. Like pressing a button and a bomb explodes far away."

At that moment, a young woman enters with a tray for Dad's roommate. "How are you doing this evening, Mr. Michaelson? I've got some nice fish for you—let me do that."

From our side of the curtain, we hear her arrange the plates on his tray. None of us say a word. It's like listening to a radio play.

"Would you rather have tea?"

I wonder if Mr. Michaelson has had a throat operation because I can't hear his voice.

"That's your dessert—What? No, the dressing is for your salad." A brief silence. "String beans." A little louder. "String beans. Would you rather have peas?" Silverware rattles on the tray. "No? The beans are okay? Want your table closer?"

Apparently, he doesn't. A black girl wearing the hospital's pink volunteer apron comes around the curtain. "Mr. Richards—" She stops in her tracks. "You're not Mr. Richards. Hi. I'm Debbie."

My father pats his chest. "Please to meet you. I'm Charles."

"Mr. Charles." She ticks off the choices on her fingers. "Breaded fish, nice and light, or the meatloaf, which is our specialty. The soup is turkey vegetable or broccoli cheddar—that's my favorite. Finally, ice cream or a berry compote. Oh, I forgot, beans or peas?"

"You've sold me on the fish and the broccoli soup. And I'll have the ice cream. When you have a chance, send in the wine list."

Frowning, Debbie appears at a loss. Then her face lights up, and she beams. "You're teasing, Mr. Charles." If she'd been closer, I think she would have poked Dad in the ribs.

"No, I'm not." He acts dead serious. "I'll have the house white, chilled, with my fish."

We hear her talking to a coworker in the hallway. "Guess what my patient said—" The rumbling of a cart drowns her out. She's still laughing when she returns with his dinner.

While Leslie organizes the tray, Dad starts with the soup. He waves at the bowl with his spoon. "Delicious. Have a taste."

Leslie shakes her head. "You finish it. How's the fish?"

Dad takes a bite and swallows. He gives her the mezza-mezza hand signal.

While he eats, we discuss the practical matters of getting his mail and cancelling the newspaper. "Don't bother cancelling it right away. They might send me home tomorrow." He stabs the beans with his fork. "And I left laundry at the cleaners." There's nothing wrong with his appetite that I can see. "You don't need a ticket. Just give them my name."

The secretary from the nurses' station comes into the room. "We're calling the doctor to let him know you're here."

"When do you think he'll—?" but I stop.

The secretary is already speaking with Dad's roommate. "Mr. Michaelson, your scan's scheduled for eight in the morning." Then she's out the door, having avoided any human interaction. I don't think she paused to breathe.

Leslie gets my attention and purses her lips. As far as she's concerned, that employee is skating on thin ice. Another curt interaction like that and Leslie will chop a hole under her. I'll avoid being around when she complains to the charge nurse. I'm no good at confrontation. I always end up thinking that somehow the problem must be my fault.

Leslie and I are silent as we watch Dad finish his dinner. After each mouthful, he uses his fork to keep each food item from encroaching on the others' territory.

Before I can stop it, my stomach growls, and both Leslie and Dad look at me. "Excuse me. Seeing the food makes me hungry."

"Mark, go home and have something to eat. I'll be fine."

I'm tempted to leave, but Leslie will stay until she sees the doctor. "I'll get something in the cafeteria. Leslie, anything for you?"

My sister stands. "I'll come with you."

"Take your time." Dad shakes his head. "There's no need to rush back on my account."

The food in the cafeteria has been picked over. I'd like some pepperoni pizza, but the oven is off, and the remaining slices look dry. I order a cheeseburger. Leslie takes a chicken Caesar roll-up to the cashier.

She sits across from me. "One of us needs to reschedule our vacation next summer. Otherwise, we'll be away for the same two weeks again this year." She snaps the plastic cover off her meal. "I forgot the dressing."

"I'll get it."

"Never mind." She picks up where she left off. "We both can't be away the same two weeks. Last summer after you left for the Cape, I stopped by to see Dad before heading to New Hampshire. He kept confirming the dates when we'd be home. I couldn't enjoy my vacation thinking about him."

"But Rachel and I were less than an hour and a half away. I called him every morning."

"I called too. That's not the point. Our being away reminds him of what it would be like if we weren't around."

This is a touchy subject that Leslie has brought up before. She and her kids have vacationed on Newfound Lake in New Hampshire for over twenty years; Rachel and I have rented the same cottage on Cape Cod for three. When our vacations end, we both reserve the same two weeks for the following year.

"I hate to ask," Leslie says, "but could you possibly change your weeks?"

Rachel oversees the vacation plans. She's fanatical about reserving the middle two weeks of July. "I'll see what we can do." I doubt we can switch weeks. I dread broaching this with Rachel.

A group of interns and nurses enter the cafeteria. They are loud, laughing, and joking with each other, unconcerned with the commotion they're causing.

"They're on an adrenaline high."

"It must have been a long procedure." Leslie watches them pile food on their trays. "*They* don't have a problem with the food."

"Rachel says interns eat anything. Leftover birthday cake a week old disappears in five minutes."

Leslie rewraps what's left of her roll-up. "I'll finish this later." She sighs, signaling a change in subject. "Dad felt guilty enjoying himself while Mom was in the nursing home, but since her death, I've hoped he'd have a new lease on life."

Leslie has tried to interest Dad in the senior center. "He says 'maybe,' but when the time comes, he has an excuse to stay home. He'd enjoy himself if he'd give it half a chance. He loves playing cards, and they provide a good lunch. They even offer transportation." She acts the part of Dad and waves her hand dismissively. "Nope. Not interested."

"The problem is he doesn't think he's old."

"In a year, he'll be eighty-seven no matter what he thinks. How can he stay alone all day?"

I look around the cafeteria at patients with their families. Each group seems to be having a party. The visitors eating without patients appear shrouded by uncertainty.

"I almost forgot. I got an appointment at Pinewood Gardens on Friday." Leslie tucks her roll-up in her purse. "It's an assisted living complex in Stoneham. I've read good reviews."

"I'll take time off and come with you."

"Great. It's better if we both visit. I'm lining up a couple of other places next week."

We carry our trays to the carousel and take the elevator back to the room. Nurse Janet is in the doorway when we arrive. "Your father's asleep. He's had an exhausting day."

"We'll sit in the visitors' lounge," I say. "Tell the doctor we're there when he comes."

"The doctor was just here. He'll see you tomorrow."

If necessary, Leslie will camp outside Dad's room to see him.

"Did he say if my father can go home tomorrow?" I ask the nurse.

"I doubt he'll be leaving anytime soon. His chest X-ray shows he has pneumonia."

"Pneumonia?" Leslie and I both speak at once.

"We've put him on antibiotics. The doctor has ordered more tests."

"What tests?" Leslie is alarmed.

"When the doctor sees you, he'll bring you up to date."

"What time will that be?"

"Sometime around ten in the morning."

We tiptoe into the darkened room to check on Dad. He's sound asleep with his head thrown back, his mouth open. He's wearing an oxygen mask, and his breathing is calm and regular. My eyes are drawn to his protruding Adam's apple. Despite the darkened room, he has more color than he did on Christmas.

In the parking garage, Leslie stops before getting in her car. "I want us both here when the evasive Dr. Quack makes an appearance." We plan to meet in Dad's room at nine.

My sister is distracted when she kisses me. I watch her drive away before I continue down to the overflow lot. Leslie believes that somehow she's failed our father.

CHAPTER 38

"The Eyes of Habit"

I'm on the road to the hospital at eight. Leslie calls to say her car has a flat and she's waiting for AAA. "I'll be in before ten."

Parking is easier because most medical offices don't schedule morning appointments until nine. In the Air Force, I was assigned to the hospital's records office. I enjoyed walking through the peaceful wards in the early morning, delivering lab results and doctor notes for patient records: the waxy smell of polished floors, every surface cleared and scoured, wheelchairs and carts stored out of sight, everything anticipating the colonel's inspection. All problems of the previous day were scrubbed away. New problems and emergencies hadn't had time to infect the building.

I wish Dad's roommate, "Good morning." He's wearing his headphones, engrossed in *Good Morning, America.* I doubt he's even aware I'm in the room. Dad's not in his bed. His test schedule must have started at daybreak. I don't expect the doctor to stop by until he has some results.

My stomach rumbles. I'd grabbed a cup of coffee at home but had planned to eat at the hospital. Dad's breakfast tray lies untouched on his table. I lift the cover and find scrambled eggs, bacon, and two slices of wheat toast. I pick up his fork and take a small bite of eggs. Lukewarm but delicious and not dry or runny. I'm like Goldilocks: "They're just right." Certainly, the hospital will bring a fresh breakfast when he returns.

I fold a piece of toast around two slices of bacon. Then two more bites of eggs, after which I push the food around to disguise the fact that some is missing.

"Is this Charles Aherne's bed?"

Startled, I almost choke on the toast. "I'm his son."

The man sticks out his hand. His fingers are thin and bony, delicate. I feel manly giving his small hand a solid squeeze. "I'm in charge of your father's care while Dr. Madison's away. We're in the same practice— Oh, I'm sorry. I didn't introduce myself. Dr. Wattly. Like the bulb." He sticks out his hand for another squeeze.

"Mark Aherne." I run my tongue along my teeth, hoping there's no food on them. "They took my father early for tests. He didn't have time to eat his breakfast."

"You were here when he left?"

"No. I must have just missed him—"

"Is this a convenient moment to talk?" He doesn't wait for an answer. The moment is convenient for him, so it *must* be convenient for me. "I see that you and your sister are designated as his health proxies. Is she here?"

"She's dealing with a flat tire. She'll be here later in the morning."

"That's unfortunate. I'd hoped to have a chance to talk with the two of you together."

I shrug as if to say, *I'm all you get.* "That sounds ominous."

"I'm sure you have many questions." The doctor gestures for me to sit in the chair beside the bed. "When did you first notice your father feeling ill?"

I tell him Dad hasn't had much energy lately but no recent change. "On Christmas, he seemed tired, so we didn't stay long. I never suspected he needed to be hospitalized."

"I'm happy he took the initiative and called the practice. By the way, I've never met your father. I hope my stepping in temporarily won't upset him. Or you."

"Oh, absolutely not." Don't sound too delighted that Madison is away. "What I mean is… I'm glad… I hoped Dr. Madison could get away for the holidays."

Wattly nods. Have I answered a question he didn't ask?

"My sister and I always wanted… I mean… it's important to get a second opinion."

The doctor says nothing and scans my father's chart. He flips a page.

"In fact, *I've* never met Dr. Madison," I say. "I've only spoken to him over the phone."

"Then *I* could be Dr. Madison for all you know." Wattly's attempt at humor is odd.

"No. I'd know by the voice. Dr. Madison is much older."

Wattly smiles. "Ah, the detective solves the crime."

"The nurse said Dad had pneumonia. How serious is it?"

"When the patient is eighty-six, any pneumonia is concerning. We've started an antibiotic, so I expect it will be under control in a few days. Is your mother at home?"

"She died about a year ago."

"Oh. I'm sorry. I must have missed that in his record." He makes a note on his pad. "Is your dad in assisted living, or does he live with someone in the family?"

"He lives alone. He's determined to stay in his apartment."

"Then you have caregivers coming in regularly." This is not a question; Wattly is confirming his assumption.

"My sister and I check on him by phone every day and see him twice a week." I'm becoming defensive.

The doctor comes to the point. "I was referring to a home health aide who comes to the apartment every day to help him bathe, dress, cook some meals—"

"Dad can do all that. He's coping very well. He walks every day. He has his routines."

"I'm sure he does, but someone outside the family who sees him daily would notice subtle changes in his health or state of mind. It's difficult for a family member to do so, in part because they don't want to believe there are any problems."

"I'm sure my sister and I would—"

"I don't mean to suggest you wouldn't, but adult children have what we call 'the eyes of habit.' We remember our parents as they were and want that memory to live on."

I only nod, realizing I'm on the losing end of this argument.

"The X-ray identified another problem that must be treated. We noticed his lungs are pooling liquid, indicating congestive heart failure."

I draw in my breath with an airy rasp.

"We need more tests, but he'll need meds to control this condition. Perhaps surgery as a last resort, but only after his health and stamina improve."

I don't want to ask the question, but I must. "Is he dying? How long—?"

"It's a serious complication but not fatal if controlled. However, age, asthma, and now pneumonia have put his heart under a great strain." Wattly closes Dad's medical records. "We'll keep him in the hospital as long as necessary, but he'll require rehab to fully recover. The hospital will help you find a place."

"How much will rehab cost?"

"With your father on Medicaid, there's no problem. The costs are covered if he's here for at least three days, which he will be." He thrusts out his hand. "Sorry to rush off."

I'm surprised he's leaving so soon. Caught off guard, I stand quickly. My chair scrapes the floor and bumps the wall. We shake hands. I'm distracted and forget the manly squeeze.

"With rehab, he could be home in a month. Meanwhile, I encourage you and your sister to check out home health services. The hospital can help you."

Wattly moves to leave, already checking his phone. "Tell your sister I'll call this afternoon. By then, I'll have more information." His smile is sad. "A lot to process, I know. You must help him understand extra help is needed at his age. It's amazing he's got this far on his own, but stubborn independence can be as dangerous as an illness."

And then he's gone. I've been abandoned. I take out my phone and dial the office to check if there are any emergencies. I'm speaking with work when Leslie comes in.

"Ta-da!" She throws open her arms as if appearing out of thin air. "I've arrived." She notices I'm on the phone and whispers, "Sorry."

I finish my call. "That was quick. Did AAA have a truck on your street?"

"Even better. My neighbor let me borrow her car, and she'll keep a lookout for the repair truck."

"Lucky you."

"Luck has nothing to do with it. I work hard to maintain my support network." She removes her hat and scarf. "Have you seen Dad? Any word on his tests?" She drapes her coat over the chair. "I'm desperate for coffee. Do you want one? I'll only be a minute. Can't miss the doctor."

"He's already been here."

"What?" Her shoulders slump in disappointment. "Damn!"

"It's a doctor subbing for Madison. He seems nice. He's young—"

"That's in his favor unless he's Doogie Howser. What did he say?"

"He says Dad's suffering from congested heart failure."

"Congestive heart failure. Rachel wondered if that was a possibility."

"She did?"

"She mentioned it at Christmas."

"She never told me." I'm ticked off. I thought *I* had the latest information. Instead, I'm scooped before I speak. "The doctor said Dad might be able to leave the hospital next week—"

"But certainly, he'll need rehab. I located an empty bed at the Silverton Nursing Center. I'll work with the hospital to make arrangements." Leslie notices my surprise. "I called them before leaving home. Just in case." She hesitates. "You don't mind, do you?"

"Of course not." Circumstances are changing so fast I must have missed something along the way. "I appreciate all you're doing."

I mean it. A quick decision is not my strong point.

When Leslie and I return with coffee, Dad is still not back. Food service has removed his breakfast tray. His bed was made by someone who doesn't know how to make hospital corners. I learned that in basic training. As the sergeant warned us, "The sheets better be tighter than a gerbil's ass. If a quarter doesn't bounce on the blanket, you fail inspection."

Leslie returns to our conversation of the day before. "We have to decide what's happening in July. Even if Dad's in assisted living, we can't both be away at the same time."

"I agreed to have Rachel check it out." I endeavor to hide my impatience.

"Don't sound so enthusiastic." Leslie takes her needlepoint out of her bag.

For the next hour, Leslie works on her pillow, and I attempt to read an article titled "Increasing SQL Transactional Efficiency," but I'm anxious about the looming problem with our vacations. When I reply to a work email on my phone, I'm distracted and accidentally reply to all. Shit! I don't want every recipient reading my snarky answer. I instantly send another email with the subject: BEWARE PREVIOUS EMAIL *** INFECTED WITH VIRUS *** DELETE WITHOUT OPENING.

I take deep breaths, hoping to relax. I don't need any more tension. I'll finagle Rachel into inviting Leslie for dinner and bring up the subject of vacations then.

Planning a vacation always creates tension and provokes minor resentments. Add in the drudgery of packing and unpacking, the tall grass waiting at home, and then the return to work to discover all the problems left behind are still problems, and I wonder if vacations are worth the trouble.

My ideal vacation? Remain at home—alone—with air-conditioning, a pile of books, a phone to order in food, and—why not?—a pool in the backyard for a dip between finishing one book and starting the next. Screw it! Just go to a luxury hotel with a spa.

I'm feeling sorry for myself. I'm worried about Dad and where he'll live. I'm nervous about missing work and falling behind. I don't want a quarrel with Leslie or Rachel about vacations.

Dozing in my chair, I have an out-of-body experience, bouncing across the ceiling like a helium balloon. I want to go home. And why not? Leslie and Rachel have everything under control. They love taking control. I'm the third wheel.

I don't go home. I walk around the floor, visit the gift shop, buy a plant for Dad's room, and then hang out in the visitors' lounge. The sun shines into the room, heating it up like a sauna. I lower the windows' sunscreens, which keeps out the UV rays but does nothing to lower the temperature. I catch myself leaning forward in my chair, half asleep but with no energy to get up. A large family speaking Spanish comes in, and I return to Dad's room.

Debbie arrives with the lunch trays. It's obvious she'd hoped to see Dad. "Where's Mr. Charles?" She looks around as if he might be hiding.

"Tests," I tell her.

"What a shame." She clicks her tongue. "He'll be worn out with all that prodding and poking and too tired to enjoy his lunch." She places the lunch tray on his bedside table. "Would you folks like a bite to eat? I've extra meals. They'll only go to waste."

"Thank you," Leslie says before I can speak, "but we're just back from the cafeteria."

"Suit yourselves." Debbie takes a last look to make sure nothing is missing and leaves.

Leslie notices my expression. "What's the matter?"

"I might have wanted a tray."

"Tell her. She's still out there."

"No, it's all right."

"For heaven's sake, Mark! Don't be silly."

"Never mind."

Leslie walks out to the corridor. "Miss? We'll take a tray. My brother is hungry after all."

Debbie returns with a wide grin on her face. Her teeth are dazzling white against her dark skin. "I thought you looked like you could eat a lunch." She hands me the tray, which I balance on my lap. She stands with her hands on her hips, enjoying the sight of me uncovering the food.

"Chicken salad and cake. Looks delicious. Thank you."

"The best chicken salad you'll ever eat. Have the nurse call dining services if your dad needs anything." She hears a noise from Dad's roommate. "Better be gone." She disappears behind the curtain. "Yes, Mr. Michaelson, I'm getting your lunch right this minute."

We hear the tinny sounds of the TV when he takes off his earphones. "What?"

"I'm getting your tray. Chicken salad."

Debbie is correct. When Dad returns to the room a half hour later, he's slumped in his wheelchair. He brightens a moment when he sees us, happy to know we're here, but seems uninterested in talking.

The orderly helps Dad into bed. Leslie goes to remove his slippers but only finds one. She plumps his pillow and pulls up the sheet.

Janet, the nurse, is behind them. "Mr. Aherne, do you feel like eating something now?"

Dad shakes his head. "I had something in the clinic. I could use a ginger ale. No ice."

"I'll get it right away." Turning back toward the door, she signals me to follow her. "Could you come back"—she lifts the watch hanging from her uniform blouse—"in about three hours?"

"He's all right, isn't he?"

"I expect he'll sleep most of the afternoon. The nurse noted he was restless last night."

Back in the room, I motion to Leslie that we should go.

"Dad?" I lean over the bed. "We'll be back later."

He opens his eyes. "Sounds like a plan." He yawns, and his eyelids flicker and close. He's falling into sleep, his face peaceful, looking waxy in the fluorescent light. I take his hand, the skim warm and soft, and

I'm reassured. For a moment, I'd remembered the death masks of famous people.

Janet returns with the ginger ale.

"He's asleep."

"I'll leave this," she whispers, putting the cup on his table. "I'll get his vitals later."

Leslie and I make plans for the afternoon. "I'll head over to his apartment," I tell her, "and pick up his mail and dry cleaning."

"If I don't get to the grocery store," she says, "I won't have anything to eat tonight."

We agree to return at four thirty.

While driving to his apartment, I call the *Globe* and put delivery on hold. Avoiding the traffic lights, I drive down Summer Street rather than Mass Avenue. I'll stop at the pharmacy to see if he has any prescriptions to pick up. He won't need them in the hospital, but if the pills remain too long in the out bin, the pharmacist reshelves them. This has happened before, and when Dad tried to reorder them, I spent a half hour on the phone convincing someone in the Philippines that Dad wasn't stockpiling pills to sell on the black market.

There are more traffic lights on Summer Street than I remember, and I don't save any time. The pharmacist recognizes me and enquires after Dad's health. I tell him he's fine. There's nothing to pick up.

"Tell him I asked after him."

On the way out, I pass a telephone booth in the corner, surprised one still exists. The pharmacist notes my curiosity. "I keep it as an antique. Kids are fascinated. They've never seen anything like it."

"I haven't seen one in years."

"There's something civilized about closing a door when using a telephone. Nowadays, people are all walking around talking on their phones." He shakes his head. "I hear them and think they're crazy people talking to themselves."

Before driving to his apartment, I pick up Dad's laundry on the corner. They wash, dry, and fold, discounted for seniors. I expect a laundry bag as large as the one I used in college. Instead the owner brings out my father's clothes in a tiny bundle. It's the weight of a child's hat liable to fly away in a breeze.

At the apartment building, I remove his mail and take the elevator. Only forty-eight hours earlier I rode this elevator with my family on Christmas Day. With the sun on the other side of the building, the apartment seems dark. I put the laundry bundle on the hall table and leave. The empty apartment terrifies me.

CHAPTER 39

"I HOPE I'LL BE HERE"

After eight days in the hospital, Dad is discharged and sent to rehab in an ambulance. That night, I drive over to see him, but the center says they have no Charles Aherne.

"Would you check again? He came by ambulance this afternoon."

Unable to find him, the receptionist calls the charge nurse. "I'm sorry. There's no one here by that name."

Thanking the receptionist, I return home. I thought I knew the location of the nursing home and didn't write down the name or address. On the way, I stop at another rehab center whose name sounds familiar, convinced this is the one. No. Never heard of Aherne.

"Where were you?" Leslie asks when I call later in the evening.

"I forgot the name of the place—"

Before I say anything else, Rachel takes the phone. "I thought I was the only one he never listens to, but apparently I'm not."

I drive over to see Dad the next evening. Leslie had arrived earlier. He's curled up on his bed in a fetal position, dressed in his clothes, looking like a visitor who became tired and had to lie down. He faces the wall, lying on the spread, childlike and vulnerable, his bare ankles above the flimsy slippers supplied by the center, slippers that are little more than cardboard, which reinforces my uneasiness since entering the facility. The place is operating on a shoestring.

I'm shocked to see him like this. Leslie is rubbing his back, leaning forward in a chair pulled up beside the bed. She acknowledges me with a discouraged expression.

A nurse brushes by to take his temperature. She taps her foot in time to the song on the roommate's radio, then removes the thermometer and holds it up to the light. "It's not going down." Turning to my father, she raises her voice. "Mr. Aherne, I'm getting a protein shake for you to drink before going to sleep." She looks at Leslie and me. Her meaning is clear: *It's up to you to see he drinks it.*

I see from my sister's expression she wants to tell me something but won't in front of our father. I can't help feeling impatient with him. Dad's supposed to be getting better. I expected to find him happy to be out of the hospital, flirting with the nurses, and planning the next time we'd go out to eat together. I want him to be like he was before Christmas.

"Dad." Leslie speaks softly. "Mark's here to visit." Her voice is hopeful that he will roll over and sit up, like Lazarus, healthy and raring to go.

He twists his head awkwardly. He's not wearing his glasses, and I doubt he'd recognize me if Leslie hadn't told him I was here. I've said nothing since entering the room.

"Hi, Mark. Thanks for stopping by." He lays his head back on the pillow.

"How are you doing?"

He doesn't bother with the hand motion. "Mezza-mezza."

Leslie bites her lip. She's emotionally exhausted.

"What's wrong?" I carry another chair over to the bed.

Leslie answers to prevent him from having to repeat everything. "He's complained about a pain in his stomach all day. He's been lying down most of the afternoon." She pantomimes that he hasn't eaten all day.

"How about some ice cream? That would go down easy," I ask.

Dad hugs his arms tightly against his chest. "No ice cream. I could do with some water."

"Of course." I jump up, happy to have something to do. "I'll be right back."

He speaks as I leave the room. I stop and go back. I frown at Leslie. "He said no ice."

In the hallway, I follow signs to the dining room. An aide is setting the tables for breakfast. "Water?"

She nods toward a corner and returns to the kitchen. The machine spouts orange juice and lemonade inside plastic containers. I'm thirsty and fill a plastic cup with orange juice, but it's watered down and thickened with something. I try another cup with lemonade, but there's an aftertaste I can't identify.

I fill another cup with water, but it's cold. I add warm water and return to the room.

Leslie is helping Dad sit up with two pillows propped behind his back and one behind his head. His eyes are closed as if moving makes him dizzy. "Is that comfortable?"

No matter how sick he's been in the past, he rarely complained. He sighs and opens his eyes, looking around like he expects the room has changed. Did he imagine for a moment he was back in his apartment?

Leslie brings the cup to his lips. Dad raises his hands to hold it, but knocks the cup, spilling some on his shirt. He slurps the water and turns his head to the side.

"Have another swallow." Leslie remembers how dehydration contributed to Mom's fast decline. She blames herself for not keeping on top of it.

He takes another sip to please her, then pushes the cup away and closes his eyes.

"Do you want to sit up or lie back down?"

"Down," is all he says. I help Leslie reposition him. At least he no longer faces the wall.

Leslie stands and takes her overcoat off the back of her chair. I notice a small vase of flowers on the bedside table. Why don't I think to do something like that? I hear Rachel's answer in my head. "Like most men, it never crosses your mind, so I suppose it doesn't much matter."

"Those are pretty." I point to the flowers.

"Aren't they? One of the nurses brought them in."

"Roberta Conley," Dad says.

Leslie continues, "She was wearing an Arlington High sweater. Her grandmother went to school with Dad."

"Aha." I attempt a little humor. "Was she a rival for your affection?"

"No, we all thought she was a lesbian."

"On that note, I'll be off." Leslie's voice is a mixture of relief and reluctance. "Mark will be here a little longer before he goes home for dinner. Okay?"

"You're staying, Mark?" He sounds like he's afraid to be alone; he wants me here, his words making me happy but also sad. For an instant, I remember how, as a child, I clung to the band of light beneath my bedroom door, dreading the darkness.

"Give me a kiss."

Leslie kisses his cheek. "A good night's rest and some oatmeal for breakfast will set you right. I'll be back around lunchtime." She hates to leave him. "I have a meeting at work." She turns to me. "I've got something of Rachel's in the car." She waves at Dad. "See you tomorrow."

Dad attempts a smile. "I hope I'll be here."

"Of course you will. But we'll get you home soon." She tips her head toward the door to make sure I follow her.

"I'll be right back." I follow Leslie out of the room.

Out of earshot, Leslie drops her cheerful tone. "Lord, I've been here since two o'clock." She sounds tired and discouraged. "I'm afraid, Mark. He's not doing well. The head nurse says she's concerned about his high temperature. If his temp isn't down overnight, they'll send him back to the hospital."

"How long has he been like this?"

"His temperature flared last night, but it's worse today."

It's been two days since I've seen him. The guilt piles higher. I'll have to cancel another meeting tomorrow if I'm to meet Leslie at lunchtime.

"He's not the same." She's close to tears. "I think he's given up."

I must look more stricken than I imagine because she puts her arm around me. "We have to have faith he'll get better."

Outside in the fresh air, she regains a positive attitude. "I've asked them to give him a shower before bed. That should help him fall asleep." She stops walking. "Try to get him to drink more water. He hates those protein drinks." She shudders at the thought. "They'll kick you out in half an hour, so they can get him ready for bed. See you tomorrow."

"Don't you have something for Rachel?"

"No, I wanted to talk in private."

She walks to her car to drive home to an empty house. My heart goes out to her, but whenever Rachel and I act concerned and invite her to dinner, she reminds us she must get home to feed her dog. "He's like a child and a lot less trouble," she says.

When I return, Dad behaves like conversation is too much effort. I have the impression that if I say nothing more, he'd be just as happy. The protein shake on his bedside table is unopened. His eyes are closed and he's rolled over to face the wall again. Until he feels better, I doubt the real world holds any interest.

One of his roommates is reading the Globe and listening to his radio.

The nurse returns with a thermometer. She's older and acts like she's seen it all before. "Let's get your temp before you start the protein drink."

Dad doesn't move.

"Roll over. I don't want you breaking my thermometer."

"It's not yours." His irritation is obvious. I'm surprised when he doesn't attempt to move. Dad always follows the nurses' instructions, if only to stay in their good graces.

"It's mine at the moment," she snaps, pausing to wait for him to roll over. "Don't make me go back and get a rectal thermometer—"

"Don't raise my hopes." For a moment, his humor reappears. He rolls over and opens his mouth.

"That works every time." She winks at me, shakes the thermometer, and sticks it under his tongue. She sees the flowers. "I heard Roberta brought those in."

He nods, the thermometer bobbing.

"She thinks you're charming."

Dad can't hide looking a little smug.

"But you don't fool me. Some of us see right through you." She laughs and takes the thermometer out of his mouth. "Down a bit. Let's hope that keeps up."

She turns to me. "Are you the younger Mr. Aherne?"

"You are correct, madam." I bow, keeping the conversation light.

"Nice to meet you. I'm Mildred, but I have to ask you to leave. We need extra time to get your dad ready for bed. A tepid bath is on the docket."

Dad groans. "I knew she'd have my pants off before she was finished."

She puts her hands on her hips. "Ha! I doubt you've got anything to shock me."

"Don't be so sure about that."

Mildred glances at me. "Big promises."

Dad ignores her and speaks to me. "Go home, Mark, and have your dinner."

"Mr. Aherne senior, you need to follow your own advice. You have a protein drink to finish after your bath."

"I'll be back tomorrow with Rachel." I lean over and hug him. "I love you."

"Let's get you ready for your bath," the nurse says as I walk away.

Outside, I drink in the night air. The air chills me, and I zip up my coat. The facility is overheated, and I'm sweating. I imagine my nostrils filled with dust. My nose itches.

———— ❖ ————

Before driving to the nursing home the next morning, Leslie and I meet to visit an assisted living facility not far from her house. The cost is more than Dad can afford, but we're determined to never have him stay in a place like the one Mom was in. We'll have to lie about the cost, since there's no way he'll agree to live somewhere that expensive.

On the way to the rehab center, I review the costs he'll save after moving. Apartment rent, food shopping, the twice-monthly cleaning lady. Leslie and I also include selling his car. We'll argue it's unnecessary because the facility provides transportation to medical clinics and a shopping center. That eliminates the cost for gas, repairs, and insurance.

To these savings, I add Dad's social-security check. He also has a pension from the engineering firm. It's nine hundred and fifty a month, which Rachel says is a disgrace. "After forty years?"

When I subtract the savings from the facility charge, my calculation identifies a gap of twenty-two hundred dollars a month. How long can he remain there with only eighty thousand in savings? A little over three and a half years, if fees don't increase, which they will. Then what?

Leslie and I agree to each contribute four hundred dollars a month. I quickly discover that's only two extra months! Mom was in a nursing home for nearly two years.

Leslie and I arrive at the rehab facility, where we find an ambulance blocking access to the parking lot behind the building. The EMTs roll a stretcher with a patient into the back, slam shut the doors, and drive the ambulance off with an ear-splitting siren. When we walk by the nurses' station, a nurse I don't recognize is looking at a patient's record. She's working alone and doesn't notice us. Entering Dad's room, I say a silent prayer that his temperature is back to normal. God will earn extra points if he's eaten breakfast.

Instead, we find Dad's bed stripped bare. Leslie gasps, her hand pressed over her mouth. I'm sick to my stomach. We have the same thought: Dad died during the night.

Leslie's cell rings. Her hands shaking, she fumbles taking it from her purse. "Hello?"

She listens. "Thank God." To me she mouths: He went to the hospital. "I was shocked to find him gone… Yes, I just arrived. I'm standing in his room… When I saw his bed stripped, I thought he was dead." Leslie glares at me like I'm a stand-in for the person she's talking to. "When?… I never received that call."

I glance at the roommate sitting on his bed. He's enjoying the excitement. He raises his eyebrows as if to say, She's a spitfire.

"Who decided it was necessary?… The doctor was late?" Leslie throws her arm up in disgust.

The roommate shakes his head in sympathy. It must be confusing when roommates appear and disappear without notice. I shrug in agreement.

"Yes, we'll stop by the nurses' station." She mouths, "Yadda, yadda, yadda." She closes her cell phone. "C'mon. He's back at Lehigh."

CHAPTER 40

"Would You Like Me to Say a Prayer?"

I'm stalled in traffic at a construction site on Route 128 at Totten Pond Road. What are they doing? A dump truck shuttles back and forth behind the barriers, its cargo covered with snow. For all anyone knows, it could be hauling snow from one end of the site to the other.

I make up time in Lexington. I've parked my car when Leslie pulls up. She rolls down her window. "I thought I was ahead of you. How come you got here before me?"

"I have a sixth sense about traffic. I hope they have him settled in a room."

"The poor guy. He won't know which end is up." She pauses. "Mark, I hate to do this, but an emergency came up at work—a coworker called—and I have to take care of it."

"Don't worry. I'll hold down the fort."

"I'll be back as soon as I can. I'll stay with him through dinner."

I wait outside the Admissions Office, checking every fifteen minutes with the receptionist, hoping the system has posted his room assignment. I'm a pest, I know; she can't do anything to speed up the process.

I sit and watch humanity ebb and flow. Most people look bored, relieved, frightened, or lost. A middle-aged woman walks through the lobby, trying but failing to hide her tears. I want to run after her and comfort her but realize she'd think I'm berserk or a predator and scream for help. But *that* would get her mind off her problems.

I notice the receptionist waving to me. Dad's in his room.

On his floor, I can see into his room across from the nurses' station. An aide holds him under his arm as Dad shuffles crabwise across the floor to his bed. I'm shocked by his unsteadiness. His bare legs appear to be nothing more than two bones covered with skin. He'll be too weak to return to his apartment after even three or four weeks in rehab. His johnny is open in the back. He's not wearing boxers, and his buttocks are flat, almost non-existent. I look away. No father should be exposed like this to his son.

I walk closer but stay out of sight behind a laundry cart. Dad struggles into bed, ignoring the aide as if tired of people fussing over him. He falls back against his pillows, looking like he's used every ounce of energy. "Ah, that's better. I'm set for the rest of the afternoon."

"Get well soon." The aide leaves and passes me in the hall.

Before I enter his room, a middle-aged woman with a large purse confronts me. I suspect she's been lying in wait. "Are you next of kin to Mr. Aherne?" When I say I am, she continues, "I'm the social worker assigned to your father. What arrangements have you made for him when he's discharged from the hospital?"

"My sister and I are looking into assisted living—"

"Too late for that." She's abrupt and hard-edged. "He needs more than assisted living. They can't provide the care he'll need."

I attempt to speak, but she continues, uninterested in what I have to say.

"We can't discharge him if he's not returning to a safe environment. We'll arrange for a nursing facility if you or your sister can't care for him in your home."

"One place we're considering has a nursing home on the grounds. When he needs that level of care, we won't have to move him to a different—"

"What place is that?"

I can tell from her tone of voice that no matter what I answer she'll find fault. "The Hilltop on the Fairway in Andover." That Dad can't afford to stay there is another matter.

"They have an opening?" She doesn't believe me. "I'm surprised. I've heard some couples have been waiting for months."

"We've already checked with them. They have a single apartment available at the end of the month."

"You'll have to find something before then."

"Then while we wait, my sister and I will care for him in his own apartment. We're not taking him to any old place." If she takes offense at my characterization of her help, too bad for her. What will she do? Pack his bag and dump him out on the curb?

"It sounds like you have it all figured out."

I suspect she'll call the Hilltop to verify my statement. "Are you working tomorrow?"

"No, I'll be out until Tuesday."

All the better. "I'll speak with someone in your office tomorrow." I smile as if I can't thank her enough for what she's done for us.

She glares at me and is gone. I hope Dad hasn't heard our conversation. I take a deep breath to calm down. I'm angry, but I don't want him to think he's the cause.

I enter his room. "Dad, how are you doing?"

"Looks like I'm back where I started." He's happier now that he's out of that rehab facility.

"You're all settled in, I see."

"Doesn't take long when all you've got is in a plastic bag."

"Have you seen the doctor? Is Madison back?"

"The hospital called him. He's back from vacation and will stop by tomorrow."

"Do you know when he's coming in?"

Dad stares off into space. "I forget. The nurse can tell you when she comes in."

"Is the young doctor who saw you last time around?"

"You mean Dr. Witless?"

I laugh. "His name is Witley... no, Wattly. What's wrong with him?" Did he tell Dad something he didn't want to hear?

"You think he's any good?"

I shrug. "I only met him once. He seemed to know what he was doing."

Dad makes a sound like *That's what you think.* "I don't like change."

"Don't worry. Madison's back. You're in good hands. They want the best for you."

Dad acts like he's lost faith in doctors. "What's the weather like out there? Cold?"

"Not bad. We're heading into a warming trend. At least they say so on TV."

"My TV's not working. Stop at the office and find out where I'm on the schedule?"

The TV, hanging off the wall, doesn't look secure at the end of its extension arm. Do any drop off like ripe fruit?

"I have your mail and paid the bills. This magazine came." The publication is *Today's Engineer.* I've glanced inside, but the articles are crowded with math and impenetrable footnotes. Deadly.

"You can chuck it."

"The store still hasn't refunded the treadmill's service contract."

"Which I never wanted in the first place. Funny how it got on the bill. I'll be dead and buried before it's resolved. That's what the store is counting on."

The department store is lucky it's not facing a lawsuit.

I accompanied Dad when he shopped for a treadmill last October. With winter coming, he couldn't walk outside if there was any ice.

A young salesman came over as soon as we entered the sporting goods department. There were no other customers. People interested in sporting goods were at work or in school. I guessed the salesman was a recent hire—too energetic and obsequious.

Despite his glowing recommendations of higher-end equipment, Dad selected a basic model and dismissed the idea of a service contract. "I get one year for free, don't I?"

"The fee for a lifetime guarantee is very reasonable." The salesman launched his sales pitch, "It covers—"

"I'm over eighty. I don't need a lifetime guarantee. This machine will live longer than me. By the way, do you have an elderly discount?"

"A discount?" The young man frowned as if he'd never heard of such a thing.

Ignoring him, Dad grabbed the sidebar and mounted the treadmill. "How do I turn this gizmo on?"

"Careful. Let the salesman help you," I said.

The young man stepped forward to show him how to stand with his feet on either side of the belt. "The main idea is to start off slow."

Behind his back, Dad gave the salesman his drop-dead look. "I'll keep that in mind."

My father was determined to show this pipsqueak that being old doesn't make you any less active. I should have foreseen what would happen next.

"And this is the emergency stop button." The salesman pointed to a red button hanging on the end of a cord. "A kill switch is also here on the dashboard."

"Got it," Dad said.

I selected *Level 1, no incline, slow speed, duration one minute.*

The salesman hovered on the other side of the machine. "Hold on to these bars."

The machine began slowly, and Dad stepped on the belt. He was startled by its unexpected speed but quickly adjusted his rhythm. I could tell he was showing off. He looked down at the dashboard with its blinking lights. "What does this do?" He poked the button with an arrow pointing up. Not once but several times.

Before either the salesman or I could react, the treadmill sped up. Dad tried to jog, but it was a losing battle. He held on for dear life, but in another second he'd have flown off the end of the machine.

The salesman hit the red button. The treadmill stopped, and Dad lurched forward. The salesman caught him before he fell. We were all too shaken to speak. The salesman looked like a pink slip had passed before his eyes. I had a vision of riding in an ambulance with Dad suffering from a broken hip and one or two limbs. Try explaining that to Leslie and Rachel.

Dad has more to say about his refund. "Give them another call and ask what's the hold-up."

"I'll do it tomorrow."

"They better get on the stick, or I'll fire off a letter to the consumer bureau."

After lunch, Dad drifts off to sleep. I buy a Coke from the machine beside the elevators and return to his room. Outside the window, the sky is darkened by low-lying clouds. Snow is falling unexpectedly, but it's light—nothing to worry about. So much for the warming trend.

Turning on a bedside lamp, I don't see any of Dad's Christmas books. I look in his bag, but they're not there. I hope he hasn't lost interest in reading, but he probably forgot to pack them at the last minute.

My stomach growls. I'm hungry. Where is Leslie? Perhaps the weather conditions are worse than they look. Her office at the top of a steep hill can be treacherous when icy.

I stand to reposition the pillow behind Dad's neck. Ever since I arrived, the crooked pillow has bugged me like a picture frame on a neighbor's wall I have no opportunity to nudge back into alignment. I quash my compulsion, afraid to wake Dad. I leave to find something to eat.

When I return to the room, Dad is awake. Leslie has just arrived. I help her out of her coat and hang it over the back of a chair. She kisses Dad. "Do you need another pillow?" She finds a spare pillow in the closet and helps him lean forward until she positions it behind his back. "That's better." The other pillow is still crooked but out of sight.

"Did you come from work?" Dad asks her.

"I stopped at the office. The dinner arrangements for the Spring Fling Golf Tournament are screwed up. Our guests will revolt if we don't hold it at the Wellesley Country Club. Then the traffic getting here!"

"They're building three thousand more apartments along 128 by the end of next year. It's insane! The highway will be non-stop gridlock."

Leslie ignores my rant and takes Dad's hand with a gentle squeeze. "How're you doing?"

"All settled in. The emergency room doctor is concerned about my high temperature."

"Have you got your appetite back?" Leslie looks at me, hoping I can confirm he's eating again. I raise my shoulders to signal I don't know.

There's a knock on the door. I expect a nurse in a white uniform, but instead it's a woman wearing a black choirlike robe and white collar. My heart sinks.

"Excuse me, I'm Reverend Brenda Livingston. I'm with the hospital chaplain's office." Of medium height with her dark hair cut short, she's on the younger side of middle age but with the exuberance of a recent university graduate. Her smile is disarming.

Polite as always, Dad ignores the religious connection, if he noticed it in the first place. "I'm Charles and this is my daughter, Leslie, and son, Mark."

"Pleased to meet you." She shakes our hands. "Forgive my interrupting your visit, but I'm looking in on patients to ask if I can do anything to help. How are you doing?"

"I've come down with old age."

"That's a disease we all hope to get someday." She has a gentle laugh.

"He's been in and out of the hospital." Leslie sighs. "Back now after two days in rehab."

"He recovered from pneumonia, but something is still going on." Should I address her as Reverend?

"When I get a cold, it always goes to my chest and stays there." Dad taps his lower chest. "I was run-down before Christmas, but that's cleared up. I still have something here."

"What's your physician telling you?"

"He'll be in tomorrow. He's been on vacation for a week." Dad looks at Leslie to verify the length of time.

"Two weeks."

"They think it's conjunctivitis."

"No, Dad," Leslie says. "It's your heart."

"I hope you're well soon and return to your normal routine."

"I've got my two kids here to help me. My two right hands."

"That's good. You're truly fortunate." Reverend Brenda pauses a moment. "I extend an invitation for someone of your religious faith to visit with you."

"We're Protestant—" I say.

"Congregationalists," Dad interrupts me as if he's trying to stump her.

She laughs. "I'm a Congregationalist minister, myself. Do you attend church nearby?"

"We're members of the Pleasant Street Church in Arlington."

"Then you know Reverend Adele Richardson? We were in divinity school together."

"I haven't been to church for several years," Dad confesses, "and the kids don't live in Arlington. We *were* active in the church when Peter Lowden was the minister."

"Well before my time. I'm a late bloomer. I went to divinity school after my divorce."

"He left after the kids graduated from high school."

"He was there when the church put on the minstrel shows," I add.

"They were very popular," Dad says. "Our couple's club put one on every spring."

Reverend Brenda shakes her head. "Those shows were big fundraisers at Congregational churches in the fifties. Looking back today, we must wonder what they were thinking."

"We learned that lesson when a black family joined the church. The blinders came off."

"I don't think many members of the church were consciously racist," Reverend Brenda says, "but they can't have considered African-Americans as equal, God forgive them."

I was thankful I hadn't mentioned Dad had a starring role in the shows.

"Before I go, would you like me to say a prayer for your recovery and safe return home?"

"I'd like that."

"Okay, let's do it." She rubs her hands as if excited about a prize fight.

We draw closer around the bed. Leslie and I each hold one of Dad's hands, while Reverend Brenda stands between us. We bow our heads.

"Dear Heavenly Father, we pray to you today for your blessing on this family. We ask for your mercy and to help Charles recover his strength and health so that he can more fully enjoy his family and his life."

For someone who's cynical about religion, I can't doubt the power of prayer. During these few moments, we're linked by the hope our prayer will be answered.

"We ask you to bless his children who have set aside their own problems and daily routines to care for their father in his time of need. We ask your blessing in the name of Jesus Christ. Amen."

"Amen." The three of us speak in unison. The words are simple, but the solace behind them is potent. I'm always amazed to find these quiet moments affect me deeply. Despite tears at the edge of my eyes, I sense a peace pervading the room that wasn't here before. Surely, God will make Dad well.

"Thank you," Dad tells her. "Just what I needed."

Reverend Brenda smiles and wishes us a good afternoon. Clutching her Bible, she leaves the room.

"I'd go back to church," Leslie says, "if she was my minister. Protestants were smart to ordain women."

"Mother and I lost interest once Lowden left the church. The guy they hired was too high-handed for his own good. Mom couldn't abide him. Said she couldn't sit there and listen to him."

"One afternoon I was watching a game show with Mom when he drove to the house," I say. "Catching sight of him coming up the walk, she became agitated and made me promise to say she wasn't home. Then she ran out the back door and hid in the garage."

"Poor Kat. He was a piece of work. We continued contributing to the church to keep him away, but that wasn't enough." Dad jabs his leg with a finger. "He wanted us in a pew every Sunday. He must have had a checklist in his hymnal."

I stand. "Okay, I'm off. I need to finish coding a program for work."

"Thanks for coming, Mark. I appreciate it. Will you be in tomorrow?"

"I'll be in after my demo in the morning, barring any emergency." I go over to hug and kiss him. "I love you. Rachel sends her love. You'll be fit as a fiddle before you know it."

"Bye, Mark." Leslie kisses me.

I walk out to the car park, relieved. I hadn't realized how tense I'd been in the hospital. I put the key in the ignition. The tears come freely. I lean my head against the steering wheel. With all my heart, I want to believe God will answer our prayer.

At home, Rachel looks up from her magazine. "How's your father doing?"

"He's weak but seems comfortable. He acts happier in the hospital, which is a bonus."

"I can't go tomorrow, but I'll come with you the day after. I haven't seen him for a while."

CHAPTER 41

"I Haven't Seen Him Yet"

The next morning Leslie texts me a message during my demo: *He's in intensive care.* I don't see it. My phone lost its charge, but I don't realize it until after lunch. When I arrive, she's waiting outside the door to the intensive care ward. I rarely see her this worried, pacing back and forth, her face drawn and eyes blinking as though she could cry with frustration at any moment.

"How's Dad?"

"I haven't seen him yet."

"Why not?"

"They say he's not ready to see anyone."

"What does that mean? He doesn't have to *see* us. *We* can look at him through a window until we go in. Why's that a problem?"

"They keep telling me it'll be soon—"

"I know what we can do."

"What?" Leslie sounds hopeful, like I've thought of a solution she's missed.

"We'll walk in and see for ourselves."

"Don't think I haven't thought of it."

A nurse approaches the door. She nods to acknowledge us. Pushing a button on the intercom, she waits a moment and then asks someone to let her in. The door unlocks with a click. Before the door closes after her, a doctor comes out. "Mr. and Mrs. Aherne?"

"I'm Mark Aherne. This is my sister, Leslie."

The doctor shakes our hands. "I'm Dr. Vargas. Your father is my patient this afternoon."

"Is his regular doctor here?" Leslie asks.

"He'll be here as soon as we get in touch with him. In the meantime, you can come in for a short visit. He's on a ventilator, but his difficulty breathing is making him anxious."

The doctor holds the door open. The room on our left has a glass wall through which we see a single bed with Dad among an array of medical machines. A nurse is watching the monitors. When the doctor leads us into this room, I notice a tall, young doctor—intern?—leaning against the wall. He's watching me closely when our eyes meet.

"Charles." The doctor leans close to Dad's ear. "Your children are here."

Dad slowly turns toward us. His glasses have been removed. He's covered with a sheet up to his neck. Several wires extend from under the sheet to monitors chirping beside the window. Two slender air tubes are in his nose. The ventilator swishes up and down. He doesn't appear agitated, but the sparkle in his eyes is gone. He smiles. At least he recognizes us.

Leslie and I stand on opposite sides of the bed. He grips our hands as if holding us will prevent him from disappearing into the mattress.

"Dad." Leslie rubs his shoulder. "How are you doing?"

"I'm having trouble"—a shallow breath—"getting enough air"—another breath—"but this tube makes it easier."

I'll bet he adds this last phrase because he doesn't want the staff to think he doesn't appreciate their help.

"Don't talk if it tires you," I say, rubbing the back of his hand with my thumb.

Dad closes his eyes, concentrates, but instead of breathing, he coughs. The monitors react with various sounds. The nurse scans the graphs and numbers. I wonder if the young intern in the corner is here to observe. Studying how to cope with a patient's grieving family?

The nurse leans over Dad and adjusts the tubes dislodged by his coughing. "That's better. Try to take slow, deeper breaths."

"I'm trying." He makes an effort to draw in a deep breath, but it's shallow and rasping. "How's Rachel?"

"She's thinking about you. Worried about you. She's coming in with me tomorrow."

Dad closes his eyes again as though he needs darkness to process what I've told him. What is he thinking? Returning to his room, hoping to leave the hospital soon, getting back in his apartment? Or is he focused only on getting his next breath?

He coughs again. The doctor motions to the nurse and then turns to us. "We need to intubate to help him breathe. He's putting too much of a strain on his heart. I recommend inserting a tube."

"My father doesn't want any heroic acts," Leslie tells the doctor.

"Oh no," the doctor assures us. "This is only to help his breathing."

"How long will he need the tube?" I ask.

"It's hard to tell."

"Dad." I bend over to make sure he can hear as well as see me. "The doctor wants to put a tube in your throat to help you breathe. Is that okay?"

His eyes can't seem to focus on me. Does he understand what I'm talking about?

"Do you think I should?" he whispers through the phlegm in his throat.

I look at Leslie, who bites her lip.

"It will help you relax." I have to put to rest any doubts he may have.

"Okay."

I nod to the doctor.

"I need you both to leave for ten minutes while we insert the tube."

Leslie and I pat Dad's hands. "We'll be right back. We're not leaving you." He follows us with his eyes.

In the hallway, the doctor points to a small waiting room. "You can wait there. I'll be out as soon as possible."

Once again, we find ourselves outside the locked door. We're the only people in the waiting area. I'm shocked to see street lamps on over the highway.

"By the way, I changed my vacation weeks." Leslie's voice is void of emotion, flat. "Someone at the lake was already trying to swap."

I gaze at her reflection in the dark windowpane.

"I can relax now knowing we won't be away at the same time..." She doesn't look relaxed.

She sits on the edge of the couch, then looks up and speaks as if checking off the last item on a to-do list. "There's one more assisted living place to check out..." She's silent for several moments—I watch her as if she has all the time in the world—and she then adds, "This one's cheaper than the Hilltop"—another long silence and a deep breath—"...but not as nice." She acts like she's lost interest in visiting any more places.

"I hope we made the right decision," I say.

Leslie is distracted. "About vacation or assisted living?"

"No, the breathing tube."

"Did we have a choice? He was fighting for every breath."

"I was afraid he'd suffer a heart attack." We should have insisted on staying in the room.

"I'm exhausted," Leslie says, sinking back on the couch. "I couldn't sleep last night."

"I'm sorry I arrived late. My phone died. I didn't see your message until charging my phone. I hate to think of you in here alone." I'll never tell her I kept finding something to do before leaving. I was afraid once I was out of the office, I'd start crying and wouldn't be able to stop before riding the subway to Wellington Station.

"We need to bring the kids in," Leslie says, standing suddenly. "Dad needs cheering up." Her sigh trembles in her throat. "We should have called them yesterday. I've forgotten there are other people involved."

"I'll contact my kids tonight. Maybe a visit the day after tomorrow? That gives Jon time to get here from New York and Dad will have a day to rest. He's had a rough couple of weeks."

"Dad will stay with me when he gets out of the hospital. He's better off there than in that depressing rehab place." Leslie starts making plans. "I have the sleep sofa in the den. He's slept there before, and the bathroom's next door. He won't need to climb the stairs. When you stop by, you can move the TV down from Palmer's room."

"He'll want to watch TV with you in the living room."

"But if he stays up late or gets up early, he'll watch the TV when he's in bed."

"Rachel will help with the cooking, and I'll do the shopping. One of us will stay with him whenever you need to get out."

"And we can hire a PT person to come in and help with his rehab—"

We're excited making plans. The door to the intensive care opens and the doctor signals us to come in. "I'm afraid he's extremely ill. He may not last the night."

Leslie sucks in her breath. "What?" She stops and looks at the doctor in shock. "I didn't know he was that bad." She reaches out and grips my sleeve. "Why didn't you tell me this earlier?" She's angry with the doctor, stunned by his words. "I waited all day to see him. And why were we told to leave the room? We need to be with him."

I put my arm around Leslie to steady her. She's trembling.

"You can come in now," the doctor says, letting us walk ahead.

My fingers are numb, and cold sweat coats my face and neck. What happened to make him worse in ten minutes? We should have demanded to stay in the room.

The doctor acts uncomfortable but says nothing. He closes the door behind us.

Except for Dad and the machines, the room is empty. Leslie and I stand on either side of the bed and take his hands in ours. His eyes are closed as if he's drifted off to sleep. The tube in his mouth makes him look even sicker. But at least his breathing is no longer a struggle. The ventilator puffs up and down.

"Dad, we're here," Leslie says. "We won't leave you."

"Have a good sleep. We'll be here when you wake up." Through the glass wall, I see the intern standing outside the door, staring at me. He's even younger than I thought.

The breathing machine is the only sound.

Dad lies peacefully.

"We made the right decision," I say. "He's not struggling like he was before."

We stand by the bed, rubbing his hands. Leslie reaches over and smooths his hair down where it sticks out at an odd angle. Neither of us says anything. Words can wait until he wakes up. It'll be a long night.

The nurse enters the room and wipes down the counter. She throws out some packaging and places several instruments in the sterilizer.

The doctor comes in and stands at the end of the bed. He takes Dad's hand from Leslie and feels for Dad's pulse. "I'm sorry. Your father has passed."

"He has?" Leslie's face is stricken. His words can't be true.

I look down at Dad. I should have known this when I came into the room. He was too peaceful. He should have been awake.

The nurse turns off the ventilator. The silence is Death. Leslie cries out and buries her face in her hands. "Dad, Dad."

The nurse and doctor leave and close the door to give us privacy.

And then I realize the heart monitor hasn't beeped once since we've been back. I cry, still holding his hand. I stroke his shoulder with my other hand. He's gone. And yet, a few minutes before he was alive and breathing, his heart beating, his memories and experiences stored in his mind. Now everything is gone. All his knowledge, feelings, desires, and fears no longer exist. All gone. I wonder if my sobbing can be heard outside the room.

Leslie is crying, saying, "Dad, Dad," over and over as if trying to call him back. I walk around the bed and put my hands on her shoulders. It doesn't comfort her. "That goddamn tube," she says bitterly. "*That's* what killed him. They killed him putting it in!"

Looking up, I see the intern has moved closer. Suddenly I *know* he's never seen anyone die before. He's transfixed by our reaction, trying to learn how to deal with death.

I remember a program on PBS about a man who was clinically dead for twenty minutes but had miraculously been brought back to life. He spoke about what he'd experienced. "What I remember most is that I wasn't afraid. From a corner of the ceiling, I saw everyone working on me. I didn't believe it was me because I wasn't down there anymore. I was at peace and happy. I wasn't in suspense wondering if they would succeed. It didn't matter to me. I would be missed, but their grief would pass."

Leslie is still talking. "He was already dead before we came back to the room. They knew he was dead. It was all a deception."

She's right, of course, but I hope she will come to believe it was better this way. I want to say they did their best, but Leslie would shake me away in anger. And do I believe it myself?

"He was sick. We couldn't see it because we didn't want it to be true. He died quietly, without pain."

"You don't know that." Her voice is a snarl, calling me a liar. Tears run down her cheeks. "How would you like that tube shoved down your throat?" Leslie's expression is one of utter despair. "I wasn't there when Mom died, and now Dad's passed, and we weren't there for him. It isn't fair. We should have been with him. We promised him."

"Leslie, he was more frightened trying to breathe. He couldn't have gone on much longer."

"I want him back. We didn't have him long enough after Mom died. He was just beginning to enjoy life again."

"But we had a year. And it was a good year," I plead with her. "We must remember the evenings we took him out for dinner, how much he enjoyed them, and the times he was with the family." I put my arm around her waist. "Leslie, come with me. There's nothing more we can do."

I'm surprised she comes willingly. She looks back at Dad, still sobbing. I can't look back. I will never forget him lying in that bed with the sheet pulled up to his neck, but I don't want to think of him this way. I want to remember him sitting in the living room of his apartment. Talking and not talking, but alive.

We leave the hospital. I walk with Leslie to her car. "If you want to come home with me and Rachel, we can pick up your car tomorrow."

She's no longer crying. "I'm going home. I need to be alone for a while. I'll be all right."

"Call us if you need to talk. Any time."

"I'll call Palmer and Elaine when I get home. She'll come and stay with me a few days."

I think about all that must be done. Tell Rachel. Call family. Notify the funeral home. Write a notice for the paper. Clean out his apartment. Tell his friends in the building.

Leslie and I walk down the garage stairs to the level where she parked her car. "We should meet at his apartment tomorrow," she decides, "and find out what needs to be done. I'll call the telephone and cable company to stop the service." Leslie is back in planning mode where she's most comfortable. This has always helped her through tough times: concentrate on what must be done, work down the list, and think about the reason for it later.

Leslie must drive the long way around in the garage to reach the exit. I cut across several aisles to reach my car. I'm opening the door when she passes me. She stares straight ahead.

I arrive home and unlock the front door. I smell the stew Rachel prepared for dinner. The television is on, and she doesn't hear me come in. Without her noticing me, I stand in the entrance to the living room. When she sees me move, she's surprised and presses *mute* on the remote.

"You were away for a while. How's your father doing?"

"He's gone."

Rachel takes a deep breath, her hand covering her mouth. "Oh God! I had no idea it was that serious." We meet in the middle of the room. She embraces me.

I'm crying again. "I feel cheated. We had one chance to be with him when he died, to hold and comfort him, and we weren't there. Leslie will never forgive herself."

"I'm so sorry." She rubs my back. "He was a wonderful man." She stands back. "And Leslie?"

"She's having a rough time."

"Let me get your dinner, and then I'll call her."

I sit in the darkened living room, watching the TV with no sound. It reminds me of intensive care, with the staff on the other side of the glass wall. I can't hear them, and on our side, there is nothing to hear. The machines are off, and Dad is gone.

CHAPTER 42

"WOULD YOU TELL YOUR FATHER?"

"Excuse me."

I'm unlocking the door of Dad's apartment when I hear a voice behind me. A tiny, elderly woman with beautiful white hair is coming out of her apartment. "Would you tell your father I found the newspaper article he's looking for? I left it on my hall table."

She scurries back into her apartment before I can speak. I don't want to tell her Dad's dead. I can hardly believe it myself and don't want to discuss it with anyone. Even sincere sympathy is an insult when measured against my sense of loss. No one can help me.

"I tried knocking several times," she speaks from inside her apartment, "but there was no answer." She returns holding a clipping with a long tail like a kite. "It took me a while to find it in the paper. I don't want him to think I'd forgotten." Standing beside me, she looks into the apartment and raises her voice. "Charles? I found the article you wanted."

"I'm sorry." Without thinking, I move to block the doorway. "My father's not here."

She frowns at me with surprise as if I said he'd moved away. "Where is he?" She glances around me to see into the apartment again.

"He's in the hospital."

"I hope nothing's wrong."

I want her to go away. "He'll be better soon."

"That's all right then." She acts like going to the hospital is a day's excursion.

I take the clipping. "I'll give this to him when I visit him tonight."

She smiles, pats my arm. "Tell him Gladys is thinking of him. He's such a nice man."

She turns and walks to the elevator. I enter the apartment and close the door. I lean against it, overcome with guilt and grief.

A soft knocking. Gladys. She has a sheepish expression, and her eyes sparkle. "I don't want you to think I have any designs on him."

In spite of myself, I smile. "I'd never think that. Thanks for the clipping."

With the door closed, the apartment is silent. Sounds from the street are muffled by the coating of snow. Stepping into the living room, I see him sitting in his recliner, happy to see his grandchildren on Christmas Day. Unable to stop shaking, I press my fists against my eyes and sink to my knees, hiding my face in my lap.

He died too quickly. We were right there outside the ward, but we never had a chance to say goodbye. We should have asked more questions, should have demanded to stay with him. But Dad was fighting for air, and we were desperate to help him.

Being with him when he passed would have been a comfort to him and made his death easier for us to accept. We deserted him. He lived for eighty-six years, and on his last day on earth we were only with him for five minutes, and even then he died alone. He suffocated with no one beside him.

My shaking subsides. He didn't deserve a death like this. If he'd been that sick, they should have encouraged us to take him to hospice. But how do you explain hospice to a loved one who is unaware Death is standing beside him? Would Dad have resisted? Or was he ready to go? He would have had a peaceful death with drugs easing him to meet his end. I imagine the expression on his face when we'd say, "We're taking you to hospice." My God! The look of disbelief in his eyes.

Quiet now, I struggle to stand, leaning on the La-Z-Boy for support. My knees creak. I concentrate on what must be done. I replace the cordless telephone in the charger on the table by his recliner. I pick up one of his Christmas books, perched like a tent on the arm of his chair. The tears flow when I recall his excitement while explaining the book to his grandkids. I replace his bookmark and then wonder when I'll stop thinking he's coming back.

There is an unpleasant odor in the kitchen. The smell reminds me of the day I arrived after Leslie first called to ask me to come to Boston. I look for the remains of Dad's breakfast from the morning when he left for the last time. Nothing. Then I remember he left in the middle of the night.

A coffee cup sits on the counter, its remaining coffee covered with a furry green mold. I pour it into the sink. The scum stretches from the lip of the cup and falls with a plop. The smell comes from the garbage disposal. I rinse the cup with hot water and turn it on.

I open the refrigerator and find the two dinners Rachel made for Dad on Christmas. He never had a chance to eat them. I remember putting the food in the fridge with the sound of the grandchildren in the living room. I half expect to hear him talking to them.

But that memory is usurped by my imagination. I hear the EMTs called by Life Alert pounding on the door. They strap Dad on a stretcher for the ride to the hospital. As they wheel him out, does he watch the ceiling and wonder if he'll ever return to his apartment? Or does he feel too ill to care? He must be grateful someone arrived to rescue him. His feeling of peace perhaps supplants any morbid thought he might have had.

I throw out the two dinners. They land with a thud on the bottom of the wastebasket. I empty the half-and-half and fat-free milk down the sink. I pull out the wilted and spoiled vegetables. Everything is tossed in the trash. Nothing has a right to exist now that Dad is dead. I'll take my grief out on anything at hand. Better I do it now before Leslie arrives. My eyes are swollen and my cheeks, raw from the cold weather, sting from the salt.

I find his laundry where I left it in the hall and carry it to his bedroom. I stop when I see his bed, the covers thrown back like he got up for a moment but will return. I wouldn't be surprised to find the sheets still warm.

I sort the laundry. Four pairs of socks. Three undershirts, one worn so thin I can see through it when I hold it up to the window. Five pairs of white boxer shorts, one pair tinged green as if washed with dark green clothes. I gather the laundry to throw it out but instead place the clothes back on his unmade bed. I'm not ready to toss any clothes away today. Bureau drawers are half empty. He started discarding clothes he knew he'd never wear again.

On the other side of the bed, a metal cabinet acts as a bedside table. His bottles of pills anchor the document listing all his financial holdings and telephone numbers. The printing is perfect, each number the same size, in perfectly straight lines. I'd recognize his handwriting anywhere. Every item on the list is duplicated on a folder in the top drawer. In an unmarked folder, I find his university diploma and his Army discharge papers.

After the German defeat, he volunteered as a parachutist in the war against Japan. "Training was perfunctory," Dad said. "What was there to teach? If you were crazy enough to jump out of a plane, all you had to learn was landing without breaking a leg." Dad knew the odds of his not returning alive. "It was all a roll of the dice: you jump, you land, you fight, and along the way, you try not to die." Why did he volunteer and give up remaining stateside in safety? Halfway across the Pacific the atom bombs were dropped on Japan.

I walk down the hall and stand for a moment in my mother's bedroom. She lived only a brief time in the apartment. I have few memories of her in this room, but I recognize her double bed and duvet, the bedside table and bureau from the bedroom they once shared. In an instant, these objects recreate the bedroom I remember with its wallpaper pattern, the windows in their familiar configuration, and the cast-iron radiators against the walls.

A summer day between fifth and sixth grade. I'm helping Mom make the bed. The radio is playing pop songs with Sinatra singing "Love and Marriage." Mom sings along.

"Why do they always sing about love?"

She smiles. "They're songs teenagers like to listen to. You'll understand in a few years."

That moment is as vivid as the day it happened. I long to go back to that summer day and relive making the bed with my innocence and with my mother at age forty. What catches a fleeting memory in its unrelenting grip?

There must be many other moments that could unlock other doors revealing what made me who I am, but I can't think of any. And what would I do with these hours of memories? How boring most of them would be, like looking at a box of photos, wondering why most were ever worth taking.

From the window, I see Leslie turn into the parking lot. I rinse my eyes in the bathroom. I'm shocked by how much older I look. My skin sags beneath my eyes, and the lines around my nose and mouth are engraved deep in my face.

I open the door to the hall and listen for the elevator. I'm thankful for the chance I had to be alone in the apartment and to discover the calm one experiences when resigned to what one must face. Now I hear the elevator motor start. I wait for the doors to open and Leslie to appear.

The last people to know me all my life are gone. I'm empty, diminished. Years of my own life have passed from the world. My father, who I once thought was so little a part of my life, is gone. Only now do I find the empty space inside me where he had always lived.

Thank you for reading
Your Father Has Something to Tell You.
If you enjoyed the book, please post a short review
on Amazon, consider telling your friends about the
book, and promote the novel at your book club.
Word of mouth is an author's best
friend and much appreciated.

Thank you, **Dave Riese**

ACKNOWLEDGEMENTS

To the friends who kept asking me when my next book was coming out and I was too embarrassed to admit I'd almost given it up;

to Sasha Knight, my editor, who advised me to make a significant revision to the novel which I stubbornly resisted to consider until I saw the error of my ways;

to my sister Anne Cucchiara who has shared my life and provided valuable insights;

to James Groves who has encouraged me to write for over forty years;

to my wife Susan who had no idea what was in store for her by marrying a writer and with whose patience over four years allowed me the time to finish the novel; and

to *all* my relatives, both living and dead whose stories inspired me while writing this novel.

A NOTE FROM THE AUTHOR

Is *Your Father Has Something to Tell You* a memoir? No, but who will believe me when, as the writer, I say most of it is fiction? While working on this novel, I saw a cartoon in *The New Yorker* that hit close to home. I paraphrase: two tortoises are talking about a third tortoise withdrawn inside his shell:

"Can you hear Junior typing on his computer?"

"Yes, and he'd better not be writing a memoir."

It's understandable that parents are uneasy when a child announces that he's writing a book; the entire family freaks out and focuses on every word. As a new manager, when I started giving performance reviews to my employees, I found, to my surprise, a single negative comment in an otherwise glowing evaluation would often upset the team member and ruin the meeting. Looking at it that way, one can sympathize with a family's paranoia.

First, a definition of memoir found on Wikipedia:

A memoir is a collection of memories that an individual writes about moments or events, both public or private, that took place in the [writer's] life. The assertions made in the work are understood to be factual ... a memoir often tells a story "from a life", such as touchstone events and turning points from the author's life.

—https://en.wikipedia.org/wiki/Memoir

The operative words are "The assertions ... are understood to be factual." Some writers, to their discredit, have called their work a memoir only to have it revealed as fiction.

Now a definition of fiction:

> A work of fiction implies the inventive construction of the imaginary world, most commonly, its fictionality is publicly acknowledged, so its audience typically expects it to deviate in some ways from the real world rather than presenting only characters who are actual people or descriptions that are factually true.

—https://en.wikipedia.org/wiki/Fiction

The operative words here are "The inventive construction of an imaginary world." For this reason, I am unable to write a memoir (or work as a journalist) because my imagination insists on introducing events and details that never happened. After reading parts of the novel, my wife and sister have asked me if such-and-such an incident really occurred. I often must admit I don't remember. Events in the novel have become more real than my memories.

Although writing a work of fiction doesn't require the writer to have had an unusual or exciting life, there's no doubt it helps, especially when the subject matter relates to a current problem in our society. Would you read a story about a middle-aged man who had a fairly normal childhood, helped his parents in their old age, and was present at their deaths? Even if the book has an impressive cover and an intriguing "blurb," the answer is probably "No."

To attract a reader, I added a secret in each parent's life, exaggerated the dysfunction between a father and son, enhanced childhood memories that blossomed from a germ of truth, and created an extreme depiction of the child's home life. One elderly beta reader said in reference to the father's confession, "Is that true? No? Take it out and let your father rest in peace." She wasn't convinced when I said that the character is not my father but a fictionalized actor with an important part to play on the stage of the novel. She also thought the description of the mother in a soiled nightgown was "too sad." I said I thought that detail helped to explain the daughter's horror at finding her mother lying on the couch.

What was the hardest part of writing this novel? Dealing with sadness. As a friend said, "Of course you're sad. What do you expect when you spend three years writing about the death of your parents!"

The biggest obstacle was deciding how to fictionalize the novel, expecting that many people will assume everything I write is true. Alas, a writer must be prepared to deal diplomatically with this assumption.

My core belief about life is that anything that has happened to me has happened to millions of other people. I hope that a reader living in the world of the novel will feel many sparks of recognition in the events and feelings of the characters' lives.

My constant concern: am I being fair to my parents and other deceased relatives? Is my story too one-sided and is fictionalizing their stories unfair to their memory? Despite the situations in the book, I had a happy childhood; most of the unhappiness was of my own making. Although a distant father or a parent's drinking don't have positive effects on a child's development, I have wonderful memories of my life with my parents. Why didn't I include more of those memories? My answer: that wasn't the book I was writing. Tolstoy was exactly right in the first sentence of *Anna Karenina:* "Happy families are all alike; every unhappy family is unhappy in its own way."

On a lighter note, an author chooses a time period in which to tell his story. In my book, I chose to begin the novel in July 1998. Just before the book went to the editor, I realized I hadn't verified the day of the week of Halloween in 1998. The actual day was Saturday, but I have it occur on

Monday. The thought of changing the weekdays for many of the novel's events seemed too risky. I decided to use my authorial license to keep the day of the week as I wrote it. I expect one or two readers will check the date and alert me to my error.

QUESTIONS FOR A
READERS' GROUP

1. In the previous note the writer discusses how he struggled with the decision to write this book. Would your decision be to write or not to write a novel based on your parents and childhood?

2. At the beginning of the novel, Mark is convinced he will escape becoming like his parents. In what ways is Mark like his mother and like his father? How is he different from each of them?

3. One of the storylines describes the mother's descent into dementia. Unfortunately, many families have relatives who experience dementia or Alzheimer's disease. Is your knowledge or experience of this condition similar to or dissimilar to Mark's?

4. Another storyline describes the relationship of father and son. Thinking about the fathers you know, in what ways has American culture since the forties and fifties changed the relationship of father and son? In what ways has it not done so?

5. Mark and Leslie are forced on two occasions to discuss their parents' drinking. Have you had this conversation with your parents? What other problematic behaviors have members of the group discussed with their parents?

6. The writer includes several memories about Mark's experiences in grammar school and junior high. In what ways has primary school

education improved since the fifties? What still requires improvement in American education?

7. The dream Mark has of his father emerging from the attic prompted beta readers to assume that Mark is sexually molested. Since this was not the intent of the scene, I had the father replace his pajamas and bathrobe with a business suit and his ever-present newspaper. This clothing reminds the reader of the situation that triggered the dream. Why does Mark have this dream and what does he need from his father?

How Can You Help Me?

If you would like to help me spread the word about my book, please consider these suggestions:

1. **Review my book on websites popular with readers.** If you enjoyed the book, please review it on Amazon.com, GoodReads. com, and other sites catering to book lovers. Write an honest review giving your authentic opinion. Remember: a review only needs to be 50–100 words with a couple of specifics as to why you like the book. Ratings and reviews factor into the Amazon algorithms that select which books are recommended to customers who buy books in that genre. Reviews give my book credibility.

2. **Gift my book.** Give or lend your copy to a friend. Encourage them to leave a review.

3. **Recommend my book.** If you like the book, recommend it to friends and family on your Facebook page and Twitter account. Like the *Your Father Has Something to Tell You* page on Facebook.

4. **Recommend my novel to your book group.** This is the best way to promote the book! If you belong to a reading group, recommend my book as your choice to read next. If you know of other book groups in your area, encourage them to select it. I'm happy to attend a group meeting in person or by Zoom.

Thank you. I appreciate your help.
Dave Riese

Email: daveriese1@gmail.com
Facebook: http://facebook.com/dave.riese   Twitter: @daveriese
Amazon Author Page: https://www.amazon.com/Dave-Riese/e/B00RXXH104
Goodreads Author Page: http://www.goodreads.com/DaveRiese

Made in the USA
Columbia, SC
22 March 2021

34852079R00233